JOHN RAWLS: RETICENT SOCIALIST

This book is the first detailed reconstruction of the late work of John Rawls, who was perhaps the most influential philosopher of the twentieth century. Rawls's 1971 treatise, A *Theory of Justice*, stimulated an outpouring of commentary on "justice-as-fairness," his conception of justice for an ideal, self-contained, modern political society. Most of that commentary took Rawls to be defending welfare-state capitalism as found in Western Europe and the United States. Far less attention has been given to Rawls's 2001 book, *Justice as Fairness: A Restatement*. In the *Restatement*, Rawls not only substantially reformulates the "original position" argument for the two principles of justice-as-fairness, he also repudiates capitalist regimes as possible embodiments. Edmundson further develops Rawls's non-ideal theory, which guides us when we find ourselves in a society that falls well short of justice.

WILLIAM A. EDMUNDSON is Regents Professor of Law and Philosophy at Georgia State University College of Law. He is the author of Three Anarchical Fallacies (1998) and An Introduction to Rights (2012) and editor of The Duty to Obey the Law (1999) and The Blackwell Guide to the Philosophy of Law and Legal Theory (2004). He is also the series editor of the Cambridge Introductions to Philosophy and Law.

John Rawls: Reticent Socialist

WILLIAM A. EDMUNDSON

Georgia State University

CAMBRIDGE
UNIVERSITY PRESS

University Printing House, Cambridge CB2 8BS, United Kingdom

One Liberty Plaza, 20th Floor, New York, NY 10006, USA

477 Williamstown Road, Port Melbourne, VIC 3207, Australia

314-321, 3rd Floor, Plot 3, Splendor Forum, Jasola District Centre, New Delhi-110025, India

79 Anson Road, #06-04/06, Singapore 079906

Cambridge University Press is part of the University of Cambridge.

It furthers the University's mission by disseminating knowledge in the pursuit of
education, learning and research at the highest international levels of excellence.

www.cambridge.org
Information on this title: www.cambridge.org/9781316625774
DOI: 10.1017/9781316779934

First published 2017
First paperback edition 2018

A catalogue record for this publication is available from the British Library

Library of Congress Cataloging in Publication data
NAMES: Edmundson, William A. (William Atkins), 1948– author.
TITLE: John Rawls : reticent socialist / William A. Edmundson.
DESCRIPTION: 1 Edition. | New York : Cambridge University Press, 2017. |
Includes bibliographical references and index.
IDENTIFIERS: LCCN 2017014849 | ISBN 9781107173194 (Hardback)
SUBJECTS: LCSH: Rawls, John, 1921-2002–Political and social views. | Justice. | Liberalism. |
Political stability. | BISAC: LAW / Jurisprudence.
CLASSIFICATION: LCC JC578 .E346 2017 | DDC 320.01/1–dc23 LC record
available at https://lccn.loc.gov/2017014849

ISBN 978-1-107-17319-4 Hardback
ISBN 978-1-316-62577-4 Paperback

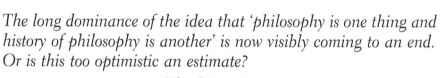

The long dominance of the idea that 'philosophy is one thing and history of philosophy is another' is now visibly coming to an end. Or is this too optimistic an estimate?

— Hilary Putnam (1997, 201)

For Lee

Contents

Acknowledgments

For favors great and small, I thank Andy Altman, David Brudney, Andrew I. Cohen, Andrew J. Cohen, Josh Cohen, Richard Dagger, Norman Daniels, Sam Freeman, Alan Gilbert, Christie Hartley, Ben Jackson, Matt Jeffers, Erin Kelly, Sharon Lloyd, Michael McPherson, Frank Michelman, Susan Neiman, George Rainbolt, David Reidy, Ben Rogers, Cheyney Ryan, Amelie Rorty, Eric Schliesser, Alan Thomas, Kevin Vallier, Bas van der Vossen, Michael Walzer, and Leif Wenar. Pam Brannon has helped me assemble the secondary materials I had to consult.

For taking on the unhappy task of plowing through the nearly finished manuscript, my deepest gratitude is owed to Jeremy Farris, Peter Lindsay, Frank Michelman, Kevin Vallier, and an anonymous reviewer for Cambridge University Press. I have tried my best to take their counsel, but of course their patience does not necessarily convey an endorsement. I do owe special thanks to Jeremy Farris for the initial suggestion that I write this book, and to John Berger, my editor, for moving it forward.

Introduction

Unlike lesser thinkers, John Rawls readily accepted criticism and openly made adjustments in his positions, while steadfastly defending what he believed could withstand criticism. Thus, both continuity and change are evident in the thirty-year interval between *A Theory of Justice* (1971) and *Justice as Fairness: A Restatement* (2001).[1] Taken together, his writings comprise the most thorough and sophisticated body of work by an individual in the history of political philosophy. This achievement was enabled by Rawls's careful study of the great work in the tradition that preceded him, by his familiarity with the literature in related scholarly fields such as economics and developmental psychology, and by his involvement in developments in contemporary philosophy more generally – notably, his elaboration of the method of "reflective equilibrium," which furthered the ascendancy of the now-orthodox Quinean/Duhemian view of theory construction.

Unlike many of the political philosophers who preceded him, and whose work he assimilated, Rawls was not personally caught up in the great social and political upheavals of his day. He served with distinction in the Pacific Theater in the Second World War, but he – unlike a number of his contemporaries – was not a conspicuous spokesperson or actor in the civil rights movement or in the opposition to the War in Vietnam. He is said to have crossed a picket line, but never (so far as I can tell) to have joined one.[2] Unlike Hobbes and Locke, he did not rely on the

---

[1] Citations to Rawls's works are abbreviated: TJ = *A Theory of Justice*, 1999 rev. ed.; PL = *Political Liberalism*, 1996 paperback ed.; CP = *Collected Papers*; LP = *The Law of Peoples*; JF = *Justice as Fairness: A Restatement*; GT = *Justice as Fairness: a Guided Tour*; LHPP = *Lectures on the History of Political Philosophy*; LHMP = *Lectures on the History of Moral Philosophy*; BI = *A Brief Inquiry into the Meaning of Sin and Faith*. Full citations appear in the bibliography. In the text, I often refer to *A Theory of Justice* as "*Theory*," to *Justice as Fairness: A Restatement* as "the *Restatement*," and to *The Law of Peoples* as "*Law of Peoples*."

[2] During the Vietnam War, Rawls was deeply opposed to the Selective Service System's policy of issuing four-year undergraduate student deferments from conscription, "quite apart from the injustice of the war itself" (Pogge 2007, 19–21).

patronage of any powerful person, and was not an advisor to any. Unlike Marx, he was not identified with a party or a movement. Unlike Hobbes, Locke, Rousseau, and Marx, he was never obliged to flee persecution. In many respects, Rawls observed the political tumult of his era from a remove as great as Kant's, in provincial Königsberg, despite the fact that the Cambridge, Massachusetts, of Rawls's time was intimately connected with the American seat of power in Washington, DC. Rawls, though very much the professional academic, admired John Stuart Mill's pursuit of a vocation as "an educator of enlightened and advanced opinion," harboring "no wish to become a political figure or a man of party" (*LHPP* 251). But, apart from adding his name to a scattered handful of petitions over the course of his years, Rawls showed no inclination whatever to play the role of public intellectual.

Given all this, it is less surprising that the development of Rawls's thinking was not directly responsive to any particular political controversies that emerged or culminated during his adulthood. The sole exceptions in his published *opera* are his few pages of criticism of the U.S. Supreme Court's campaign finance jurisprudence, particularly the 1976 decision in the *Buckley v. Valeo* case, and his analysis of the question of justifying civil disobedience – a hot topic in the 1960s – which mainly preceded the appearance of *A Theory of Justice*, in 1971.

The two most conspicuous, and commented-upon, changes in his 1971 view were an extension of the account of justice to the international case and an overhaul of the account of the stability of a well-ordered society. The former change was responsive to the widely voiced criticism that his focus on the question of justice of a self-contained, economically advanced society left out of account the more pressing issues of the day: those of global justice and the inequalities of life prospects that flow from the happenstance that some are born in rich countries and others in poor ones. The publication in 1999 of *The Law of Peoples* fulfilled the promise in *A Theory of Justice* to extend the theory to the international case. As it turned out, the extension drew even greater criticism than the omission, much of it exasperatedly negative rather than constructive; but that is not the subject of the present book. Here, the focus is on the theory of justice for an idealized, self-contained society, and on the roads to achieving such a society.

The latter of the two prominent changes was the adjustment in the account of stability, and the coordinate emphasis on a political rather than a comprehensive form of liberal theory. Unlike the first change, this one seems to have been almost entirely self-motivated. Rawls was scrupulous about crediting critics for forcing him to clarify or adjust his positions, but in the Introduction to *Political Liberalism* no one is credited with having pointed out to him the "serious problem internal to justice as fairness, namely ... the fact that the account of stability in part III of *Theory* is not consistent with the view as a whole" (*PL* xvii–xviii). (Rawls does thank his Harvard colleague Burton Dreben for helping him find his way along this path, once he had taken it.) It is remarkable that this major inconsistency had not been pointed out in the already extensive critical literature. Perhaps this is a clue that Rawls's concern about a deep inconsistency was merely valetudinarian; or, more charitably, it could be seen as further evidence of the depth of his insight. Rawls's continuing focus on stability also led him, in *Justice as Fairness: A Restatement*, to reconfigure the argument for the two principles of justice as fairness, in ways that have not yet been sufficiently remarked.

The subject of this book is a related, equally significant development in Rawls's thinking. This is his express insistence that *welfare-state capitalism* cannot satisfy the two principles of justice as fairness. The significance of this change is underscored by the fact that numerous commentators had understood *A Theory of Justice* to have been designed to serve as a defense of welfare-state capitalism. Rawls's Harvard colleague Hilary Putnam recalled that "the publication of *A Theory of Justice* ... coincided with enormously important debates in American public life about the rightness or wrongness of the welfare state" (Putnam 1997, 189). Americans had by that time become accustomed to thinking of their nation *as* a welfare state, and work such as Daniel Patrick Moynihan's *The Negro Family: The Case for National Action* (popularly known as "The Moynihan Report" [1965]) was widely taken as a solemnly irreverent challenge to the received wisdom of remaining a welfare state – even to the morality of remaining so. The relatively minor portion of *A Theory of Justice* devoted to certain questions of "non-ideal theory" contains passages that strongly suggest that Rawls considered the United States circa 1971 to be a "reasonably just" or "nearly just" state (*TJ* 308, 309). So, for these and many similar reasons, it was easy to view the work as a "transcendental deduction" of welfare-state capitalism – that is, as a defense of the basic justice of a society that allows a normally only lightly regulated market to determine prices, wages, and capital investment, and which makes separate provision to attend to those whose participation in the labor market is impossible or insufficient to meet their needs.

In 1988, Richard Krouse and Michael McPherson (1988, 79 n.1) compiled an impressive list of scholarly commentators who understood Rawls this way: Robert Paul Wolff, Brian Barry, Allen Buchanan, Barry Clark, Herbert Gintis, Norman Daniels, Amy Gutmann, Carole Pateman, Alan Ryan, and David Schweikert. Krouse and McPherson cite but one writer, Arthur DiQuattro (1983), as having perceived that *justice as fairness*, the theory Rawls advanced in *A Theory of Justice*, is unfriendly to capitalism. DiQuattro himself had already listed the names of C. B. Macpherson, Benjamin Barber, Robert Amdur, and Kai Nielsen on the roll of non-perceivers of Rawls's antipathy to capitalism. Austrian economist and free-market champion Friedrich Hayek was satisfied that *A Theory of Justice* is not properly interpreted "as lending support to socialist demands" (1984, 113). Even the sympathetic Marxist Rodney Peffer wrote that "Rawls *presumes* that a democratic form of welfare state will best conform to ... the requirements of social justice" (2014 [1990], 378; reordered, but emphasis in the original).

DiQuattro rightly pointed out that the word "capitalism" does not occur at all in *A Theory of Justice*. But the expressions "private-property economy," "private-property society," "private-property regime," and "private-property democracy" are used, and are used in explicit contrast to "socialism" (*TJ* 235–236, 239, 242). Rawls is quite clear that his theory of justice – I will call it "justice as fairness," as was Rawls's practice, or "the two principles"[3] – regards economic inequality as an inescapable fact of life. Justice as fairness is designed to make extensive use of a labor market, and it legitimates wage and salary differentials as incentives that are necessary to achieve economic efficiency. Rawls took the trouble to show how "a properly organized democratic state that allows private ownership of capital and natural resources" could "fit the two principles of justice" (*TJ* 243–251). In a properly designed private-property economy, with "background justice" assured, and so long as there is also a "social minimum" safety net, "the distribution of wealth that results is just whatever it is" (*TJ* 249). And Rawls ruled out by all but name the Communist or "command" socialist economies that were familiar, at least in broad outline, to contemporary readers, on the ground that they infringe the "important liberty of free choice of occupation" (*TJ* 242), not to mention the equal political liberties. The many commentators who took Rawls as a friend of welfare-state capitalism were not guilty of any crude misreading of the text.[4] It is not straining to read Rawls's social minimum and difference principle as intended to serve as sufficient correctives of the inequalities inevitably generated by a just market system of private ownership.[5] Classifying the theory as a defense of welfare-state capitalism was an easy mistake to make, if indeed that is what it was.

---

[3] Throughout *A Theory of Justice*, Rawls also refers to the theory developed therein as "the contract theory." I will not do so. Rawls later emphasized that justice as fairness is not unique in being a theory of justice supported by contractualist methods of theory-building, and he stopped referring to the theory of *Theory* as "the contract theory."

[4] Crude misreadings tended instead to lead the opposite way. Sociologist Daniel Bell, for example, saw *A Theory of Justice* as "the most comprehensive effort in modern philosophy to justify a socialistic ethic" (1972, 72). But note Bell's reading of the difference principle:

> We have here a fundamental rationale for a major shift in values; instead of the principle "from each according to his ability, to each according to his ability," we have the principle "from each according to his ability, to each according to his need." And the justification for need is fairness to those who are disadvantaged for reasons beyond their control.
>
> (1972, 57)

In fairness to Bell, I note that he was writing for an educated but not a specialist readership, and was attempting to weave Rawls's then very recent big book into a broad account of the intellectual history behind an affirmative-action debate that was then also new. Conflating Rawls's difference principle with Marx's prescription for the "higher phase of communist society" (1978 [1875], 531) would not ordinarily be excusable.

[5] Political philosopher Michael Otsuka takes Rawls as an exemplar of "liberal egalitarianism" i.e., as avowing a stringent right of control over one's own mind and body but denying any "very stringent right to all of the income that one can gain … on one's own or though unregulated and untaxed exchanges" (2003, 15 n.17). "Liberal egalitarian capitalist" is not an oxymoron.

Rawls accepted responsibility for this misunderstanding. In the 1987 preface to the French translation of A *Theory of Justice*, Rawls confessed that he would now "distinguish more sharply the idea of a *property-owning democracy* . . . from the idea of a welfare state . . . [which is] quite different" (*CP* 419; emphasis added). He warned that a welfare state "*may allow* large and inheritable inequalities of wealth incompatible with the fair value of political liberties . . . as well as large disparities of income that violate the difference principle" (*CP* 419; emphasis added). This passage was repeated in the preface to the revised edition, published in 1999 (*TJ* xv). The "may allow" could be read as merely cautionary, or – as his colleague and "tutor" Burton Dreben might point out – it could also be read as intimating in a cramped, muffled way that capitalism, in both its laissez-faire and its welfare-state guises, tends inevitably toward injustice.

> Burt was doing what he could to make me be clear, to write forcefully and sharply, to be less guarded and muffled, a term he often used. He wanted me to find my own "voice," as we sometimes say. He would often comment by name on other people who were extraordinarily bright and knowledgeable but failed to express themselves clearly and with vigor. Their style was muffled and cramped, somehow they held back.
>
> (Rawls 2000a, 426)

It is fairly certain that Dreben had no opportunity (if he had the desire) to press Rawls to be more vigorous in this particular connection.

Finally, only shortly before his death in 2002, Rawls for the first time declared in print, in *Justice as Fairness: A Restatement* (2001), that welfare-state capitalism *could not* realize justice as fairness even in the best of circumstances (*JF* 135–138). It is a "serious fault" (*JF* 139 n.5) of *Theory* that it does not emphasize that welfare-state capitalism is not among the private-property regimes that might satisfy the two principles. Put bluntly, capitalism in all its guises is unjust. But the *Restatement* did not excite the curiosity of the educated public, or even of specialists, to the same degree as A *Theory of Justice* had, nor even as much as had the *Restatement*'s predecessors, *Political Liberalism* (1st ed. 1993) and *The Law of Peoples* (1999). The often astute Cambridge political philosopher Raymond Geuss, for example, wrote that *Law of Peoples* is Rawls's "last systematic work" (2005, 33).

Possibly this diminution of interest was symptomatic of a general "Rawls fatigue" that was accumulating – along with the enormous secondary literature – over the thirty years since 1971.[6] Jeremy Waldron, the former Chichele Professor in Social and Political Theory at Oxford, wants "to encourage young political theorists to understand that there is life beyond Rawls" (2016, ix). Waldron means no disrespect, but his advice spells relief for theorists of all ages: it was hard even for sympathetic

---

[6] This literature's growth owed in part to debates premised in part on other misreadings of Rawls, as philosopher Elizabeth Anderson, his former student, recounts (Anderson 1999; Anderson forthcoming; see also Scheffler 2003).

readers to keep up with the spate of Rawls titles issued by Harvard shortly before his death, including the revised edition of A *Theory of Justice, Collected Papers,* and *Law of Peoples* of 1999. Set aside first editions, and the *earliest* of Rawls's books is the expanded edition of *Political Liberalism* that came out from Columbia in paperback in 1996, fully a quarter-century after the first edition of *Theory*.

Rawls did not exploit the obvious moment to advertise his wholesale rejection of capitalism. His confession of "the more serious faults" of *Theory,* tendered in the preface to the *Restatement,* does not even mention the "serious fault" in *Theory* that enabled his misclassification as an apologist for welfare-state capitalism. Nor does the preface cite his rejection of welfare-state capitalism as one of the "main changes" (*JF* xvi) the *Restatement* performs. It is therefore not at all surprising, much less, inexplicable, that the reputation of "John Rawls, apologist for welfare-state capitalism" persists.

And persist it does. Consider these two recent, dismissive references to Rawls, the apologist for late capitalism. According to the Swiss political philosopher Christoph Henning (2014, 461),

> The moment the individuals in the original position begin to make concrete decisions, the institutions they create resemble those of the USA down to the smallest detail. A *Theory of Justice* needs therefore to be read as a transcendental deduction of the USA [circa 1971].

"Bourgeois practical philosophy" is the category to which the "Philosophical Gourmet," Brian Leiter, assigns Rawls. Although he approves Rawls's focus on the basic structure of society rather than on individual choices, Leiter assumes that "the basic structure does not include capitalist relations of production" (2015, 32 n.15), and concludes that

> while Rawls … endorsed intuitions that had implications for basic social and economic policy in capitalist societies, his theory was neither presented nor understood as threatening capitalist relations of production, a fact surely central to any explanation of how it could become so influential in capitalist democracies, at least in the universities.
>
> (Leiter 2015, 31)

Not only is Rawls an apologist for capitalism, Leiter alleges, Rawls also owes his influence as a philosopher to his being an apologist for capitalism. My view differs. I am confident that Rawls's influence will not suffer when his theory's profound hostility to capitalism is appreciated. Rawls's theory not only does not legitimate the institutional status quo in the United States, as it was in 1971 or as it is today; it condemns it as fundamentally unjust and demands a radical reconstitution.

Readers whose primary acquaintance with Rawls comes from *Theory* and *Political Liberalism* may not be aware that the *Restatement* also represents an unheralded and complex reformulation of the argument for the two principles of justice as fairness. In the introduction to the paperback edition of *Political Liberalism,* Rawls conceded that certain alternatives to the two principles of justice as fairness – for example, liberal conceptions that reject the difference principle – can count as reasonable liberal political conceptions (*PL* xlviii–xlix; cf. Metz 2002, 619). This could have been misunderstood as a sign of surrender rather than the mere bracketing of the issue. In the *Restatement*, Rawls returns to the affirmative. He responds to criticism by economists John Harsanyi, Kenneth Arrow, and others by making more careful and sparing use of the "maximin" criterion of decision under uncertainty. In its place – taking up the slack, as it were – Rawls relies much more than he does in *Theory* on "such ideas as publicity and reciprocity" (*JF* xvii). It will emerge that stability, publicity, and reciprocity also figure centrally in the argument for socialism that Rawls adverts to but never detailed.

To recapitulate very, very briefly, and solely as a reminder of what many readers will rightly feel they already know by heart: *A Theory of Justice* presented a "working up" of ideas already pronounced in the political culture of modern constitutional democracies, enabling an ideally rational and reasonable chooser to derive two principles of justice from the "original position," the device for assuring that the choice of principles not be warped by bias. Those principles, as initially stated, are:

> First: each person is to have an equal right to the most extensive scheme of equal basic liberties compatible with a similar scheme of liberties for others.

> Second: social and economic inequalities are to be arranged so that they are both (a) reasonably expected to be to everyone's advantage, and (b) attached to positions and offices open to all.

> (*TJ* 53)

The two principles operate in what he calls a lexical order: satisfying the first principle has an absolute priority over the second, such that first-principle liberties – although to be adjusted to fit together – are not to be sacrificed to further second-principle values. Rawls made refinements and adjustments in the two principles, in ways that will be relevant later in the book.

In the *Restatement*, Rawls gives greater prominence to the division of the argument for the two principles into two parts (*JF* 87–89; 180–181; cf. *TJ* 124–125, 464–465). One reason for the division is to simplify the task facing the choosers in the original position, by freeing them from concern with what he calls the "special psychologies" of the persons the choosers represent. In Part One, the parties choose principles without knowing that the persons whom they represent are prone to "be envious or spiteful, or to have a will to dominate or a tendency to be submissive, or to be peculiarly averse to uncertainty and risk" (*JF* 180). Part Two of the argument takes the two principles as provisionally established, and the parties return to the problem of stability. The parties

> now consider the special psychologies by checking whether those who grow up under just institutions (as the principles adopted specify them) will develop a sufficiently firm sense of justice with respect to those attitudes and inclinations.

> (*JF* 184)

That is to say, the choosers must ask whether citizens in a well-ordered society will

> acquire a sufficiently strong and effective sense of justice so that they normally comply with just arrangements and are not moved to act otherwise, say, by social envy and spite, or by a will to dominate or a tendency to submit. (*JF* 181)

If the choosers can satisfy themselves that the principles of justice support a sense of justice sufficient to resist the "destabilizing special attitudes" (*JF* 181), then "the outcome of the first part of the argument is confirmed and the argument for the two principles is complete" (*JF* 181).

After the derivation of the two principles of justice, but before introducing the special psychologies, Part One of the argument outlines a "four-stage sequence" that proceeds from the original position, to a constitutional stage at which the parties "decide upon the justice of political forms and ... design a system for the constitutional powers of government and the basic rights of citizens" (*TJ* 172), to a legislative stage, where majority rule is introduced, to a final, administrative *cum* judicial stage. In the *Restatement*, Rawls introduced a new task at the second, constitutional stage. For the first time, he considered five "ideal-types" of regime as candidate institutional forms for realizing justice as fairness:

laissez-faire capitalism,
welfare-state capitalism,
one-party "state" socialism,
property-owning democracy, and
liberal (democratic) socialism (*JF* 136).

Part One of the original position procedure is not complete until this is undertaken:

> It is ... important to trace out, if only in a rough and ready way, the institutional content of the two principles of justice. We need to do this before we can endorse these principles, *even provisionally*.
>
> (*JF* 136; emphasis added)

By "even provisionally" Rawls is acknowledging that checking the "institutional content" is necessary in both Part One of the original position procedure, where the citizens' special psychologies are not known to the parties, and in Part Two, where the parties then take the special psychologies into account, and focus again on the question of stability. The "realist" critics, dissatisfied with Rawls's focus on "ideal theory," had insisted that political philosophy ought to stress "the evaluation and comparison of institutions and regime types, not only principles" (Galston 2010, 408); what Rawls offered could be taken as a response to this challenge, but Rawls presented it as already required in ideal theory by the procedure of reflective equilibrium.

After setting out the list of five ideal regime types, Rawls itemized four questions that arise with respect to any of them. One: whether it would be "right and just" on the assumption that it could be "workably maintained." Two: whether its "institutions can be effectively designed to realize its declared aims." Three: "whether citizens, in view of their likely interests and ends as shaped by the regime's basic structure, can be relied on to comply" with its institutions and rules – a question that includes "the problem of corruption." Finally, four: "there is the question of competence: whether the tasks assigned to offices and positions would prove simply too difficult for those likely to hold them" (*JF* 136). Rawls sets aside all but the first question. The three further questions will have to be dealt with in both parts of the original position procedure. Rawls is thus, in effect, limiting his "illustrative and highly tentative" (*JF* 136) survey of the five regime types to scrutiny under Part One on the assumption that each can "be effectively and workably maintained," which is an assumption that still must be scrutinized under Part One and, again under Part Two.

Rawls asks: "When a regime works in accordance with its ideal institutional description, which of the five regimes satisfy the two principles of justice?" (*JF* 137). By making the further assumption that "if a regime does not try to realize certain political values, it will not in fact do so" (*JF* 137), Rawls quickly dismisses one-party socialism and laissez-faire capitalism. One-party socialism does not protect equal political liberty or freedom of occupation, and laissez-faire capitalism does not aim to secure the fair value of political liberty and fair equality of opportunity. No "invisible hand" possibility is entertained.

This much was easily foreseeable; what is new is that Rawls went on to reject welfare-state capitalism. Welfare-state capitalism cannot realize the two principles of justice as fairness because it does not express reciprocity between citizens as free equals, it is not serious about fair equality of opportunity, and it does not guarantee, or even try to guarantee, the fair value of the political liberties. The *Restatement* makes more prominent the importance Rawls had placed, in *Theory*, on the fair value of political liberty as a prior, first-principle guarantee of reciprocity between citizens as free equals (cf. Wall 2006).

So, now having dismissed welfare-state capitalism, command-economy socialism, and laissez-faire capitalism, "this leaves ... property-owning democracy and liberal socialism: their ideal descriptions include arrangements designed to satisfy the two principles of justice" (*JF* 138). Rawls states that he does not believe that justice as fairness can decide at this point between the two remaining ideal-types of regime: property-owning democracy and liberal socialism.

> When a practical decision is to be made between property-owning democracy and a liberal socialist regime, we look to a society's *historical circumstances*, to its *traditions of political thought and practice*, and *much else*. Justice as fairness does not decide between these regimes but tries to set out *guidelines* for how the decision can reasonably be approached.
>
> (*JF* 139; emphases added)

This is disappointing, insofar as Rawls's task is "to see whether we can resolve the impasse in our recent political history; namely, that there is no agreement on the way basic social institutions should be arranged if they are to conform to the freedom and equality of citizens as persons" (*PL* 300).[7] At least since 1848, the most intractable impasse in political thought, by far, has concerned the ownership of socially significant assets – the means of production – and the competing claims made for state and for private proprietorship. The central thesis of this book is that, despite Rawls's seeming disclaimers, he was aware that his ideal theory does in fact contain sufficient resources to resolve this central impasse, and to resolve it in favor of liberal democratic socialism. This becomes evident when the question of stability is addressed, and pursued under both Part One and Part Two of the original position procedure.

The "historical circumstances" and "traditions of thought and practice" referred to in the block quotation above are already among the facts revealed to the parties at the constitutional stage. The "much else" is presumably a reminder of the "highly controversial" and "intricate" questions about "public funding of elections and political campaigns, different kinds of property ownership and taxation" (*JF* 136) that he did not want to take up either. The "guidelines" Rawls refers to are not further specified, but presumably they are the "guidelines of public reason" essential to a political conception of justice, which are adopted in the original position as companions to the two principles (*PL* 223–225). Rawls's desire is that these guidelines, taken together with the substantive content of justice as fairness, be "complete":

> This means that the values specified by [the political] conception [of justice] can be suitably balanced or combined, or otherwise united . . . so that those values alone give a reasonable public answer to all, or nearly all, questions involving the *constitutional essentials* and *matters of basic justice*.
>
> (*PL* 225; emphasis added)

"Constitutional essentials" are matters not included in the two principles, but they "concern questions about what political rights and liberties, say, may reasonably be included in a written constitution, when assuming the constitution may be interpreted by a supreme court, or some similar body." By contrast, what Rawls terms "matters of basic justice" are subjects that "relate to the basic structure of society and

---

[7] Rawls said even less on the subject in the 1989 *Guided Tour*, breaking off after merely noting that property-owning democracy and liberal socialism were alone left standing (*GT* 112). It is therefore a fair inference that Rawls had either given no further thought to the question of deciding between these two surviving regime types, or was not yet ready to put forward, in written form, what he thought. Rawls is said to have written and circulated the *Guided Tour*, as a photocopy, for the benefit of Harvard Law students. With few changes, it was ultimately published as the *Restatement*.

so would concern questions of basic economic and social justice and other things not covered by a constitution" (*PL* 1 n. 23).

Rather than carry the project through, citing a desire to be brief, Rawls broke off his investigation. I will argue in the chapters ahead that a settlement on the issue of property in the means of production is a "constitutional essential" and, as such, that the settlement is a presupposition of, and not thus not subject to revision by, ordinary majoritarian legislation. I argue, moreover, that the guidelines of inquiry, taken along into Part Two of the original position procedure, do yield the answer that Rawls did not pursue or was too reticent to announce.

I restrict myself to the question whether justice as fairness decisively favors either of these two surviving ideal regime types, "without considering whether something else might be better" (Krouse and McPherson 1988, 80). In defense of this, I rely on the general reasons Rawls gives in favor of the "historical list" approach in political philosophy, against critics who reject it as "makeshift" and insufficiently general and comprehensive (*PL* 292–293). In introducing property-owning democracy, Rawls refers to "other alternatives to capitalism" (*JF* 136 n. 3, *citing* Elster and Moene 1989) but says nothing about them. As I will try to show, Rawls's conception of property-owning democracy as an ideal regime type is itself an artifact of his trying to imagine "something else," that is, a variation on a socialist theme. Justice as fairness was never presented as a completed theory; but it did not disavow the need and ambition of completeness.

> Let us suppose that we have found a list of basic liberties which achieves the initial aim of justice as fairness ... [viz., to] provide a better understanding of the claims of freedom and equality in a democratic society than ... utilitarianism, ... perfectionism, or ... intuitionism. This list we view as a starting point that can be improved by finding a second list ... This process can be continued indefinitely, but the discriminating power of philosophical reflection may soon run out. When this happens we should settle on the last preferred list and then specify that list further at the constitutional, legislative, and judicial stages, when general knowledge of social institutions and society's circumstances is made known .... Thus, as a matter of method, nothing need be lost by using a step-by-step procedure.
>
> (*PL* 292–293; reordered)

It is important not to overlook Rawls's awareness that where a specific liberty comes in makes a huge difference. It is crucial whether a given liberty is recognized as a "matter of basic liberty" or as a non-basic liberty that is subject to "the calculus of social interests" that is always "on the table, so to speak" in a majoritarian legislature. The central purpose of this book is to demonstrate that, as to the choice between liberal democratic socialism and its alternatives, the argument deployed in the *Restatement* (and the discriminating power of political philosophy) does not run out quite as soon as Rawls might appear to be willing to let it.

Rawls never completes the argument for justice as fairness. He leaves Part Two of the original position procedure unfinished. This means that his argument for justice as fairness is unfinished also. By saying this I do not mean to repeat Rawls's own point that it is practically impossible to run every conceivable principle through the original position procedure, pitting it against the two principles of justice as fairness. Nor do I mean to repeat the point that there may be ideal regime types other than the five Rawls identified that might realize justice as fairness as well as or better than any of them. The point is that the regime types that survive scrutiny in Part One must be rechecked in Part Two, to determine whether they are capable of stabilizing a well-ordered society in the face of the "special psychologies" that citizens will exhibit. Rawls never got around to doing this, but he dropped at least two hints that, at this final stage, liberal socialism could have a decisive advantage over property-owning democracy. I will complete this step, comparing property-owning democracy and liberal socialism in Part Two of the original position procedure, where the special psychologies come into play. When that step is complete, liberal socialism emerges as the sole regime type capable of realizing justice as fairness.

The later Rawls regarded justice as fairness as but one of a family of political conceptions of justice that might reasonably stabilize a well-ordered liberal constitutional democracy. "Any conception that meets the criterion of reciprocity and recognizes the burdens of judgment is a candidate" (*PL* xlix). At first thought, it can seem that other members of the family might better be realized by property-owning democracy than by liberal socialism. Each member of this family must, however, regard society as a fair system of cooperation between free and equal citizens (*PL* 167). Therefore,

> if the liberal conceptions correctly framed from fundamental ideas of a democratic public culture are supported by and encourage deeply conflicting political and economic interests, and if there be no way of designing a constitutional regime to overcome that, a full overlapping consensus cannot, it seems be achieved.
>
> (*PL* 168)

Rawls acknowledged the tendency of a property-owning democracy to encourage such conflicts (*JF* 178). This does not necessarily mean that a liberal socialist regime would not do so as well, even if to a lesser degree. I will complete my argument, and Rawls's system, by showing how a liberal socialist constitutional regime can be designed to assure stability in conditions of reasonable pluralism.

Shortly after *A Theory of Justice* appeared in print and its impact began to be felt, Rawls's critic and Harvard colleague Robert Nozick (1974, 183) wrote, "Political philosophers now must either work within Rawls's theory or explain why not." I have chosen to work within Rawls's theory. I have done so in part because I can no longer explain why I would not, and in part because I can explain why I will. The most compelling reason is that Rawls's theory furnishes a common language in which people who are concerned enough about justice to want to understand it, and to bring it about, can communicate. It is a theoretic lingua franca having few precedents: one precedent being the dominance of the Marxian framework in Germany, Russia, and, to a somewhat lesser degree, in other European countries on the eve of the First World War. Rawls's regard for "natural piety" (*TJ* 15) is apt here: he saw himself as someone continuing the nineteenth-century discursive tradition rather than as one trying to abstract away from it. The catastrophe that was the first half of the twentieth century seemed certain to kill political philosophy, yet Rawls was able almost single-handedly to resuscitate it.[8] The perfusive influence of Rawls's terminology and conceptualizations creates a "world-historical" opportunity for real progress – despite the Babel of conflicting viewpoints of the kind that he envisages as a permanent threat to the stability of a just liberal democracy, should one ever be achieved.

So, the framework assumed throughout is Rawls's ideal theory of a just basic structure, which he contrasts to a "theory of the political system" (*TJ* 199) or a detailed design of government. Evidently he did not regard the choice between the five ideal-types of regime to belong to the latter if ideal theory itself contains sufficient resources to decide it. The task of the first chapters of this book is to show, by an "immanent critique" of Rawls's overall view, that it does contain those resources, and that his view commits him to socialism – and to socialism of the traditional and familiar type that demands public ownership of the means of production. Consider:

> The two principles ... specify an ideal form for the basic structure in the light of which ongoing institutional and procedural processes are constrained and adjusted. Among these constraints are the limits on the accumulation of property (*especially if* private property in productive assets exists) that derive from the requirements of the fair value of political liberty and fair equality of opportunity, and the limits based on considerations of stability and excusable envy, both of which are connected to the essential primary good of self-respect. We need such an ideal to guide the adjustments necessary to preserve background justice.
>
> (*PL* 284; emphasis added)

The ambition of this book is simply to unfold what Rawls packed into this and similar passages. The claim is that the "especially if" in the phrase "*especially if private property in productive assets exists*" denotes a risk of a type – as Rawls and Rawlsians already agree – that prudent parties need not and would not take.

To give the reader a sense of what is to come, I provide a brief description of the contents of the chapters that follow.

---

[8] As philosopher of language Simon Blackburn (2001, 11) put it, "During the first two thirds of the twentieth century, had anyone suggested that the most important work of philosophy produced in the final third would be a work of political philosophy, they would have been laughed to scorn ... [Yet A *Theory of Justice*] is not only the most important work of philosophy, but arguably of the humanities, in the past thirty years."

Chapter 1 sets out Rawls's distinction between personal property and property more widely conceived in terms of rights in the means of production. Further distinctions between different aspects of ownership explain why Rawls held that the right to hold personal property is protected by the first-principle guarantee of equal basic liberties, while the right to hold property in the wider senses is not.

Chapter 2 clarifies what Rawls understood the fundamental difference between property-owning democracy and liberal socialism to be. To do this, I explore some of the political history of the resources Rawls had to drawn on in formulating these two ideas as competing ideal regime types.

Chapter 3 explains the (sometimes underappreciated) significance of the priority, in Rawls's system, of the fair value of the specifically political liberties. The term "the fact of domination" is introduced to summarize a set of facts that led Rawls to insist on the fair-value guarantee to counter the Marxian criticism that liberal political equality is merely formal and not real.

Chapter 4 details the progression, within ideal theory, of the four-stage sequence from the original position to constitutional structure to ordinary legislation to routine governance. The importance of outlining the institutions of a just society needs no comment; but for Rawls it is especially important to do so in order to support his crucial claim that economic inequality in a well-ordered society is a matter of pure procedural justice – the actual distribution of wealth is to be accepted as just, whatever it happens to be, once background justice is assured. This chapter also explains why, since the fair value of political liberty is a prior, first-principle matter, an institutional guarantee is likely to count among the "constitutional essentials."

Chapter 5 outlines Rawls's view of politics as a regulated rivalry played out in the shadow of the fact of domination. Rawls laments the fact that the history of constitutional democracies shows a lack of concern to establish structural safeguards of fair value. Rawls gives various indications that the constitution is assigned the task of giving public assurance that the fair value of the political liberties is secure, but he also hints at the possible adequacy of a merely legislative "insulation strategy."

Chapter 6 outlines a fairly extensive reconfiguration, in the *Restatement*, of the central argument for justice as fairness. Rawls makes more sparing use of the maximin criterion than in *Theory* by dividing the argument against utilitarianism into two "fundamental comparisons." The first comparison is between justice and fairness and the principle of utility, but the second comparison is between the two principles and a mixed conception called the principle of restricted utility, which is formed from justice as fairness by replacing the difference principle with the principle of utility confined to the same lexically posterior position. The maximin criterion of decision under uncertainty is thus inapposite in the second comparison, and ideas of stability, reciprocity, clarity, and publicity come to the fore. This shift of emphasis will prove decisive in determining how to compare ideal regime types.

Chapter 7 explains Rawls's division of the original position procedure into two parts. In Part One, the parties (and those they represent) take no interest in the interests of others. The reason for this restriction is to counter the charge – typically heard from conservatives and libertarians – that egalitarianism is motivated by envy. The principles derived in Part One are not shaped by envy, spite, or other of the "special," other-regarding psychological attitudes; but the stability of those principles, and the institutions and regime types that realize them, must survive scrutiny, in Part Two, where the special psychologies are now in play.

Chapter 8 begins with a review of the textual hints Rawls gave that socialism might be more stable, for the right reasons, than alternative institutional realizations of justice as fairness. It proceeds then to locate the question of regime type within Rawls's architectonic. The task is complicated because the original position procedure involves two unconnected relaxations of the veil of ignorance. One lifting coincides with the four-stage sequence; the other introduces Part Two of the original-position procedure. The fact of domination, and the fact that measures to correct for disparities in fair value "never seem to have been seriously entertained" in constitutional democracies, are both known at the constitutional stage. It is therefore also known that structural safeguards are a "constitutional essential," and that a regime type that supplies them is to be preferred, especially if they survive the stability tests of Part Two of the original-position procedure without contravening the strictures of public reason.

Chapter 9 prepares the ground for the argument in Chapter 10 by specifying what is common ground between property-owning democracy and liberal democratic socialism. The method consciously models itself on the "second fundamental comparison" between justice as fairness and the principle of restricted utility. Once the common content is factored out, the residual differences will be more palpable.

Chapter 10 is a long and dense chapter. It is the wall that is built from the elements defined in the earlier chapters; and, like a masonry wall, it is larger than any of its proper parts. My hope has been to emulate Rawls by already making it plain what assumptions are in play and what defense each of them can be given. Applying the results of the earlier chapters, the argument, in précis, is that if (1) society is conceived as a cooperative enterprise for mutual advantage; (2) fair value is a demand of equal liberty; (3) publicly assured reciprocity is a condition of stability, then, within Rawls's apparatus; (4) preservation of fair value is a constitutional essential; (5) a choice between ideal-types of regime can and must be made if one among them is superior to the others in this and other relevant respects; and (6) socialism "dominates" property-owning democracy at each of the points of comparison that Rawls is committed to making. These points of comparison include amenability to public reason, workability, and sufficient public assurance of reciprocity to stabilize a well-ordered society. At each point of comparison, liberal socialism better, or alone, satisfies Rawls's desiderata.

Chapter 11 addresses the natural question to ask next: Why was Rawls so reticent to state the conclusion – which is inescapable in his mature system – that justice requires socialism? The answer I give draws on biographical material, including his undergraduate thesis, and structures itself in parallel with Joseph Schumpeter's account of Mill's evolving attitude toward socialism. In particular, I describe three stages: a youthful stage, an analytical stage, and finally a corrective stage, which in Rawls's case is consummated in the *Restatement*.

The book concludes with Chapter 12. Rawls's staunch anti-totalitarianism within ideal theory does not settle the question of his posture, in non-ideal theory, toward revolutionary methods of achieving a well-ordered liberal socialist society. For Rawls, socialism is not only a "realistic utopia" but one whose peaceful historical chances have and do come. Given a political will unfettered by notions of "false necessity," those chances can be seized when they come again.

1

Conceptions of Property in the Original Position

A *Theory of Justice* (1971) and its revised edition (1999) do not take up the question of ideal types of regime – and the specific question of capitalism versus socialism – in the terms in which it is later posed in *Justice as Fairness: A Restatement* (2001). But the socialism-vs.-capitalism question is fundamentally a question of who shall own what; and the question of individual rights of ownership is taken up in A *Theory of Justice*, which holds only that the basic liberties include "freedom of the person, which includes freedom from … physical assault and dismemberment (integrity of the person) [and] the right to hold personal property" (*TJ* 53). In the first edition, the "personal" in "personal property" appeared in parentheses: "the right to hold (personal) property" (*TJ* 1st ed. 61) – his dropping the parentheses indicates that Rawls meant to emphasize the limitation. Beyond this, Rawls recognizes a right of ownership of one's "natural assets" as entailed by the "basic liberty protecting the integrity of the person" (*TJ* 89). Rawls's framework regards the possible existence of some natural, pre-political right to property as an irrelevance, as far as his theory of justice is concerned.

In the 1982 essay "The Basic Liberties and Their Priority" (*PL* 289–371) Rawls explains that choosers in the original position would insist on "the right to hold and to have the exclusive use of personal property … to allow a sufficient material basis for a secure sense of personal independence and self-respect, both of which are essential for the development and exercise of the moral powers" (*PL* 298; see also *JF* 114). This accords with Rawls's considered approach to sorting the basic liberties from all others.

> The proposed criterion is this: the basic liberties … are to guarantee equally for all citizens the social conditions essential for the adequate development and the full and informed exercise of their two moral powers [viz. capacity for a sense of justice and capacity for a conception of the good].
>
> (*JF* 112)

This criterion assures not "the most extensive scheme," but rather a "fully adequate scheme of equal basic liberties, which scheme is compatible the same scheme of liberties for all" (*JF* 42). *Theory*'s first-edition formulation called for "the most extensive" (1971, 60) scheme but as early as 1980, Rawls had amended this. Perhaps the *most* extensive scheme of compossible liberties would not allow for ownership of anything, even personal ownership of one's own body. A world in which everyone enjoys a Hohfeldian privilege to use everything, and no one has a right to exclude anyone else's use of anything, is a conceivable world. And it seems in a sense to be a world of at least as "extensive" liberty as a world partitioned into separate, exclusive holdings – unless extensiveness is given a more precise signification than Rawls thought wise to attempt (see *PL* 331–34), or if the case were somehow made that the overall package in the latter world is more *extensive*, and not merely fully adequate.

A fully adequate scheme, Rawls stated, will include a right to own personal property, but it need not specify anything as to two "wider conceptions of property":

> One conception extends this [ownership] right to include certain rights of acquisi-
> tion and bequest, as well as the right to own means of production and natural
> resources. On the other conception, the right of property includes the equal right to
> participate in the control of means of production and natural resources, which are
> to be socially owned.
>
> (*PL* 298)

In a footnote, Rawls references, "as an elaboration of this paragraph," the passages in *A Theory of Justice* in which he discussed "the question of private property in a democracy versus socialism" (*TJ* 239–242, 247–249), adding that the "two principles of justice by themselves do not settle this question" (*PL* 298 n. 14). This indicates that Rawls understood the two wider conceptions of ownership to line up with the two types of "systems," "societies," or "regimes" identified, respectively, as "private property" and "socialism." Similarly, the parties in the original position do not insist on either of the wider conceptions that address the means of production – the first guaranteeing a right of private ownership, the second guaranteeing the first's opposite, a right of social ownership. In fact, they "are to be avoided" (*PL* 298).

> These wider conceptions of property are not used because they cannot, I think, be
> accounted for as necessary for the development and full exercise of the moral
> powers. The merits of these and other conceptions of the right of property are
> decided at later stages when much more information about a society's circum-
> stances and historical traditions is available.
>
> (*PL* 298; cf. *JF* 114)

In summary, a fundamental principle of justice guarantees a right to "personal property," but no fundamental principle guarantees a right to own natural resources or the means of production (*JF* 138). A right to own personal property is necessary to provide a "fully adequate system of equal liberty," because the "adequate development and exercise of" the first moral power – a capacity for a sense of justice – and the second moral power – the ability to form and pursue a conception of the good over a complete life – demand it. Without a right to acquire and own personal property – including "at least certain forms of real property, such as dwellings and private grounds" (*JF* 114 n. 36) – a citizen would lack "a sufficient material basis for personal independence and a sense of self-respect," and the second moral power would be unacceptably squelched.

But this is not argument. It is announcement. Abstractly, it is not obvious that a society that required all citizens to live as tenants of state-owned dwellings situated amid public grounds would be inimical to the development and exercise of the moral powers (cf. Williamson 2015, 412). It could be that it is a general, psychological truth that ownership of real property forms a social basis of self-respect, despite the fact that nomadic peoples have thrived and some few still thrive. That would, however, constitute a truth too controversial to be available behind the veil of ignorance. What would be available, however, is the truth that in certain cultures homeownership has been prized to such a degree as to become a "social basis of self-respect." A chooser in the original position will not know whether those she represents dwell in such circumstances, in which case she will also not know whether or not the right to become a homeowner constitutes part of a constituent's conception of the good – one which it would not be unreasonable to hold. Therefore, a chooser in the original position might add a right to own real property to the bundle of rights that are basic liberties. This raises the question: Why is what is sauce for the homeowner not also sauce for the factory owner?

WHY NOT CAPITALISM?

We recall that the choice problem in the original position is that of settling on principles of justice to govern society conceived as a fair cooperative scheme for free and equal citizens. The representative citizen, on whose behalf the choice is to be made, is one who possesses the two moral powers: a sense of justice and a conception of the good. Although the precise content of what is to be registered by the sense of justice is shared by all, the conception of good is not.

> [C]itizens view themselves as free [in that] they regard themselves as self-authenticating sources of valid claims ... as being entitled to make claims on their institutions so as to advance their conceptions of the good (provided these conceptions fall within the range permitted by the public conception of justice). These claims citizens regard as having a weight of their own apart from being derived from duties and obligations specified by a political conception of justice, for example, from duties and obligations owed to society [or] the general interests of society.
>
> (*JF* 23–24)

In the original position, if the chooser does not know whether she represents aspiring captains of industry, like Steve Jobs, and if a world in which such persons were deprived of an opportunity to live that dream would not be acceptable to them, the chooser could not fail to choose a principle guaranteeing not only a right to own personal property but a right to own natural resources and means of production (subject, of course, to adjustment to other basic rights and liberties, to achieve the best overall system of them).

One passage (*PL* 141–142) suggests that the parties in the original position do not even know what comprehensive conceptions there are that citizens might wish to adopt. If that were Rawls's meaning, the parties would not know that an entrepreneur's conception of the good was "on offer." The better reading is that, while the whole range of conceivable comprehensive conceptions is not – and cannot be – known to the parties, they must have a general knowledge of kinds of conceptions citizens might hold. The parties could not, for example, assign a priority to liberty of conscience if they were oblivious to the possibility that conscience might figure importantly in a comprehensive conception held by a citizen. As Rawls says,

> [O]ne should keep in mind that the parties seek to secure some particular fundamental interest, even though, given the veil of ignorance, only the general nature of this interest is known to them, for example, that it is a religious interest. Their aim is not merely to be permitted to practice some religion or another, but to practice *some definite religion, that is, their religion, whatever it turns out to be.* In order to secure their unknown but particular interests from the original position, they are led, in view of the strains of commitment, to give precedence to the basic liberties.
>
> (*TJ* 475; emphasis added)

The "strains of commitment" refer to the fact that "the parties cannot agree to a conception of justice if the consequences of applying it may lead to self-reproach should the least happy possibilities be realized" (*TJ* 371). The principles chosen must protect the fundamental interests, come what may, because a party in the original position is conceived as "a person is choosing once and for all the standards which are to govern his life prospects" (*TJ* 153). Thus the parties, as rational and reasonable, "cannot enter into agreements that may have consequences they cannot accept[: t]hey will avoid those that they can adhere to only with great difficulty" (*TJ* 153).

What is true of a religious interest must also be true of any other fundamental aim. From the standpoint of a diligent representative, Steve Jobs's right to own productive means ought to be "recognized as non-negotiable, so to speak" (*PL* 311). "[T]he parties agree to those principles which they believe are best for those they represent as seen from these persons' conception of the good"; and to do so they must have some awareness of the range of conceptions of the good, at least "so far as the parties can know these things" (*PL* 305). The parties "do the best they can to advance the determinate good of the persons they represent" (*PL* 305), whatever that good might be, so long as that good is within reason.

Rawls constructs the idea of "primary goods" to make the choice problem more determinate, but no reason appears why "means of production" would not naturally be understood to belong among them, alongside "free choice of occupation" and "all-purpose means . . . needed to achieve directly or indirectly a wide range of ends, whatever they happen to be" (*PL* 308). Although the parties "do not know the particular final ends and aims these [represented] persons pursue,"

> the parties do know the general structure of rational persons' plans of life (given the general facts about human psychology and the workings of social institutions) and hence the main elements in a conception of the good . . .. Knowledge of these matters goes with their understanding and use of primary goods.
>
> (*PL* 310)

Moreover, the parties' exposure to the "short list of alternatives given by the tradition of moral and political philosophy" (*PL* 305) would itself indicate the kinds of ends – vocational, spiritual, and social – that persons might wish to pursue within a just basic structure. A party in the original position is not held in ignorance of the fact that there are persons who might wish to produce things and to control the means of doing so, any more than a party is held in ignorance of the fact that there are persons who affirm "religious, philosophical, and moral views of our relation to the world." As Rawls might say, "the parties must allow for this possibility" (*PL* 306).

By contrast, no one who has a desire simply to dominate others is represented in the original position until Part Two of the original position procedure, where the problem of stability is pressed further, and the veil of ignorance is lifted enough to expose the "special psychologies" – "vanity and greed, the will to dominate and the desire for glory" (*JF* 36) – that must be adjusted for. So, in Part One, in choosing fundamental principles of justice, no represented person regards public ownership of natural resources and means of production as a primary good, nor does any represented person require it – given a background of fundamental justice – as necessary to avoid an unacceptable outcome for herself. Josef Stalin is not represented; Steve Jobs is.[1] Even though a property-owning economy deprives Stalin of a chance to live his dream, his conception of the good is excluded from

---

[1]   A Charles Fourier or Robert Owen or Henri de Saint-Simon will have representation. But state ownership of the means of production generally is not their dream, nor is it necessary to live it. A comment by Kevin Vallier stimulated me to address this case, and Jeremy Farris pressed my initial response. What about a utopian whose dream is to live in a way that is only possible where the means of production on a wider, non-associational scale are jointly owned? Rawls's view is that such a person would not be represented as such, for she would be taking an interest in the interests of others in a way that Part One of the original position procedure is constructed to avoid.

representation. So there is not really a stalemate a between a wide-private-property-owning system and a wide-social-property system at the stage at which fundamental principles are chosen. The wide-private-property-owning system wins, hands down.

As I will elaborate, the reasons the chooser will not agree to defer the decision to the legislative stage (where majority rules) are much the same as those that incline the chooser to eschew utilitarianism in favor of the two principles: "[T]he parties would prefer to secure their liberties straightaway rather than have them depend upon what may be uncertain and speculative actuarial calculations" (*TJ* 138–139). The "strains of commitment" tend also to rule out the option of deferring the issue of private ownership of productive means to the legislative stage. Rawls writes that parties in the original position

> cannot enter into agreements that may have consequences that they cannot accept. They will avoid those that they can adhere to only with great difficulty. Since the original agreement is final and made in perpetuity, there is no second chance . . .. A person is choosing once and for all the standards which are to govern his life prospects.
>
> (*TJ* 153)

This caution is especially acute given that the parties choose not only for themselves but for their offspring:

> We are more reluctant to take great risks for [our descendants] than for ourselves; and we are willing to do so only when . . . the probable gains, as estimated by objective information [i.e., at this stage, "general facts of human psychology"] are so large that it would appear to them irresponsible to have refused the chance offered even though accepting it should actually turn out badly.
>
> (*TJ* 146–147)

So, a chooser will have to estimate the chance that maintaining a well-ordered society will prove inimical to private ownership of productive means. The chooser will have to estimate the importance of guaranteeing the right to such ownership to descendants whose conception of the good cannot be realized without control of productive facilities. And the chooser will have to, after comparing the two, conclude that the risk to her descendants is not great enough to guarantee them that right – if Rawls is right about this.

Of course, the choosers are willing to accept certain risks of frustrating those whom they represent.

> To be sure, any principle chosen in the original position may require a large sacrifice for some. The beneficiaries of clearly unjust institutions (those principles that have no claim to acceptance) may find it hard to reconcile themselves to the changes that will have to be made.
>
> (*TJ* 154)

A party who must reckon on having a Josef Stalin as a descendant will have no apology to make to him for agreeing to principles that rule out his pursuit of his dream. Proto-Stalin's personal sacrifice, though great, was of a benefit he could enjoy only under clearly unjust principles. There was never a chance that Proto-Stalin's dream of domination would turn out well. His interest is entitled to zero weight. But Proto-Jobs's dream is nothing at all like this.

Another general psychological truth (available behind the veil of ignorance) strengthens the case for choosing a private right to own productive means as a basic liberty. This is what Rawls calls the "Aristotelian Principle":

> [O]ther things being equal, human beings enjoy the exercise of their realized capacities (their innate and trained abilities), and this enjoyment increases the more the capacity is realized, or the greater its complexity.
>
> (*TJ* 374)

For this reason, one proficient at both checkers and chess will prefer chess, and a person having a mathematical bent will rather study algebra than arithmetic. But, by the same token, a person with an entrepreneurial bent will prefer running a factory than a shop, and building computers to building radios. "[I]n the design of social institutions a large place has to be made for [the Aristotelian Principle], otherwise human beings will find their culture and form of life dull and empty ... a tiresome routine" draining them of the "vitality and zest" that enables them to gratify the material needs of society (*TJ* 377). As a "principle of motivation" (*TJ* 375), it tells us that "whenever a person engages in an activity belonging to some chain [of increasingly more inclusive sets of activities] ... he tends to move up the chain" (*TJ* 377). Thus, the smallholder will naturally seek to manage larger and more complex holdings. The businessperson will naturally strive to reach larger and more inclusive markets. And the entrepreneur will naturally seek to master the details of her enterprise and to bring it under her synoptic control. In doing so, she will of course tend to require the assistance of others, in increasing numbers, and they too will respond to the prompting of the Aristotelian Principle, at least up to the point that "the increasing strains" and "burdens of further practice" (*TJ* 376) have counterbalanced it.

Rawls variously describes the Aristotelian Principle as a "postulate," a "principle of motivation," a "psychological law," a "natural fact," a "tendency," and as a "deep psychological fact" that is "susceptible to an evolutionary explanation" while also fitting into a larger account of "our considered judgments of value." Although Rawls stops short of asserting its truth, and acknowledges possible (but merely fanciful) exceptions, he assigns it an important role:

> [B]y assuming the principle we seem able to account for what things are recognized as good for human beings taking them as they are. Moreover, since this principle ties in with the primary good of self-respect, it turns out to have a central position in the moral psychology underlying justice as fairness.
>
> (*TJ* 380)

The Aristotelian Principle, if available to parties in the original position, would encourage the parties to assure for those whom they represent a right to own productive means that is wide enough to satisfy the entrepreneurial genius of a Steve Jobs.

RAWLS'S NON-RESPONSE TO THIS ARGUMENT

What explains Rawls's neglecting to respond to this line of argument? It was not an oversight; in *Political Liberalism* he writes:

> [E]ven if by some convincing philosophical argument – at least convincing to us and a few likeminded others – we could trace the right of private or social ownership back to first principles or to basic rights, there is a good reason for working out a conception of justice which does not do this.

(*PL* 338)

The reason he gives is that it would be better "to look for bases of agreement implicit in the public political culture and therefore in its underlying conceptions of the person and of social cooperation" (*PL* 339). But this begs a crucial question, for it assumes that there is no convincing argument capable of being worked up from that restricted basis, which consists anyway of conceptions that "are obscure and may possibly be formulated in various ways" (*PL* 339). And besides, if Rawls believed that some such "convincing philosophical argument" was possible, why did he not at least sketch how it should go – as, for example, he had sketched how Mill's argument for "plural votes" for the educated would have to go – if it were to be grounded in the conceptions implicit in the public political culture?

A RAWLSIAN EXPLANATION

Although Rawls does not give any, an explanation exists. He was convinced that the incidents of property in productive means could be decomposed into an "entrepreneurial," command-and-control element and a "rentier" economic-rent element. A rent-maximizer's conception of the good could be excluded from representation in the original position as unreasonable, on much the same ground as that on which a world dominator's conception is excluded. Because wealth, in terms of capital and liquid assets, is per se meaningless outside of a distribution of some kind, a citizen whose conception of the good is simply to accumulate as much money as possible would not be represented in Part One of the original position procedure. As Rawls later puts it,

> [A]ssuming that the people in the original position desire wealth does not imply that they desire to be wealthy …. In fact, by postulating the absence of envy and supposing that the parties care only about their absolute share of primary goods and have no concern for their relative place in the distribution of wealth, the desire

to be wealthy is excluded ... the desire for income and wealth is distinct from the desire to be wealthy, and being wealthy is not a primary good.

(*CP* 273)

A party could not take on that representation without violating the stricture, which is in force in Part One of the original position procedure, against taking an interest in the interests of others, and thus also the exclusion of spite as a motive. It makes little sense to want to have as much money as one can without wanting to have more than others. Wanting to have as much money as one can accumulate just for the sake of having that accumulation makes as little sense as, in a related Rawlsian example, indulging a passion for counting all of the blades of grass on one's lawn (*TJ* 379–380).[2] We should exclude pathological explanations of such surprising interests before we concede that, indeed, they constitute the good for the person who is fixated on accumulation.

Another indication that the rentier component of ownership is not a maximand is found in Rawls's remarks about the "socially strategic" nature of primary goods: "if these goods are justly distributed ... then other injustices are unlikely to occur" (*CP* 276). This makes it reasonable to assume

as a general psychological fact, that strong or inordinate desires for more primary goods on the part of individuals and groups, particularly a desire for greater income and wealth and prerogatives of position, spring from insecurity and anxiety. And the same is true for the desire to be wealthy (to have more wealth than others).

(*CP* 277)

In a stable, just society, the Aristotelian Principle will not serve to inflame the desire for wealth for its own sake, and the pursuit of wealth for the sake of dominating others is already ruled out.

But what about a conception of the good that is not essentially comparative, for example, a conception that seeks to maximize ownership of primary goods in absolute terms?[3] I think Rawls's first response would be that "primary goods are clearly not anyone's idea of the basic values of human life and must not be so understood,

---

[2]   The undergraduate Rawls was impressed with Philip Leon's distinction between "egoism" and "egotism":

Egoism for him means a biological striving for a concrete process, for a definite object or state of affairs. By egotism he means something totally different, such as the craving for position, desire for fame and supremacy, and so on. The egotist seeks processes not in themselves, as in the case of pure appetition, but he seeks them as symbols for his superiority and for the sake of his superiority.

(*BI* 150)

Sitting on a cozy pile of cash, viewed intrinsically, can be no more gratifying than sitting on a cozy pile of old newspapers. Assuming that every biological need is assured, the egotist is satisfied with either. The egotist insists on the latter only because of the imagined status the greater accumulation confers.

[3]   Bas van der Vossen pressed me on this point.

however essential their possession" (*PL* 188). Rawls's further response would be that any reasonable conception of the good implicitly or explicitly accepts that there is some adequate or satisfactory level associated with any quantity it might like to maximize. This is what he refers to as "the guaranteeable level," which is stipulated to be "quite satisfactory" (*JF* 98–100). Although "never expressly stated" (*JF* 100 n. 21) in A *Theory of Justice*, it is an assumption that is "crucial for the argument" (*JF* 100) against utilitarianism. Moreover, it is implicit in his replacing the first principle reference to a "most extensive scheme" with a "fully adequate scheme."

A conception of the good consisting solely in the entrepreneurial component of ownership, on the other hand, could not be excluded from representation in the original position.[4] The ability to command and control productive resources is intimately connected with the conditions for exercising the second moral power, the capacity to form and pursue a (not unreasonable) conception of the good. Rawls's argument for "at least minimal" private ownership works equally well for productive as for non-productive objects. In fact, it works even better for productive means.

Here, I take issue with Rawls's distinguished student and interpreter, Joshua Cohen, who writes, "While it is plausible that the right to personal property is a requisite for individual autonomy and the independence required to participate in public deliberation, there is no similarly plausible case that links the right to own the means of production with such participation" (Cohen 1989, 38). If this is intended to supply the argument Rawls failed to give, it is wide of the mark. It downplays the importance of the power to form and pursue one's personal conception of the good, and coordinately elevates the "common good" as the focal topic of democratic deliberation. Why personal property is a prerequisite to autonomy and independence is not explained. Explanations surely exist, but, again, they seem equally available to property in productive means as a prerequisite. Moreover, although the citizen of a well-ordered society must possess a "sense of justice," Rawls plainly states that having a sense of justice is not inconsistent with opting out of political participation altogether.

But Cohen is correct about what Rawls's view was, if not as to why it had to be what it was. Rawls conceived the entrepreneurial or control aspects of ownership as inhering not in capital assets, but in the acquired skills and "natural assets" exercised in marshaling and managing capital assets. To say that a doctor has a basic right to own a stethoscope is to obscure what is important, namely, the excellence that a competent doctor manifests in skillfully making use of a stethoscope and other tools of the trade. A right to have use of a stethoscope in this sense is an aspect of the basic right to occupational choice, which choosers in the original position already recognize as a basic liberty. The right to profit from the sale or lease of medical instruments is another matter. In this sense of ownership, "ownership is not a productive activity," as

---

[4]   The argument here parallels John Tomasi's (2013) case of Amy's Pup-in-the-Tub. See also Gaus 2011.

Cambridge economist Joan Robinson (1966) put it. Rawls coined the term "pure ownership" (*LHPP* 350) to capture the idea.[5] Rawls evidently believed that property ownership in this latter sense was not essential to the exercise of the two moral powers. The distinction between these two aspects of ownership underlies and clarifies Rawls's understanding of socialism, as we will see in the next chapter.

---

[5] Rawls seems to have considered the *Restatement* and the *Lectures on the History of Political Philosophy* as comprising a single work, for in his Introductory Remarks to the latter he writes: "Because the *Restatement* has now been published, I am not including those lectures in this book" (*LHPP* xvii). The *Lectures on the History of Political Philosophy* were not published until 2007, five years after Rawls's death. Editor Sam Freeman's remarks indicate how Rawls's thinking had been evolving:

> The Marx lectures evolved perhaps more than others over the years …. Rawls's interpretation of Marx's Labor Theory of Value seeks to separate its outmoded economics from what he regards as its main aim. He construes it as a powerful response to … liberal and right-wing libertarian conceptions which regard *pure ownership* as making a tangible contribution to production.
>
> (*LHPP* x–xi; emphasis added)

The "outmoded economics" Freeman refers to would more accurately be described as an "outmoded interpretation" of Marx's aim in *Capital*, vol. I. Rawls, instead, followed the interpretation advanced by economist William Baumol (*LHPP* 330, citing Baumol 1974). Against such critics as Paul Samuelson, Baumol argued that *Capital* vol. I was not intended as a theory of price, but as a critique of the Ricardian view of ownership as a productive activity. Rawls was no doubt aware of, and certainly not in agreement with, Mill's suggestion that an owner's decision not to hoard, destroy, or consume a capital asset constitutes a productive activity.

2

Property-Owning Democracy versus Liberal Socialism

Rawls identifies five competing ideal types of regime in Part One of the original position procedure. This comes at the constitutional stage of the four-stage sequence that is needed to assess the workability of the two principles of justice as fairness. More will be said about the four-stage sequence in Chapter 4. The task of this chapter is to inquire into the precise natures of, and the differences between, the two surviving regime types: liberal (democratic) socialism and property-owning democracy. Laissez-faire capitalism, command-economy "state" socialism, and welfare-state capitalism – having failed to make the cut – will be consulted only insofar as they can provide the side-light needed to throw certain features of the two surviving regime types into relief.

This may sound like a straightforward task but it is not. Much of what Rawls says about property-owning democracy is said by way of contrasting it to welfare-state capitalism. His effort is to make the case that, while welfare-state capitalism cannot realize justice as fairness, property-owning democracy can do so. In particular, Rawls takes care to build the case that the economic inequalities property-owning democracy allows can be kept from undermining the fair value of political liberty, which enjoys a priority as a member of the family of basic first-principle liberties. Welfare-state capitalism is, by definition, unconcerned with fair value, and so Rawls helps himself to the assumption that what a regime type is not aiming to achieve it will not achieve. Strictly speaking, all that is needed is the more plausible assumption that by choosing a regime type that excludes a certain goal, while pursuing competing goals, one incurs a greater risk that the excluded goal will not be achieved. There are other aims that welfare-state capitalism lacks: a concern with reciprocity between citizens conceived as free equals, and a concern with fair equality of opportunity, as opposed to the less egalitarian aim of "careers open to talents." But Rawls chiefly concerns himself with making it at least plausible to think that property-owning democracy can secure the fair value it aims for. Rawls sometimes appears to suggest that there is something in the nature of property-owning democracy, as an ideal type, that bolsters fair value – but in fact what he argues is merely that certain pro-fair-value measures are available in a property-owning democracy that are fair-value enhancing. Rawls never states or suggests that these same measures would not be equally available or would be less effective under liberal socialism.

As will emerge in this chapter, Rawls says nothing directly to compare liberal socialism with welfare-state capitalism, in any respect. What he says is that liberal socialism, as an ideal type, can possess the same advantages over welfare-state capitalism that property-owning democracy can. I would not want to suggest that property-owning democracy functions, in effect, as Rawls's stalking-horse for socialism. That would not be a well-founded suspicion. Rawls was, I believe, sincerely holding a place open for some alternative both to socialism in the strict sense and to capitalism: some sort of "third way" that is tempting but not illuminating to analogize to certain post-Thatcher "New Labour" sloganeering.[1] Rawls was also, I will show, uneasy about "fetishizing" the socialist emphasis on common ownership of the means of production. Before getting to these matters, there is the difficult business of nailing down as precisely as possible what Rawls meant by the two terms: liberal socialism and property-owning democracy.

WHAT RAWLS MEANT BY "LIBERAL DEMOCRATIC SOCIALISM"

The ideal regime type that Rawls calls "liberal democratic socialism" is a socialist regime that is both liberal and democratic. Rawls was familiar with, and in accord with, Joseph Schumpeter's thesis that there is no necessary connection between socialism and democracy: a democratic regime need not be socialist, nor need a socialist regime be democratic, much less, need it be liberal (Schumpeter 1950, 250–296; cited at *TJ* 317 n. 18). Conversely, a socialist regime may be both liberal and democratic. In Rawls's view, there is nothing in socialism itself that is inimical either to liberal rights of the individual or to democratic governance. Although he was clear that a socialist regime could be a liberal democratic regime, he was less than clear about what he understood to be the essence, or the essential elements of, socialism itself.

---

[1] Rawls never discusses or mentions either Anthony Giddens or Hugh Gaitskell's protégé Anthony Crosland, both of whom promoted the idea of a "third way" lying somewhere between but alternative to both capitalism and socialism. Ben Rogers reports that Crosland and other British politicians, namely Shirley Williams, David Owen, and Roy Hattersley, invoked *Theory*. But "the Commission on Social Justice, which articulated the thinking behind New Labour's social and economic policies, was quite explicit in rejecting Rawls's strictures against letting individuals profit from their natural skills and endowments" (Rogers 1999, 6). In Rogers's account, the Commission omitted the further qualification "– except insofar as the least-advantaged benefit from resulting inequalities" that is needed to avoid misstating Rawls's view. Gordon Brown, "more interested in theoretical reflection than [Tony] Blair," was careful, later, to avoid this omission (Nuttall 2006, 162); but, in any case it is evident that New Labour did not draw its inspiration from John Rawls.

Socialism is an idea that has a long history, and it has been at the center of both intellectual and political controversy for at least a century and a half. This makes the term "socialism" a familiar one, but its very familiarity makes it less easily to specify its meaning. As Eduard Bernstein, the German social democrat, said at the end of the nineteenth century,

> If we asked a number of people of any class or party to give a brief definition of socialism, most of them would be in some difficulty .... In any case, the most precise characterisation of socialism will be the one that takes the idea of cooperation as its starting point ... a movement toward, or the state of, a cooperative order of society.
>
> (Bernstein 1993 [1899], 98)

Bernstein's remark is suggestive, but it is neither sufficiently precise nor as precise as it might be. Certainly, Rawls took the idea of cooperation as his starting point, but that is hardly enough to warrant counting him as a socialist. Conceiving justice in terms of an agreement upon fair terms of cooperation indeed enables a powerful argument in favor of socialism. This is especially so if this conception of cooperation is one that is already latent in the publicly political culture of constitutional democracies, and thus need not be introduced from an exogenous source. But the idea of socialism itself cannot usefully be identified with whatever theory might be supported in this way.

Unlike capitalism, socialism is mentioned by name in *A Theory of Justice* (*TJ* 235, 239–242, 247–249). Rawls states that "under socialism the means of production and natural resources are publicly owned" (*TJ* 242). But other remarks suggest that socialism, in his view, need only consist of a much larger "size of the public sector ... as measured by the fraction of total output produced by state-owned firms and managed either by state officials or by workers' councils" (*TJ* 235), remaining vague about how far this must go, beyond state ownership of public utilities and transportation. From this passage it is easy to conclude that for Rawls, "[t]he key difference between a liberal socialist state and a property-owning democracy is that the former has much more extensive public ownership of the means of production and natural resources than the latter" (MacLeod 2014, 181 n. 3). Rawls does refer to a "classical distinction" of this kind (*TJ* 235), by way of making the point that socialism as he understands it is not inimical to the use of markets. For this reason, it is not unfair to fault Rawls for having failing to stick to a precise definition of what socialism is (cf. Schweikert 1978, 1).

The desultoriness of Rawls's discussion of socialism in *A Theory of Justice* accounts for a number of separate misunderstandings about what Rawls understood it to consist in. For example, his rumination about the possibilities of workplace democracy have led some to conclude that Rawlsian socialism is "anti-statist" to the extent of making a "rigid demand for universal worker self-management" (Taylor 2014, 437 n. 19, 451; Gray 1989, 175). Some Rawlsians may make this demand (e.g., Joshua Cohen 1989, 40), but Rawls himself does not.

True, where Rawls conjectures, in *Theory*, that "a liberal socialist regime can also answer the two principles of justice," he says that "[w]e have only to suppose that the means of production are publicly owned *and* that firms are managed by worker's councils say, or by agents appointed *by them*" (*TJ* 248; emphases added). And, in the *Restatement*, he says that "[w]hile under socialism the means of production are owned by society, we suppose that, in the same way that political power is shared among a number of political parties, economic power is dispersed among firms, *as when, for example*, a firm's direction and management is elected by, if not directly in the hands of, its own workforce" (*JF* 138; emphasis added). In the latter passage, Rawls is mixing up several distinct ideas. One is of an economy featuring numerous independent firms, none of them dominant. Analogizing this situation to a system of political parties is highly misleading. If no party has an outright majority, coalitions between parties are necessary and desirable. Coalitions between firms in the economy, however, stand on an altogether different footing. A majority coalition in parliamentary politics is called a government. In the business sector, a majority coalition is called a cartel. Aside from this, workplace democracy within firms has no tendency, by itself, to disperse economic power across firms.

In any event, when placed in context, these remarks about management cannot state a demand of firms that stand upon the economy's "commanding heights" (to make this image precise, more will follow). On those heights, Rawls could not have intended as great a degree of firm autonomy as the language could suggest. A moment's reflection on what an "anti-statist," worker-managed financial sector would look like indicates that Rawls had no such thing in mind. His remarks, then, can best be understood as illustrative of various ways in which a socialist regime might organize itself democratically.

It is not credible that Rawls intended a strict demand for worker management anywhere other than the commanding heights, either, as essential to a socialist regime satisfying the two principles of justice. Think of a simple case: a farmer needs the help of two laborers. It is preposterous to think that the justice of the basic structure of society demands that the laborers be able to outvote the farmer who has hired them for the season. Rawls repeatedly states that the principles of justice "may not work for the rules and practices of private associations or ... less comprehensive groups ... voluntary cooperative arrangements [or] contractual agreements" (*TJ* 7). Rawls recognizes that certain types of private associations that constitute part of basic structure, such as the family, tend to impede the realization of justice. They are not on that ground necessarily to be abolished or to be internally governed by the two principles of justice as fairness. In any case, Rawls cannot be read as regarding worker management at any scale as essential to socialism *generally*, for it is not a necessary feature of the variety of socialism Rawls referred to as "state socialism with a command economy" (*JF* 136). In socialist societies of this kind, the means of production are socially owned but they are directed by a central bureaucracy or its delegates.

Industrial, or "shop-floor," democracy – which is more properly associated with the syndicalism of Proudhon, Sorel, and Bakunin – is an ideal that many socialists also hold, as Rawls was no doubt aware. In one passage – perhaps resonating to Schumpeter's (1954, 454–457) term, "associationist socialism" – Rawls even refers to "associational socialism" (CP 277) as the contrasting counterpart to property-owning democracy. But Rawls was not a socialist of this kind. Rawls was likely familiar with dismissals of syndicalism as unworkable utopian nonsense (e.g., Schumpeter 1954, 456–457), but this is beside the point. Even at the level of mid-sized enterprises, a demand for universal worker self-management would impinge upon first-principle liberties of occupational choice and association, and would impair the division of labor that Rawls recognizes as necessary in order to achieve efficiencies. Of course, the first-principle liberties are a family, and no member within the family is absolute. Each is subject to adjustment for the sake of the full adequacy of the package. There are, admittedly, passages in which Rawls could be mistakenly thought to have suggested that freedom of occupational choice and freedom of association might, given certain facts, have to yield space to a competing, first-principle "equal right to participate in the control" of the enterprise in which one works. In addition to those discussed above, here is another:

> [There are t]wo wider conceptions of the right of property as a basic liberty .... One conception extends this right [of personal property] to include ... the right to own means of production and natural resources. On the other conception, the right of property includes the *equal right to participate in the control* of the means of production and natural resources, which are to be socially owned. (PL 298; emphasis added)

But, again, the participation in control that is the citizen's equal right, on this latter conception, is not stated to be necessarily any more direct than participation in representative democracy at the governmental level. Nor is it necessarily exercised at the level of the economic unit or firm in which the citizen is employed. Recall that passage, cited earlier, that refers to socialist firms "managed *either* by state officials *or* by workers' councils" (TJ 235; emphasis added).

Rawls also did not equate public ownership with state ownership in the sense of unmediated central control. He shared James Meade's (1964, 67) confidence that the allocative efficiencies of "free" markets can be had without compromising core socialist commitments. Rawls expressly stated his conviction that all of the valuable aspects of markets are fully consistent, at least in theory, with public ownership of the means of production (TJ 239–241; JF 239–240). Rawls was familiar with Marxian economist John Roemer's (1994a, 1994b) proposal that private goods and wages be allocated by market pricing, and private goods be produced by profit-maximizing firms, whose net earnings are distributed as a social dividend to all rather than retained privately: the state supervises these aspects and manages the financial "commanding heights" by offering easier credit to democratically preferred enterprises.

The essence of socialism is public ownership of the means of production. It is so central that the preeminent historian of Marxism, Lesek Kołakowski, marked the mercurial variety of pre-Marxian socialist thought with reference to social ownership of the means of production as socialism's defining tenet:

> At the time when Marx came into the field as a theoretician … socialist ideas already had a long life behind them. If we sought to provide a general definition of socialism in historical as opposed to normative terms, i.e. to identify the common features of the ideas that went by that name in the first half of the nineteenth century, we should find the result extremely jejune and imprecise …. Beyond the general conception of equality, socialist programmes and ideas differed in every respect. *Not all of them even proposed to abolish private ownership in the means of production.*
>
> (Kołakowski 2005 [1978] 150–151; emphasis added)

The absence of unanimity on what is essential is what led Kołakowski to observe the uselessness of a historical rather than a prescriptive definition.[2] With whatever fervor a doctrine embraces equality as an ideal, if it leaves the means of production in private hands, it is not socialist.

An emphasis on common ownership of the means of production is coeval with the spread of socialism in the 1830s, when the Saint-Simonists called for state control of the allocation and direction of *"les instrumens du travail,"* the means of production, implying outright ownership. It was their activity that propagated the idea of socialism throughout the educated classes of Europe (Kołakowski 2005 [1978] 156–158; Gray 1968 [1946], 4, 163–166, 168; Huberman 1968, 51–52). Mill, writing in 1848, traced the origin of the term farther back:

> The word Socialism, which originated among the English Communists, and was assumed by them as a name to designate their own doctrine, is now, on the Continent, employed in a larger sense: not necessarily implying Communism, or the entire abolition of private property, but applied to any system which requires that the land and the instruments of production should be the property, not of individuals, but of communities or associations, or of the government.
>
> (Mill 2006, 203)

Rawls was a careful reader of Mill and recommended Mill's writings on socialism to students in his course on Modern Political Philosophy (*LHPP* 314).

Marx and Engels, of course, posited public ownership of the means of production as the foundation stone of socialism (Kołakowski 2005 [1978] 357–358). (As the historian of socialism, Anthony Gray, remarked, "The post-Marxian development

---

[2] In the course of summarizing the politics of Wilhelmine Germany, Rawls remarks, "[T]he social democrats [i.e., the Socialist party] *always* insisted on the nationalization of industry and dismantling of the capitalist system" (*LHPP* 9; emphasis added). The point here touches the nature of socialism, not on intransigence as a parliamentary tactic, which Rawls deplored. Chapter 12 deals with Rawls's view of the problem of transition.

of socialism has been entirely conditioned by Marx (1968 [1946], 6).) This was the tenet that was central to defining socialism for socialists in the United States during Rawls lifetime: socialism "is a system in which, in contrast to capitalism, there is common ownership of the means of production" (Huberman 1968, 51). Taking common ownership of the means of production to be the focal concept best accords with the procedural role Rawls assigns to the major traditional positions represented in the modern history of political philosophy. It is simply not possible, at the outset, to assemble an exhaustive list of all possible conceptions of property, or all possible ideal types of regime, any more than it is to assemble an exhaustive list of all possible conceptions of justice itself. Rawls's resort to the device of "simply taking as given a short list of traditional conceptions" (*TJ* 106) and proceeding to evaluate them pairwise is the natural, and perhaps the only manageable, order of business.[3]

The "Means of Production"

"The means of production" is a concept that is often assumed to have been original with Marx and Engels (1978 [1849], 207–208), rather than the Saint-Simonians, but Rawls does not acknowledge a source or elaborate the idea.[4] The proximate source might just as well have been Clause Four of the constitution of the British Labour Party, drafted by the Fabian socialist Sidney Webb, and adopted in 1918, which aimed

> [t]o secure for the workers by hand or by brain the full fruits of their industry and the most equitable distribution thereof that may be possible upon the basis of the common ownership of the means of production, and the best obtainable system of popular administration and control of each industry or service.
>
> (Elliott 1993, 34)

In passing, I note that the phrase "full fruits of their industry" seems to be an implicit reference to a Marxian surplus-value conception of exploitation, which regards the capitalist's profit as the difference between the value the worker creates and the wage the capitalist pays. Rawls discusses but nowhere endorses this tenet, or any

---

[3] There is an assumption that the relative merits of, say, ideal regime type A and ideal regime type B will remain what they are even if some other ideal regime type C is introduced. Noting this does not constitute an objection to Rawls's procedure until some C is specified. Some – Kevin Vallier (2014) and Christian Schemmel (2015), for example – have argued that Rawls gives short shrift to welfare-state capitalism, and this points up the possibility that Rawls, on further reflection, would have given greater weight to the arguable efficiency advantages of welfare-state capitalism, which, possibly, property-owning democracy could match better than socialism can. These possibilities cannot be excluded, but for reasons of economy of exposition I have to dismiss them from further discussion here.

[4] Although not referring specifically to Rawls, Marxian political economist Wolfgang Streek observes that "the academic-political establishment of the leading capitalist power in the 1950s and 1960s thought it natural to draw on key concepts (whether correctly or incorrectly understood) of Marxian political economy" (2014, xv–xvi n. 16).

transaction-specific corrective to the implied injustice of the wage relation, as essential to socialism as he conceives it. In fact, he claims that the objection by "some socialists" to the labor market as "inherently degrading" is answered by any regime that is well-ordered by the two principles of justice as fairness: "[G]iven the requisite background institutions, the worst aspects of so-called wage slavery are removed" (*TJ* 248). Furthermore,

> *It seems improbable* that the control of economic activity by the bureaucracy that would be bound to develop in a socially regulated system (whether centrally directed or guided by agreements reached by industrial associations) would be *more just* on balance than control exercised by means of prices (assuming as always the necessary framework). To be sure a competitive scheme is impersonal and automatic in the details of its operation; its particular results do not express the conscious decisions of individuals. But in many respects this is a virtue of the arrangement; and the use of the market system does not imply a lack of reasonable human autonomy.
>
> (*TJ* 248; emphases added)

It would be a mistake to read this passage as a Rawlsian conjecture that market wages are at least as "just on balance" as wages in planned economies. Bear in mind the stipulation: "assuming as always the necessary framework," namely institutions and a basic structure that realize justice as fairness. As I will argue subsequently, Rawls did not simply assume that formally democratic liberal constitutional regimes are equally likely to satisfy the demands of justice as fairness. What Rawls is concerned to do here is to suggest that the notion of a "fair wage," like that of a "fair price" generally, is a will o' the wisp that it would be foolish to recruit a bureaucracy to pursue. Rawls was not a Marxist;[5] even so, Rawls was impressed enough by Marx's analysis of the wage relation to struggle with the question of its interpretation (*LHPP* 328–332).

Historical Digression

Now, an insufficiently brief historical digression will set the context of, and suggest some possible influences on, Rawls's thinking. Social ownership of the means of production is commonly taken in the sense of the "nationalization" of major industries – with or without compensation. In Great Britain, nationalization of industry was for decades a goal of the Labour Party, as the natural implementation of Clause Four of its constitution. Whether or not Britain was heading toward nationalization

---

[5] "Marxist" is a label that Marx himself is said to have disavowed. "Accusing Guesde and Lafargue of 'revolutionary phrase-mongering' and of denying the value of reformist struggles, Marx made his famous remark that, if their politics represented Marxism, *'ce qu'il y a de certain c'est que moi, je ne suis pas Marxiste'* ('what is certain is that I myself am not a Marxist') www.marxists.org/archive/marx/works/1880/05/parti-ouvrier.htm (last accessed December 24, 2016).

of the major means of production anyway, World War II frog-marched it in that direction. In 1941, George Orwell (1941, 73) wrote, "the drowsy years have ended ... .. We cannot win the war without introducing Socialism, nor establish Socialism without winning the war." What was it, this socialism toward which history was leading Britain? "Socialism is usually defined as 'common ownership of the means of production'. Crudely: the State, representing the whole nation, owns everything ... This does *not* mean that people are stripped of private possessions such as clothes and furniture, but it *does* mean that all productive goods, such as land, mines, ships and machinery, are the property of the State. The State is the sole large-scale producer" (Orwell 1941, 48; emphasis in the original). The ultimate aim is a classless society, and common ownership of large-scale productive assets is the means. "Once that is done it becomes possible to eliminate the class of mere owners who live not by virtue of anything they produce but by the possession of title-deeds and share-certificates" (Orwell 1941, 76–77). The two conceptions – common ownership of the means of production, and a classless society – are more closely related than means and end. They are, as it were, two sides of the same coin. A classless society, in the socialist sense, is a society in which the means of production are commonly owned. A society free of exploitation, in the relevant sense, is a society in which no one is forced to sell their labor power to another who is able, through the institution of private property, to exact a rent from them as a condition of their access to the means they need in order to live productively (Shaw 2006 [1884], 15–45).

Austrian economist Joseph Schumpeter, writing in 1938, outlined a socialist program for Britain in greater detail than Orwell did, but along the same lines:

> In [present] conditions a policy of socialization is conceivable that, by carrying out an extensive program of nationalization might on the one hand accomplish a big step toward socialism and, on the other hand, make it possible to leave untouched and undisturbed for an indefinite time all interests and activities not included in that program .... The following departments of business activity could be socialized without serious loss of efficiency ....

> First, the banking apparatus of England is no doubt quite ripe for socialization .... Second, the insurance business is an old candidate for nationalization .... Third, few people would be disposed to make great difficulties over railroads or even trucking. In land transportation is in fact the most obvious field for successful state management. Fourth, nationalization of mining .... Fifth, the nationalization of the production, transmission and distribution of electric current .... Sixth, socialization of the iron and steel industry .... Seventh, ... building and building materials .... This is not necessarily all. But any step beyond this program would have to justify itself by special, mostly non-economic reasons – the armament or key industries, movies, shipbuilding, trade in foodstuffs being possible instances.

> (Schumpeter 1950, 229–231)

The question that springs to any reader's mind is: Where does it end? Schumpeter (1950, 231) counseled that "those seven items are enough to digest for quite a time to come, enough also to make a responsible socialist, if he gets so much done, bless his work and accept the concessions that it would at the same time be rational to make outside of the nationalized sector."

Labour came to power in 1945, and under Clement Attlee – socialism's least appreciated hero – Orwell's and Schumpeter's prescriptions for nationalization of the railroads, banking, electrical power generation, steel, trucking, and coal became realities. At the end of 1946, Anthony Gray, who had just completed decades of work on a history of socialism, was not content merely to voice "a humble and hesitant doubt as to whether the social and industrial build-up which we are now realising is socialism at all" (Gray 1968 [1946], xvi). He went further: "[D]o not let us call this strange jungle of 'autonomous' corporations by the name of Socialism, or delude ourselves into imagining that the new order of things which we are fashioning, without any clear perception of what it is we are fashioning, would in any way represent the realisation of the socialist dreams and visions of the past" (Gray 1968 [1946], xvii). Dreams of revolutionary rather than evolutionary change were disappointed, of course. But Gray's doubts had to do with the democratic bona fides of the administrative structure of the new British order, rather than as to whether common ownership had been effected. True, one might worry whether a factory manager who dictates her own salary is effectively extracting the same kind of rent as a private owner; but the members of the Coal Board were never so free as that. In any case, the derogatory expression "creeping socialism," coined by right-wing ideologues in the United States, seemed to fit.

Schumpeter – avowedly not an advocate of socialism – was confident until his death in 1951 that the process of digesting the seven sectors he named would proceed undisturbed (Schumpeter 1950, 417). But the British voting public grew wearier of continued austerity measures, such as rationing, as general economic conditions improved. Labour's loss of power in 1951 was seen by "revisionist" leaders in the party as an indication that further nationalization along the lines of Clause Four was an issue that favored the Tories, who, once back in power, had defied Schumpeter's forecast by promptly denationalizing trucking and steel. Other Labourites wanted nationalization to proceed. The 1952 party congress was torn over the issue whether to draw up a list of industries to be nationalized over the next five years, along with renationalizing of steel and trucking. It was assumed that the Tories would continue to denationalize. This did not happen, not immediately anyway, nor did the economic downturn that Labourites expected would follow.

Labour's loss again in 1955 saw the ascendency of the revisionists, including Hugh Gaitskell, who became party leader. After yet another loss in 1959, Gaitskell denounced Clause Four as itself an anachronism and a hindrance to returning to power. This assured that Clause Four would be an issue of continuing controversy (especially for those who read it – with unnecessary rigor – as stating "a commitment to the eventual abolition of private enterprise in total" [Coates 1975, 76–80, 93]).

Where was John Rawls, about this time? After the war he married Margaret ("Mardy") Warfield Cox and finished his Ph.D. And then, after intensive postdoctoral reading of economic theory in Princeton, he took a Fulbright fellowship at Christ Church College, Oxford, for the academic year 1952–1953 (Pogge 2007, 16). This coincided with the tail end of Labour's "halcyon days of 1945–51" (Elliott 1993, 22). During this year-or-so interval of British history, Elizabeth II ascended to the throne upon the death of George VI, the rationing of tea and sweets ended, Britain detonated its first thermonuclear bomb (three years after Stalin detonated his), the "Cambridge spies" Guy Burgess and Donald Maclean defected to Moscow, the Great Fog killed thousands of Londoners, Watson and Crick announced the discovery of the double-helical structure of DNA, and Marshal Josip Tito of Yugoslavia became the first Communist head of state to be received officially in the United Kingdom. Any perusal of the common-room periodicals and any explanation of British politics at high table would have familiarized Rawls with the Clause Four controversy, and also with the dissension within the Labour Party over further nationalization of industry, and the Tory determination to roll it back.[6]

It would be interesting to know whether Rawls kept an eye on this specific issue in British politics after his return to the United States. His year at Oxford was "one of the most formative of his long career" (Freeman 2007, 3) and "the philosophically most important for Rawls since … his first year as a philosophy student" (Pogge 2007, 16). Rawls returned to Oxford to lecture in 1978, 1986, and 1993. He took a keen interest in the English social and political context of Hobbes's and Locke's political philosophizing, and he takes particular care to argue that their theories cannot otherwise be understood.

> The early twentieth-century philosopher R. G. Collingwood said: "The history of political theory is not the history of different answers to one and the same question, but the history of a problem more or less constantly changing, whose solution was changing with it." This interesting remarks seems to exaggerate a bit, since there are certain basic questions that we keep asking, such as:
> What is the nature of a legitimate political regime?

---

[6] Rawls had long-standing friendships with socialist-minded philosophers J. O. Urmson and Stuart Hampshire. They may very well have passed along their views of the significance of the tumultuous Labour Party conference at Morecambe in September 1952. At the conference, Attlee was unable to suppress controversy between two factions, the Bevanites – followers of the Welsh firebrand Nye Bevan – who favored pressing onward with further nationalization, and the Hugh Gaitskell camp, the "consolidationists," who did not. But the consolidationists did not favor denationalization, even to appease the United Kingdom's American creditors. Both parties were frustrated by the fact that nationalization per se had not reduced inequality, for the nationalizations had been compensated, not confiscatory (Jackson 2007, 159–163, 208). After a surprise Bevanite sweep in the vote for leadership offices, Gaitskell denounced Communist influence at the conference and ridiculed the Bevanites – who included future prime minister Harold Wilson – as "a group of frustrated journalists." It was, in the words of future Labour leader Michael Foot, "rowdy, convulsive, vulgar, splenetic, threatening at moments to collapse into an irretrievable brawl" (Harris 1982, 503ff).

What are the grounds and limits of political obligation?
What is the basis of rights, if any? and the like.

But these questions, when they come up in different historical contexts, can be taken in different ways and have been seen by different writers from different points of view, given their political and social worlds and their circumstances and problems as they saw them. To understand their works, then, we must identify those points of view and how they shape the way the writer's questions are interpreted and discussed.

(LHPP 103)

In his conception of a property-owning democracy, Rawls draws on the work of a twentieth-century British thinker: economist James Meade, whom I will shortly turn to. Meade wrote with the circumstances and problems Britain faced at mid-century paramount in his thinking – defining his point of view, although not, of course, fully determining his answers. But in Rawls's published work there is scarcely any reference to the politics of twentieth-century (or even post-Victorian) Britain. One perhaps significant exception is Rawls's passing reference to the fact that "a liberal socialist regime . . . was envisaged by the English Labor [*sic*] party and the German Social Democrats" (*LHPP* 150 n. 12). Possibly, he believed that these "political and social worlds" and his own were so similar that the reader of the future, who finds Rawls instructive, will understand that his world and Meade's – and even Marx and Mill's – were sufficiently similar that a common set of problems, and a common context, would be sufficiently evident. Whatever the case, Rawls was surely aware that the phrase "ownership of the means of production" is heavily freighted with historical and emotional associations.

The "Commanding Heights" of the Economy

In his use of the phrase "the means of production," what Rawls surely had in mind was only the "commanding heights of the means of production," a term that can be traced to Lenin's New Economic Policy in the 1920s.

> What is the plan or idea or essence of [the New Economic Policy (NEP)]? (α) Retention of the land in the hands of the state; (β) *the same* for all commanding heights in the sphere of means of production (transport, etc.); (γ) freedom of trade in the sphere of petty production; (δ) state capitalism in the sense of attracting private capital (both concessions and mixed companies).

(Lenin 1971, 585–587; emphasis in original)

As such, the means of production would not include means applied in small-scale production. This is consistent with Orwell's commonsense notion of the socialist state as owner of the "large-scale" productive assets.

In the introduction to the French translation of *A Theory of Justice* (1987), Rawls writes that "justice as fairness includes . . . no natural right to private property in the means of production (although it does include a right to personal property as necessary for citizens' independence and integrity)" (*CP* 420). Rawls can only mean *major* means of production here because, obviously, the same grounds for a basic right to personal (and real) property are a fortiori grounds for a basic right of a worker to her tools.[7] I will use the term "means of production" without always repeating this restriction: it is to be understood.

Rawls (not unlike Marx) was outspoken about the advantages of markets in allocating social resources. The market "allows the decisions of households to regulate the items to be produced for private purposes" (*TJ* 272), and in that way a competitive market for consumer goods indirectly determines the allocation of productive resources without requiring the massive informational bureaucracy that a centrally planned economy needs. But Rawls did not conceive of socialism as inherently averse to markets. He made it explicit that market devices are equally available to both socialist and property-owning regimes, and keyed on the difference between the allocative and the distributive function of market prices, including those for labor. The allocative function uses market pricing to achieve efficiency, while the distributive function concerns "determining the income to be received by individuals in return for what they contribute" (*TJ* 241).

> Since under socialism the means of production and natural resources are publicly owned, the distributive function is greatly restricted, whereas a private-property system uses prices in varying degrees for both purposes.
>
> (*TJ* 242)

Understanding "the means of production" in the "commanding heights" sense, we see that Rawls means that socialism does not permit a private rent to accrue from pure ownership of major productive assets, ever, at all. The distributive function of capital ownership is "greatly" restricted, that is, restricted entirely to petty production.

Taking the term "the means of production" in the "commanding heights" sense is the only plausible reading of Rawls. We cannot assume that Rawls was aware of the role that the "commanding heights" qualification played in the running debates within the Labour Party in the 1950s and 1960s; but that debate disclosed implications and complications built into the concept itself. Peter Sedgwick writes:

> The manner in which the Clause Four question was handled (at the 1960 Conference) was to set the tone for the consistent fudging and befuddlement that characterized Labor [*sic*] Party policy decisions in the later Sixties. For Clause Four was not, in the end, removed from the constitution; it was permitted to remain, with a parallel statement of aims declaring for "an expansion of common ownership sufficient to give the community power over the *commanding heights*

---

[7]   As Kevin Vallier points out, this is an "important failure of Rawls's, because the term 'means of production' is a very open-ended term. My education is a means of production, and so is [a] shovel [or] my lawnmower if I mow my neighbor's yard for money. I think Rawls has in mind something like the 'commanding heights' of capital in the economy" (Personal communication).

of the economy" – a commitment loose and vague enough to please everybody and leave the leadership with the maximum latitude in interpretation.

(Sedgwick 1970, 79–80; emphasis added; see also Miliband 1973, 344–349)

This much is informative, but Sedgwick continues:

The phrase "the commanding heights" typifies, in its pregnant vacuity, its slippery indefiniteness and its trancelike, Utopian quality, the entire bent of Labor policy-language in the present epoch. It was proposed, at a meeting of Labor's Executive in 1960, by Harold Wilson. Evasion as a political style was laid down by evasion's master, shortly to become the Party leader.

(Sedgwick 1970, 80)

The implicit comparison between Wilson and Lenin is, I assume, one that Sedgwick did not intend. Interestingly, the 2015 selection of Jeremy Corbyn as Labour Party leader revived the Clause Four controversy in the United Kingdom.[8] In any case, my purpose here is to defend neither the utility nor the precision of the terms "means of production" and "commanding heights." Rather, it is to show what role these ideas might have to play in Rawls's thinking. In certain respects, Rawls might have counted the alleged "pregnant vacuity ... slippery indefiniteness and ... trancelike, Utopian quality" possessed by the concept to be features rather than bugs. One of the hallmarks of Rawls's theorizing is an unwillingness to insist on regimenting usefully loose conceptions prematurely or unnecessarily, for example: "[A]dmittedly the concept of the basic structure is somewhat vague ... but it would be premature to worry about this matter here" (*TJ* 8). The concept of the basic structure remained imprecise enough to ascertain whether it could be fitted together with the other fundamental ideas (cf. *JF* 12, 57). The "commanding heights of the economy" and "basic structure of society" are notions whose vagueness is forgiven to the extent that the overall theory to which they belong is one that, on reflection, we find to be a success.

In this connection, it is important to appreciate that the term "the commanding heights" – and thus also the term "the means of production" – does not have a fixed designation. They, like "the least advantaged" members of society, are not Kripkean "rigid designators" (cf. *JF* 59 n. 26). Scale, natural resources, existing infrastructure, and comparative advantages, and technological development would be relevant to applying the concept in particular places at particular times. The British coal industry in 1950 stood on the commanding heights: it has ceased to do so. One fixed point, however – which I will simply state as too obvious to require argument – is the place of banks and related financial institutions on those commanding

---

[8] Compare "Jeremy Corbyn suggests he would bring back Labour's nationalising clause IV," *The Guardian*, August 9, 2015 03:59 EDT with "Jeremy Corbyn denies he would bring back Labour's nationalising clause IV," *The Guardian*, August 9, 2015 07:05 EDT.

heights.[9] Paradigm examples are the too-big-to-fail or "systemically important finan-cial institutions," which in the United States are singled out as subject to certain regulations under Section 113 of the Dodd-Frank Act. Put abstractly, the command-ing heights of the economy are those areas that most citizens, most of the time, must have access to in order to be productive, cooperating members of society, and are therefore likely to be unfair to allot to any private person or entity as a source of rent. I say "likely to be unfair" because an argument is needed. If there is a sufficiently good argument, judged in reflective equilibrium, then the incentives that are allowed under the difference principle cannot consist in or be convertible into ownership of this type of asset.

RAWLS'S UNDERSTANDING OF "PROPERTY-OWNING DEMOCRACY"

Rawls credits James Meade, winner of the Nobel Memorial Prize in Economic Sciences, and Oxford, LSE, and Cambridge economist, for the term "property-owning democracy" (*TJ* 241–242; *JF* 135 n. 1) and "some of its features" (*CP* 419 n. 7). Rawls clearly intends it to be understood as "an alternative to capitalism" (*JF* 135–136) and also, as he rather belatedly made clear, as an alternative to welfare-state capitalism, the type of capitalism he is taken by many to be defending.

In his first lecture on Marx, Rawls says, "I focus on his ideas about right and justice, particularly as they apply to the question of the justice of capitalism as a social system based on private property in the means of production" (*LHPP* 320). Once capitalism is defined this way, a reflex reaction is to ask how property-owning democracy could fail to be a species of – rather than an alternative to – capitalism. The answer to this begins by noticing that property-owning democracy *permits*, but is not *based on*, private ownership of productive means. Property-owning democracy permits private ownership of the means of production only in limited – but never specified – circumstances. But even where such ownership is permitted, society is not *based* on it. The question a Rawlsian has to ask is how private ownership of the major means of production is to be tolerated as an expedient without being allowed to shape society so extensively as to become its basis. This question is the focus of Chapter 10.

Property-Owning Democracy as an Alternative to Capitalism

Compared to capitalism and socialism, property-owning democracy was not in 1971 and is not now as widely known a conception. The term "property-owning

---

[9] I set aside the question of what else stands on those heights now. Extraction industries such as Exxon and Gazprom are obvious candidates. Also obvious, but requiring subtler analysis, are cases like Wal-Mart, Amazon, Google, and Facebook. "Big" does not necessarily mean "a means of production," so Coca-Cola, MacDonald's, and big tobacco raise different questions, which might not be questions of justice in Rawls's sense.

democracy" has a history, which I will set out in the following section. That history does little to illuminate Rawls's meaning. In his most extended discussion, in the *Restatement*, Rawls proceeds to define property-owning democracy by contrasting it to welfare-state capitalism. He says little by way of contrasting property-owning democracy with socialism, beyond telling us that in a property-owning democracy the means of production need not be socially owned, although they may be.

Rawls says that welfare-state capitalism and property-owning democracy "allow private property in productive assets. This may tempt us to think they are much the same. They are not" (*JF* 139), and in a footnote he adds: "As I have said, a serious fault of *Theory* is that it failed to emphasize this contrast" (*JF* 139 n. 5; presumably referring to *JF* 8 n. 7). But what is the contrast?

> One major difference is this: the background institutions of property-owning dem-
> ocracy work to disperse the ownership of wealth and capital, and thus to prevent a
> small part of society from controlling the economy, and indirectly, political life as
> well. By contrast, welfare-state capitalism permits a small class to have a near
> monopoly of the means of production.
>
> (*JF* 139)

Private ownership of the means of production is permitted under property-owning democracy, but its "background institutions" do not permit "a small class" to "have a near monopoly" of the means of production. The "background institutions" do this by dispersing "ownership of wealth and capital." Welfare-state capitalism, by contrast, allows a near monopoly to arise, and thus allows "a small class" of owners to control not only the economy but "political life" as well. If the problem were one of monopoly or near monopoly, presumably welfare-state capitalism would already, to preserve its contrast to laissez-faire capitalism, include institutional safeguards. But Rawls overlooks this point and moves immediately to the question of the means by which property-owning democracy blocks the tendency of capital accumulation to monopolize both economic and political life.

> Property-owning democracy avoids this, not by the redistribution of income to those
> with less *at the end of each period*, so to speak, but rather by ensuring the
> widespread ownership of productive assets and human capital (that is, education
> and trained skills) *at the beginning of each period*.
>
> (*JF* 139; emphases added)

The idea of introducing "periods" of time in this way is a curious innovation (one might even say "epicycle") in Rawls.[10] I will have more to say about it later. In the present context, it serves to mark two distinct ways of viewing the less fortunate.

---

[10] Compare the time-related principle of rationality Rawls calls the principle of continuity: "[S]ince a plan is a scheduled sequence of activities, earlier and later activities are bound to affect one another. The whole plan has a certain unity, a dominant theme. There is not, so

Note here two very different conceptions of the aim of the background adjustments over time. In welfare-state capitalism the aim is that none should fall below a decent minimum standard of life, one in which their basic needs are met, and all should receive certain protections against accident and misfortune, for example, unemployment compensation and medical care. The redistribution of income serves this purpose when, at the end of each period, those who need assistance can be identified.

(*JF* 139–140)

To interject: Rawls should not be understood to be making the odd suggestion that it cannot be known that a person needs insurance against risk until that risk has befallen him. He is, rather, working toward formulating a difference in the expressive content of two different institutional orientations. In a welfare-state capitalist society,

> given the lack of background justice and inequalities in income and wealth, there may develop a discouraged and depressed underclass many of whose members are chronically dependent on welfare [and which] feels left out and does not participate in the public political culture.

(*JF* 140)

The "lack of background justice" refers here to welfare-state capitalism's rejection of fair value of political liberty as a value. Welfare-state capitalism is not concerned to prevent the political disengagement of such an underclass. Its only concern is "at the end of each period" to identify who is in need of public assistance and to redistribute sufficient resources to meet basic needs. The attitude of a property-owning democracy is, so to speak, proactive rather than reactive, to "from the outset, put into the hands of citizens generally, and not only of a few, sufficient productive means for them to be fully cooperating members of society on a footing of equality" (*JF* 140). But a defender of welfare-state capitalism would interject two thoughts. First, it is not the intention to deprive anyone of productive assets in the ideal description of this type of regime. Second, being put in possession of means at the beginning of a period is not itself a guarantee that they will be used successfully: at the end of each period, there will be winners and losers. Rawls confesses as much: in a property-owning democracy, "we hope that an underclass will not exist; or, if there is a small such class, that it is the result of social conditions we do not know how to change, or perhaps cannot even identify or understand" (*JF* 140). Might not a welfare-state capitalism avail itself of the same consolation? It cannot: for, unlike property-owning democracy, it cannot say that "it has at least taken seriously the idea of itself as a fair system of cooperation between its citizens as free and equal" (*JF* 140). Quite unlike a welfare-state capitalist society, in a property-owning democracy,

to speak, a separate utility function for each period. Not only must effects between periods be taken into account, but substantial swings are presumably to be avoided." (*TJ* 369)

[t]he least-advantaged are not, if all goes well, the unfortunate and unlucky – objects of our charity and compassion, much less our pity – but those to whom reciprocity is owed as a matter of political justice . . . . although they control fewer resources, they are doing their full share on terms recognized by all as mutually advantageous and consistent with everyone's self-respect.

(*JF* 139)

The importance of manifesting reciprocity is unmistakable here. It must be placed alongside the dedication to the fair value of political liberty (see Chapter 3) as a crucial distinction between welfare-state capitalism and property-owning democracy. Both reciprocity and fair value are integral to taking seriously Rawls's master idea, that of society as a fair system of cooperation between free equals.

The Political History of the Term "Property-Owning Democracy"

Although Rawls credits Meade, the catch-phrase "property-owning democracy" in fact had been coined much earlier, in the 1920s, by the Tory MP Noel Skelton, and it was a popular slogan of the Conservatives in the wake of its loss to Attlee's Labour Party in 1945 (Jackson 2005, 419; see also Ron 2008). The term was taken up by Meade and other "revisionist" Labour economists in order to gain or retain the allegiance of an electorate emerging from postwar austerity into the relative affluence of the 1950s. Further nationalization of industry was regarded as unwise – in no small part because of the aggressive disapproval of Britain's American creditors – and the popular desire to acquire personal private property was regarded as not inconsistent with breaking up the massively unequal holdings of the wealthy. As Ben Jackson tells the story, the Labour Party was not adroit enough to take advantage of many Britons desire for homeownership, and this issue was quickly captured by the Tories. In contrast, few of the revisionist Labour economists' proposals had any impact at all on Labour Party policy, much less government policy. Jackson writes:

> Scholars of British political history are of course familiar with the continued vitality of the Conservative variant of the idea of a "property-owning democracy", since it was appropriated by Margaret Thatcher to characterize the new Britain that would emerge from privatization of public sector assets, with greater home and share ownership being used to foster a new culture of personal responsibility and entrepreneurship. There was no egalitarian purpose behind this agenda, and indeed both income and wealth inequalities increased as a result.

(Jackson 2005, 438)

Needless to say, Rawls would not have been altogether at ease with the political history of the term "property-owning democracy," were he ever acquainted with it. Rawls's 2001 addition of ownership of "dwellings and private grounds" (*JF* 114 n. 36) as a basic right might possibly have been a (tardy) move to co-opt the popular appeal of the homeownership theme. But, in fact, it is unlikely that he had any knowledge at all of this historico-conceptual "backstory," and meant to refer only to what can be found within the pages of Meade 1964.[11]

Meade, a leading economist in Attlee's Labour government, did not intend property-owning democracy as an alternative to Clause Four's emphasis on public ownership. The concept of property-owning democracy came into play only as the posited starting point – brought about "as by the wave of some magic wand" (Meade 1964, 40) – in a thought experiment exploring how one might prevent gross social inequality from eventuating if one began at an initial starting point of strict equality. Meade's rather technical discussion noted that starting from the diametrically opposite position, total state ownership – which he did not advocate either – would offer an important efficiency advantage in resolving problems of "combining an efficient level of the real wage rate with an equitable distribution of income" (Meade 1964, 66). Meade took the public ownership of railways, electrical power generation, and those industries "bound in any case on technical grounds to be monopolies" (Meade 1949, 13) as a given. The revisionist group of Labour economists to which he has been assigned also believed in "'providing basic services generally through the state,'" free of charge at the point of service (Jackson 2005, 430). Such services would naturally include health care and old-age, disability, and unemployment insurance, primary and secondary education, and perhaps post-secondary education as well.

What Meade proposed, in the work Rawls drew on, was a hybrid strategy combining the diffusion and equalizing of property owned privately with an *increase* of state ownership in the British economy as a whole (Meade 1964, 38–68). What Meade and the other revisionists intended by the term "'property-owning democracy' ... was not offered as an alternative to the welfare state [*sic*]. It was rather offered as the next stage in the battle against inequality in addition to the great social achievements of 1945–51" (Jackson 2005, 440). Those achievements included the National Health Service, British Rail, the National Insurance Act, the Bank of England, and the National Coal Board – all publicly owned means of production.[12]

Meade did not appear to attach special significance to ownership of real property and capital assets. He had this to say about the advantage that accrues to those who own property:

---

[11] Alan Thomas (2016) misrepresents Meade as having been hostile to state ownership in 1964 when he published *Efficiency, Equality and the Ownership of Property*. The Meade that Rawls was familiar with defended social ownership of the means of production, and proposed property-owning democracy as a supplement, rather than an alternative, to socialism and indicated respects in which socialism would be preferable to a pure regime of property-owning democracy (Meade 1964, *passim*; and see Jackson 2014, 45–46).

[12] See also Meade 1950, 116: "M. de Jouvenel realises clearly (unlike some American Senators and some British Members of Parliament) that the nationalisation of coal, transport, gas, electricity and even iron and steel is almost completely irrelevant to the solution of our most immediately pressing problems such as the balance of payments deficit" – i.e., the fact that "we are living now on American charity" (Meade 1949, 14).

A man with much property has great bargaining strength and a great sense of security, independence, and freedom; and he enjoys these things not only vis-à-vis his propertyless fellow citizens but also vis-à-vis the public authorities. He can snap his fingers at those on whom he must rely for an income; for he can always live for a time on his capital. The propertyless man must continuously and without interruption acquire his income by working for an employer or by qualifying to receive it from a public authority.

(Meade 1964, 39)

What is true of an owner of "much property" is true also, to a degree, of one who owns some property, if less. But the enhancement of the sense of independence cannot be as significant in a well-ordered Rawlsian society, where the basic liberties, including the fair value of the political liberties, are already assured, as is fair equality of opportunity, a basic minimum income, and whatever benefits accrue by the operation of the difference principle.

The sense of independence Meade speaks of – the ability to snap one's fingers at authority – may have seemed to Rawls (and perhaps also to Meade) to be assured by property ownership in a distinctive way. But, in the work cited, Meade's attention reverts to the owner's power to get a stream of income.

Rawls would have disagreed with Meade on at least one point. Meade believed that this independence also assured a decent minimum income that would allow free exit from the labor market (Meade 1964, 39; see also Krouse and McPherson 1988, 92). Although Rawls was concerned to mitigate "the worst aspects of so-called wage slavery" (*TJ* 248), he made it increasingly plain that justice as fairness will not underwrite such independence: "Surfers must somehow support themselves" (*JF* 179), he writes, and so "would not be entitled to public funds" (*CP* 455 n. 7). The priority of liberty prohibits compelling anyone to work (*JF* 64), but Rawls was not willing to subsidize exit. This is not merely an expression of a Calvinistic aspect of Rawls's psyche: it flows immediately from his conception of society as a cooperative *productive enterprise* for mutual benefit. Meade, in contrast, was looking forward to the disappearance of work as essential to making a living, and imagined property-owning democracy as a way-station in that direction. Marx's conception of a "full communist society" was, in Rawls's account, a conception of a society "beyond justice" (*LHPP* 371). In full communism, conflicts disappear because classes have disappeared; and no "sense of justice" would be needed. Meade's conception of a leisure society, from Rawls's point of view, would not necessarily count as "beyond justice," because Meade did not suggest that social conflict would disappear along with the necessity to work for a living. But Meade's conception does envisage a society beyond the circumstances of justice that are the setting of a society conceived as a scheme of fair cooperation between productive citizens as free equals; and so Meade's conception is, to that extent at least, "beyond justice."

AMBIGUOUS INDICATIONS

At this point, it is worth pausing to ask why Rawls so obviously preferred to discuss property-owning democracy rather than socialism. After all, the difference between them is essentially in the position each takes toward the allowability of private ownership on the commanding heights of the economy. Rawls never states unambiguously that in a property-owning democracy all manner of productive assets might be allowed to be privately held. The idea of a critical core akin to the commanding heights is not absent from Rawls's characterization of property-owning democracy. An ideal property-owning democracy is

> a democratic regime in which land and capital are widely though not presumably equally held. Society is not so divided that *one fairly small sector controls the preponderance of productive resources.* When this is achieved and distributive shares satisfy the principles of justice, many socialist criticisms of the market economy are met.

> (*TJ* 247–248; emphasis added)

Of course, the banking and credit system is in a sense a "fairly small sector" that will, in a modern economy, inevitably control "the preponderance of productive assets." But it would not be charitable to construe this language as *itself* excluding private ownership of what thus stands on the "commanding heights" of the economy. Rawls did not intend to meet socialist criticisms by advocating socialism *sans phrase.*

But if property-owning democracy is not, for Rawls, simply socialism in soft focus, it becomes more rather than less puzzling why he had so little to say about socialism itself in the *Restatement.* Suggestions that he saw the two as to some degree interchangeable are present in his posthumously published *Lectures on the History of Political Philosophy,* in the three lectures on Marx. Rawls began lecturing on Marx in 1984 and continued to do so after the dissolution of the Soviet Union in 1991.

> It may be thought that with the recent collapse of the Soviet Union, Marx's socialist philosophy and economics are of no significance today. I believe this would be a serious mistake for two reasons at least.
>
> The first reason is that while central command socialism, such as reigned in the Soviet Union, is discredited – indeed it was never a plausible doctrine – the same is not true of liberal socialism. This illuminating and worthwhile view has four elements:
>
> (a) A constitutional democratic political regime, with the fair value of the political liberties.
> (b) A system of free competitive markets, ensured by law as necessary.
> (c) A scheme of worker-owned business [*sic*], or, in part, also public-owned through stock shares, and managed by elected or firm-chosen managers.
> (d) A property system establishing a widespread and a more or less even distribution of the means of production and natural resources.

Of course, all this requires much more complicated elaboration. I simply remind you of the few essentials here.

(LHPP 323)

Of these "essentials," only (c) and (d) call for comment. Item (c) is somewhat opaque but it can be read consistently with what I said above about Rawls and syndicalist industrial democracy. Item (d) is likewise somewhat opaque. It obscures the distinction between major and non-major means of production. As a result, it blurs the distinction between property-owning democracy and liberal socialism that Rawls evidently thought worth drawing. In fact, the lecture seems to personify Marx as a skeptical critic of both:

> When I say that we focus on Marx's critique of liberalism, I mean that we examine his criticisms of capitalism as a social system, criticisms that might seem offhand *to apply as well to property-owning democracy, or equally to liberal socialism.* (*LHPP* 320; emphasis added)

Rawls never corrects this offhand seeming, that is to say, he does not proceed to show that Marx's critique cuts differently as to the members of the pair. That said, in his Introductory Remarks, Rawls states that the lectures are not systematically connected to his other work. Therefore, I think it is best to take his characterizations in the lectures as something of an amalgam put forward to present a common front against Marx's line of criticism of liberalism, rather than a definitive statement of the essentials of liberal socialism specifically.

The collapse of Soviet communism had other sequelae. After years as the focus of controversy within the Labour Party, Clause Four was ultimately abandoned in 1995, under Tony Blair's leadership, and replaced with the following:

> The Labour Party is a democratic socialist party. It believes that by the strength of our common endeavour we achieve more than we achieve alone, so as to create for each of us the means to realise our true potential and for all of us a community in which power, wealth and opportunity are in the hands of the many, not the few, where the rights we enjoy reflect the duties we owe, and where we live together, freely, in a spirit of solidarity, tolerance and respect.

If one ignores the phrase "democratic socialist," it is tempting to align the original Clause Four with Rawls's definition of liberal socialism, and the Blair replacement with Rawls's property-owning democracy. *The Independent*'s contemporaneous account read:

> On the central question of public ownership, the current Clause IV commitment to "common ownership of the means of production, distribution and exchange" is replaced by an economy "where those undertakings essential to the common good are either owned by the public or accountable to them" ... [it] accepts the "enterprise of the market and the rigour of competition" – even if combined with "the forces of partnership and co-operation."

This speaks more to political control than to the dispersal of ownership, or its nature as public or private.[13] It would be interesting to know whether Rawls was following this closely enough to register what it meant for the Attleean Britain of his youthful acquaintance. By fits and starts, New Labour continued the Thatcherite policy of privatization, bringing the National Health Service and the Royal Mail into discussion – pausing at last with the (re)nationalization of Northern Rock and other banks in the wake of the collapse of the world financial system in 2008.

SUMMING UP

In summary, the best understanding of Rawls is that the fundamental difference between a property-owning democracy and liberal socialism is to be conceived in terms of rights privately to own major, socially significant means of production. Under socialism, the socially vital means of production are owned by society. Property-owning democracy allows, though it does not guarantee, a private right to acquire and exercise such ownership (*CP* 420; *LHPP* 321). Liberal socialism forbids private ownership of the means of production, but guarantees every citizen's right to participate democratically, through representative government, in the overall control and direction (though not in the routine management) of productive means that are, always, socially owned.

By "guarantee," here and throughout this book, I mean guarantee in the same strong sense as that in which justice as fairness guarantees a right to own personal property: as something so essential to a secure sense of self-worth that it is a component of, or best implementation of, the lexically prior first-principle of equal liberty. Worker involvement in management is not excluded, and may very well be desirable – even demanded – on other grounds, but it is not essential to socialism, as Rawls understood socialism. *Liberal* socialism, for Rawls, is a socialism intended to assure background justice by its integration with liberal constitutional democratic institutions.

Under socialism, citizens, whether or not working in an enterprise that makes use of socially vital means of production, enjoy all the incidents of joint ownership – in

[13] The American "New Left" of the 1960s similarly tended to speak of democracy rather than of ownership. According to the 25,000-word "Port Huron Statement" of the Students for a Democratic Society (1962), "[T]he economy itself is of such social importance that its major resources and means of production should be open to democratic participation and subject to democratic social regulation ... [meaning,] increased worker participation in management decision-making, strengthened and independent regulatory power, *balances of partial and/or complete public ownership*" (emphasis added). Elsewhere, the Statement suggests criteria defining a "public domain": "1) when a resource has been discovered or developed with public tax revenues, such as a space communications system, it should remain a public source, not be given away to private enterprise; 2) when monopolization seems inevitable, the public should maintain control of an industry; 3) when national objectives contradict seriously with business objectives as to the use of the resource, the public need should prevail" (www.lsa.umich.edu/phs/resources/porthuronstatementfulltext; last accessed July 14, 2016).

particular, an equal say in how the rents that accrue to these means of production are to be set and to be distributed. Those incidents of ownership that are rents, and thus not the fruit of productive activity, are not for private accumulation. Only the people as a collective body are pure owners of the productive means that are central to being a cooperating member. This cuts deeper than majoritarian democratic regulation of the means of production. It does not apportion an assured rent to a private owner, as is the case with regulated utilities in, for example, many states of the United States. Management is due a salary for its productive activity, but rents are for the public. As a further measure, these rents may be set at zero, as when essential services are provided without charge to the public and are subsidized by revenues otherwise generated and collected. Moreover, the citizen's joint-ownership share, like her right to vote and her right to life itself, is intended to be inalienable.

3

Fair Value and the Fact of Domination

The preceding chapters have discussed Rawls's narrow and wider conceptions of property in the original position, and how they relate to his understanding of the essential difference between property-owning democracy and liberal democratic socialism. The discussion showed how Rawls's thinking in A *Theory of Justice* underlies and shapes the way he posed the choice, in *Justice as Fairness: A Restatement*, between the five ideal types of regime.

The choice among the five ideal regime types is not the only thing to emerge in sharper and clearer form in the course of the evolution and reorientation of Rawls's thinking. Another is his insistence on the fair value of the political liberties. In this instance, A *Theory of Justice* plainly states that fair value has both a first-principle priority and a distributive import. Two things about fair value became clearer over time (see Brighouse 1997, 155–156). One, which Rawls emphasized, is that the prior guarantee of the fair value of political liberty plays a key role in the defense of the difference principle. Another, which Rawls elaborated with increasing urgency and even dismay, is the nature and extent of structural measures required to secure fair value. This chapter explores these themes, in preparation for the discussion of the later chapters.

There is a difference between merely formal political equality and real, meaningful political equality. The value of a citizen's equal right to free speech, for example, will be significantly greater if she happens to own a newspaper, and coordinately lesser if she hasn't got the leisure time needed to look at one. Compare the young Marx:

> The contradiction which exists between the [tremendous] effective political power of the Jew and his [formally denied] political rights, is the contradiction between politics and the power of money in general. Politics is in principle superior to the power of money, but in practice it has become its bondsman.
>
> (Marx and Engels 1978 [1843], 50)

The advantage in the value of liberty that accrues to wealth pervades the political process. This is the gist of the Marxist charge that parliamentary democracy is merely the public instrument by which a wealthier class maintains its dominant position in society. The charge is a serious one, in Rawls's view, and to rebut it he insists on a guarantee of the fair value of the political liberties: principally, the equal right to participate in political discussion and to vote, and of fair equality of opportunity, which includes a "fair chance" to occupy "public offices" (*JF* 43).

> The fair value of the political liberties ensures that citizens similarly gifted and motivated have a roughly equal chance of influencing the government's policy and of attaining political authority irrespective of their economic and social class.
>
> (*JF* 46; cf. *TJ* 197)

Fair value gives – or simply *is* – this assurance. It is defined in terms of chances to *influence*, not merely to participate. Importantly, it includes "a fair chance to add alternative proposals to the political agenda for public discussion" (*TJ* 198; citing Dahl 1956). An equal say in deciding on proposals that have been set by others for a vote is not enough. The public agenda too must be one that all have an at least roughly equal chance to set.

The comparison corrects for differences in gifts and motivation. So defined, fair value might seem to be trivially satisfied in circumstances in which citizens of lower economic and social classes generally lack the gifts or the motivation possessed by citizens in the upper classes. But Rawls must be understood to intend that the principles of justice will have already disrupted any regular correlation between gifts and motivation on one hand and class on the other. If the citizens who occupy the lower orders lack sufficiently developed gifts of articulateness and persuasiveness, or are unmotivated to participate in public life, that circumstance will already be an indictment of a basic structure's failure to assure background justice. Rawls's awkward discussion of eugenics embarks from an acknowledgment that "the distribution of natural assets . . . is bound to be affected by the social system" (*TJ* 92), and thus should not be accepted simply as a natural fact. "In the original position, then, the parties will want to insure for their descendants the best genetic endowment (assuming their own to be fixed)" (*TJ* 92). The parties would have no good reason to ignore the distribution and effect of human capital, and so would also want to ensure their progeny the best endowment in that sense as well. Bowles and Gintis's (2002) work on the "assortative mating" function of higher education in the United States illuminates this point.

The fair-value guarantee operates on two levels. One, citizens of different classes have a roughly equal chance of possessing the motivation and skill to influence policy. Two, citizens who in fact possess in similar degree the relevant motivation and skill have roughly equal chances of exerting political influence and of holding public office. Rawls sometimes seems reluctant to disturb any settled association between motivation, skills, and family circumstances (*TJ* 265), but other remarks express optimism that the tendency of justice will be to break up any such associations – which, looked at in isolation, would suggest abolishing the family altogether (*TJ* 448). No citizen will "withdraw into apathy and resentment" because she is skeptical that she has the means to exercise a "fair degree of influence" over public affairs (*TJ* 198). Henceforth, when I refer to fair value, I mean that of both the formally equal political liberties and of formally equal opportunities to influence policy agendas and outcomes and to hold public office.[1]

I set aside the awkward and possibly irreconcilable position Rawls assumes in *The Law of Peoples*, according to which a "substantial" and "meaningful" political role for citizens is consistent with the denial of both formal and fair political equality (*LP* 63, 64). A Rawlsian "decent" people

> secures for all members of the people what have come to be called human rights [which include] the right to life (to the means of subsistence and security); to liberty (to freedom from slavery, serfdom, and forced occupation, and to a sufficient measure of freedom of religion and thought); to property (personal property); and to formal equality as expressed by the rules of natural justice (that is, similar cases be treated similarly).
>
> (*LP* 65)

A decent people may conduct its political affairs according to a "decent consultation hierarchy" even though "all persons . . . are not regarded as free and equal citizens, nor as separate individuals deserving equal representation" (*LP* 71). Human rights "express a special class of urgent rights" (*LP* 79) that "are recognized as necessary conditions of any system of social cooperation" (*LP* 68); but respect for human rights, as Rawls sees the matter, "does not require acceptance of the liberal idea that persons are citizens first and have equal basic rights as citizens" (*LP* 66). This means, for example, that "one religion may legally predominate in state government, while other religions, though tolerated, may be denied the right to hold certain positions . . . [thereby] permitting 'liberty of conscience, though not an equal liberty'" (*LP* 65 n. 2). Rawls affirms that "[h]uman rights, as thus understood, cannot be rejected as peculiarly liberal or special to the Western tradition [or as] politically parochial" (*LP* 65). The negative pregnant here is that both formal and fair-valued political liberty *can* be rejected. Whether or not Rawls meant to suggest this (I do not believe he did – cf. Wenar 2004), the important matter is the significance Rawls assigned to political liberty – and its fair value – for liberal political justice in the central, domestic case.[2]

---

[1]   I note that a condition in which no individual can have any non-negligible influence over politics is, trivially, also a condition in which fair-valued political equality exists. Such a condition is not what Rawls had in contemplation, however. Although political participation cannot be mandatory, it is a welcome inevitability that some individuals, in conditions of reasonable pluralism, will find fulfillment of their personal conceptions of the good life by engaging in policy discussions and serving in public office (*JF* 144–145). The reward for public service is not to be greater than roughly equal political influence.

[2]   In §82 of *Theory*, Rawls rejects something like a "decent" but unequal provision for political liberty in the domestic case (*TJ* 479–480).

The fair-value guarantee became hugely important to Rawls's mature position. Because fair value is a political value, any comprehensive political or moral view that rejects fair value as a first-principle value fails to satisfy the test of reciprocity, and is pro tanto unreasonable (cf. *CP* 586, discussing autonomy). Although reasonable differences may arise as to the proper adjustment between fair-valued political liberty and other basic, first-principle liberties, a reasonable point of view must agree that fair-value is lexically prior to the difference principle (or any reasonable substitute distributive principle). This means that the least-advantaged may not be told that they must accept their lesser political influence on the ground any greater influence they had would come at the expense of their enjoyment of primary goods. Although such a claim might be couched in an argument "of the required form," as Rawls said of Mill's contemplation of plural votes for the intelligentsia, it is unreasonable to propose once the parties "go beyond the general conception of justice as fairness" (*TJ* 204) and agree to the priority of the basic equal liberties. For "once the required social conditions and level of satisfaction of needs and material wants is attained, as they are in a well-ordered society under favorable circumstances, the higher-order interests are regulative from then on ... and reveal their prior place" (*TJ* 476). The political liberties are essential guardians of the higher-order interests.

The fair-value guarantee serves not only to parry the Marxist critique of parliamentary democracy but also to forestall a standard objection to the difference principle.

> It is sometimes objected to the difference principle as a principle of distributive justice that it contains no restrictions on the overall nature of permissible distributions. It is concerned, the objection runs, solely with the least advantaged.
>
> (*JF* 46 n. 10)

What Rawls is referring to is the difference principle's exclusive focus on whether a given material inequality benefits the least-advantaged group in absolute terms. The difference principle is insensitive to the relative gap that it allows to open between the more advantaged and the least advantaged. So long as the least advantaged receive some small material advantage they would not otherwise get, it does not matter how great a material gain the more advantaged enjoy. "But," Rawls answers, "this objection is incorrect":

> [I]t overlooks the fact that the parts of the two principles of justice are designed to work in tandem and apply as a unit. The requirements of the prior principles have important distributive effects.
>
> (*JF* 46 n. 10)

The prior principles will themselves not allow relative inequality to grow to any objectionably great degree: a constraint on distributive inequality is already provided before the difference principle ever "kicks in." As Norman Daniels (1975, 280) put the point: "it is the First Principle, rather than the Second, which carries the

egalitarian punch" (accord with Brighouse 1997; see also Tomasi 2012, 250). In the
Restatement, Rawls asks us to

> [c]onsider the effects of fair equality of opportunity as applied to education, say, or
> the distributive effects of the fair value of the political liberties. We cannot possibly
> take the difference principle seriously so long as we think of it by itself, apart from its
> setting within prior principles.

(JF 46 n. 10)

The tone is emphatic, as though Rawls himself is ready to scoff at the very suggestion
that the difference principle might possess much stand-alone appeal, or to be
capable of redeeming an infringement of each citizen's basic right to a fair, equal
share of political power. The "social surplus" that the difference principle operates
upon is presumed to be what is generated by a society that already guarantees the fair
value the political liberties. And yet Rawls seems also to be taking care to speak only
of "distributive effects" and not of a "distributive task."[3]

Although "the collective activity of justice is the highest form of human flourishing"
(TJ 463), the fair-value guarantee does not entail a civic duty of political participation.
The citizen "is expected to vote" and thus "expected to have political opinions" *(TJ* 205),
but these expectations are not coercively enforceable. Just as Rawls rejects the idea that
political activity is a necessary part of a reasonable conception of the good, he also
rejects the thought that political liberty is consistent with compelled participation:
"[T]he extent to which we make engaging in political life part of our complete good
is up to us as individuals to decide, and reasonably varies from person to person"
(JF 144). True, "we cannot afford a general retreat into private life," but luckily "some
will find . . . their good importantly in public life . . . . It is to the good of society that this
be so . . . . The idea of a division of labor (rightly viewed) applies here as elsewhere"
(JF 144–145). Given the fact of reasonable pluralism, it is most unlikely that every citizen
will in fact equally influence political decisions. The fair-value guarantee thus has a
counterfactual component: those who opt out of politics would, nonetheless, have
roughly equal influence were they to opt in. The option itself serves to "enhance the
self-esteem and the sense of political competence of the average citizen. His awareness
of his own worth developed in the smaller associations of his community is confirmed
in the constitution of the whole society" *(TJ* 205). Those shut out of public office "would
be right in feeling unjustly treated even though they benefitted . . . [for] they were
debarred from experiencing the realization of self which comes from a skillful and
devoted exercise of social duties . . . one of the main forms of human good" *(TJ* 73).

This raises a host of questions. What does fair value require? Rawls speaks of a
"rough" equality of ability to influence political outcomes. Krouse and McPherson

---

[3] Rawls is not uniform in this avoidance. "The two principles of justice assess the basic structure
    according to how it regulates citizens' shares of primary goods" *(JF* 59).

(1988, 89) acknowledge the "considerable egalitarian bite" that fair value lends to the first principle (especially in combination with fair equality of opportunity), but they also correctly emphasize that "rough equality" can only be that, and that an "egalitarian collapse" would be incompatible with other Rawlsian commitments (Krouse and McPherson 1988, 85). "Egalitarian collapse" would occur if fair value were to impinge upon the "central range" (*PL* 358) of application of the other basic, first-principle liberties, such as freedom of speech and of association. Those citizens who are more charismatic or more eloquent, for example, cannot be silenced to preserve the fair value of the political liberty of those less gifted.

Fair value of political liberty requires rough equality of political influence. How is political influence to be objectively measured? Unless subject to objective assessment, fair value does not satisfy a liberal political conception's demand that matters of first-principle priority be free of those doubts and controversies that are grist for the mill of ordinary majoritarian legislation. What kinds of measures are allowed or required in order to secure fair value? At a minimum, a "deliberative" democracy implies "the public financing of elections, and the providing for public occasions of orderly and serious discussion of fundamental questions and issues of public policy" (*CP* 580). Is this all? Public debate must satisfy a "criterion of reciprocity" (*CP* 574), but how is that to be applied? Does reciprocity favor institutional arrangements additional to public financing of elections and subsidized public forums? Answers to these questions have to be collected from Rawls's writings, and in some instances inferred from theoretical commitments that do not directly involve fair value.

Rawls acknowledges a connection between better life prospects generally and better access to political power:

> To accomplish [fair equality of opportunity] certain requirements must be imposed on the basic structure . . . . A free market system must be set within a framework of political and legal institutions that adjust the long-run trend of economic forces so as to prevent excessive concentrations of property and wealth, especially those likely to lead to political domination.

> (*JF* 44)

Here, Rawls speaks of measures to prevent accumulations of wealth, rather than of allowing them while insulating political institutions and processes from their influence. And Rawls was impressed with, if not won over to, the Marxian idea that a just distribution presupposes social ownership of productive means:

> [W]e are likely to think that justice in distribution can be improved more or less independent[ly] from the relations of production. This tempts us to look for the best account of distributive justice to guide us in doing this. But distribution is not independent from the relations of production, which are, Marx thinks, fundamental.

> (*LHPP* 358)

These "relations of production" centrally include ownership.[4] For Rawls, distributive – as opposed to merely allocative – justice is to be accomplished by a "public system of rules [that] determines what is produced, how much is produced, and by what means" (*TJ* 76). The question is how far down Rawls meant those rules to reach.

Rawls does not expect a guarantee of a decent social minimum to be enough to guarantee also the fair value of equal political liberty (and this is regardless of whether the social minimum guarantee is given priority to the two principles). And the difference principle, being posterior to the first principle guarantee of equal basic liberty, would not suffice either. In fact, he emphasizes that the fair value of the political liberties must be assured by a principle that is lexically prior to the difference principle or any acceptable substitute principle for distributing the social product (*JF* 42–43, 149). The priority rules have a significance that Rawls explains this way:

> [T]he priority of the first principle over the second ... rules out exchanges ("trade-offs," as economists say) between the basic rights and liberties covered by the first principle and the social and economic advantages regulated by the difference principle. For example, the equal political liberties cannot be denied to certain groups on the grounds that their having these liberties may enable them to block policies needed for economic growth and efficiency.
>
> (*JF* 47; cf. *PL* 293–294, using the same example, but stating the priority in terms of "absolute weight")

Pro-growth policies cannot justify denying equal political liberties, but, inferably, pro-fair value policies *can*. "Denying" is not the right word, however. The first-principle liberties are to be conceived as a package, and liberty of political speech can be restricted for the sake of greater overall equal political liberty. The priority of first-principle liberties is inapplicable within the package, so long as the central

---

[4] Gerald Doppelt is critical of Rawls on the ground that

> [f]rom his standpoint, the sole question posed by capitalism and socialism is which system in some definite circumstances yields a more efficient economy and thus allows the democratic state to maximize the income of the worst-off ... these two social systems emerge as nothing but two alternative technical means for producing wealth with no fundamental differences in ethical or political principle between them.
>
> (1981, 293–294)

But Rawls does emphasize that a well-ordered society is a "productive scheme of social cooperation for mutual good" (*CP* 279) and that "moral relations between persons [are those of] members of a joint undertaking" (*CP* 217). Distribution is secondary. See Dan Brudney (2014) for a deft exploration of the charge that Rawls wrongly focuses on distribution rather than on production. A possibly unconscious modulation of Marx and Engels (1978 [1875/1891], 531) can be heard in Rawls's dictum that responsible citizens choose ends that "can be pursued by the means they can reasonably expect to acquire in return for what they can reasonably expect to contribute" (*PL* 34). (Surfers off Malibu, take note.)

range of application of each is respected. Fair value is a first-principle matter, but one that directly registers concerns about relative social and economic advantage. It is for this reason that Rawls finds legislation that limits campaign spending unproblematic, even though it is very much a matter of regulating both social and economic advantages and the first-principle basic right of free speech.

Rawls rejects any guarantee of the fair value of the other basic liberties. What is it about the political liberties, in contrast to the other liberties, that makes them special in this way? Rawls characterizes the political liberties as "the liberties of the ancients," which have "in general less intrinsic value" than "the liberties of the moderns," such as liberty of thought and conscience and the liberty to pursue one's own conception of the good outside the political arena. It may seem incongruous that the less significant political liberties are guaranteed their fair value while the other, more significant liberties are not. Rawls says:

> The role of the political liberties is perhaps largely instrumental is preserving the other liberties . . . . But even if this view is correct, it is no bar to counting certain political liberties among the basic liberties and protecting them by the priority of liberty. For to assign priority to these liberties they need only be important enough as essential institutional means to secure the other basic liberties . . . . And if assigning them this priority helps to account for the judgments of priority that we are disposed to affirm after due reflection, so far so good.
>
> (PL 299)

Although Rawls is evidently confident of this justification for selectively guaranteeing the fair value of only the political liberties, his "even if this is correct" is not meant to signal a concession.

> [E]qual political liberty is not solely a means. These freedoms strengthen men's sense of their own worth, enlarge their intellectual and moral sensibilities, and lay the basis for a sense of duty and obligation upon which the stability of just institutions depends.
>
> (TJ 206; cf. PL 404 n. 39)

These virtues do not flow from merely formal political equality. "Equal political liberty when assured its fair value is bound to have a profound effect on the moral quality of civic life . . . the effect of self-government where equal political rights have their fair value is to enhance the self-esteem . . . of the average citizen" (PL 205). Contrariwise, to the extent that the fair value is diminished, the less advantaged will tend to regard the conduct of public discussion with "apathy and resentment" (TJ 198); and – because the principle of reciprocity is coordinately dishonored – "[a]ll desire and activity becomes empty and vain, and we sink into apathy and cynicism" (TJ 386). Insofar as "self-respect is secured by the public affirmation of the status of equal citizenship for all" (TJ 478), it follows that a public policy that rejects or consciously undermines fair value can rightly be resented by the less advantaged as an assault upon their self-respect.

The importance and priority of the fair-value guarantee, and its role as a distributive constraint – if not a distributive formula – were clear in A *Theory of Justice*, if seldom remarked. The question naturally arises: What measures does justice require to be taken to realize the fair value of political liberty and to assure that the criterion of reciprocity is honored? The following chapter prepares the ground for a crucial aspect of the discussion: Are fair value and reciprocity to be protected by entrenched constitutional provisions or by legislative measures that a majority might adjust, strengthen, weaken, or even rescind altogether? Or is some hybrid of constitutional and legislative measures sufficient? Is guaranteeing fair value and reciprocity consistent with private ownership of any sector of the commanding heights of the economy, those major means of production that compose the engine of the productive cooperative enterprise that Rawls conceives society to be? Finally, does the institutional design assure the stability of a well-ordered society, conceived as an ongoing productive enterprise, continuing from generation to generation, and intended never to "wind up its affairs" (*PL* 18)?

Let me introduce a term to refer to the set of general facts that warrants Rawls's guarantee of the fair value of the political liberties, and the political liberties alone. I will call it *"the fact of domination."* The fact of domination includes, but is not merely the tendency toward, inequality of wealth, which Rawls already sees as an inevitable aspect of the workings of the basic structure of society. Nor is it merely the tendency of social and economic inequalities to be reflected in inequality of political influence.[5] Rather, it also takes in the tendency of unequal political influence (whether or not born of unequal social and economic advantages) to do two things. One, those in possession of greater political influence tend to entrench and extend that influence. Two, those in possession of greater political influence tend to exert that influence to gain, secure and extend other advantages, economic and social, and to promote via coercive state power comprehensive conceptions of the good that others might reasonably reject. For Rawls, the tendency is self-reinforcing (cf. Daniels 1975, 256–257). An actor in possession of social and economic advantages tends to possess and exercise a greater political influence, which in turn leads to greater social and economic advantages, which in turn ... etc.[6] Rawls adds this in his third lecture on Rousseau:

---

[5]   But to register this tendency is, already, to move beyond mere liberalism, for as political theorist John Dunn (1984, 9) points out, "in contrast with liberalism at least, socialism is principally a doctrine about the political implications of economic organization."

[6]   Joshua Cohen distinguishes *"structural constraints,"* i.e., the fact that "private control of investment importantly limits the democratic character of the state by subordinating the decisions and actions of the democratic state to the investment decisions of capitalists," and *"resource constraints,"* i.e., the fact that "unequal distribution of wealth and income ... limits the democratic character of politics by undermining the equal access of citizens to the political arena" (Cohen 1989, 28–29). The fact of domination is intended to encompass both of these types of constraint.

> A[nother] reason for controlling political and economic inequalities is to prevent a
> part of society from dominating the rest. When those two inequalities are large, they
> tend to go hand in hand . . . . [This] allows the few, in virtue of their control over the
> political process, to enact a system of law and property ensuring their dominant
> position, not only in politics, but throughout the economy. This enables them to
> decide what gets produced, to control working conditions and the terms of employ-
> ment offered, as well as to shape both the direction and volume of real saving
> (investment) and the pace of innovation, all of which in good part determines what
> society becomes over time.
>
> (*LHPP* 245)

Dominance over the productive process tends to become dominance in the background culture as well; he is speaking for Rousseau, but Rawls could as readily be
heard as speaking for Marx.

The tendency plays itself out across generations if left unchecked; but, as Horatio
Alger, rags-to-riches examples attest, a dominant position is attainable within a
generation. Coordinately, the less advantaged, as rational actors anticipating the
opposition of the more advantaged, increasingly tend to curtail their investment in
political effort.

The Marxist critique of parliamentary democracy emphasizes the roles of ideology and social classes: similarly, Rawls sometimes claims that the most advantaged
either can (*JF* 150) or tend generally to (a) share a certain self-interested political
viewpoint and (b) affiliate politically in order to further a common agenda (see, e.g.,
LP 139).[7] Rawls elsewhere disavows reliance on the affiliation claim (*PL* 360–361);
and nothing beyond what is already implied by "purely strategic, or game-theoretic"
(*JF* 125) behavior on the part of the well-off is essential to Rawls's position. The
special psychologies of envy and spite, which enter into account in Part Two of the
original position procedure, have not been invoked, either. In any case, recent
empirical work supports the commonsense idea that the very well-off exert dispro-
portionately great influence over government policy in the United States – an
influence that is independent of, even if more powerful in combination with, the
influence of business-oriented interest groups (Gilens and Page 2014; cf. Stepan and
Linz 2011). There is also empirical evidence that very wealthy Americans tend to be
very active politically and do, in fact, tend to share a certain self-interested political
viewpoint, especially on issues of taxation and economic regulation, a viewpoint that
is widely variant from the views of the vast majority (Page, Bartels, and Seawright
2013).

One might object that Rawls cannot justify a special place for the fair value of
political liberty on the basis of instrumental considerations. Political philosopher
Stephen Wall, for example, has argued the following:

---

[7] Kevin Vallier and Bas van der Vossen have convinced me that these two claims are too
controversial to rest on an appeal to commonsense.

> [T]o establish that the fair value of the political liberties is an indispensable
> condition for the justice of the political process it is not sufficient to argue, as Rawls
> sometimes does, that the current distribution of wealth in the United States
> undermines the justice of the political process in this country.
>
> (Wall 2006, 251)

Rawls never states or implies that the status quo in the United States, taken by itself,
suffices to establish the fact of domination. Wall continues,

> But, in fact, it is not even necessary to insist on this point. One need only follow
> Rawls in observing the limited scope of political philosophy. Whether the link in
> question here is tight or loose is an extremely complex and controversial empirical
> issue. Like the issue of what institutional arrangements would best satisfy the
> difference principle, it is not one that political philosophy can resolve.
>
> (Wall 2006, 251)

Rawls's basis for concluding that there is what Wall calls a "tight" link between fair
value and political justice is the set of facts that I have summarized as the fact of
domination. Rawls indeed does insist on the limited scope of political philosophy.
But he never states or suggests that the set of facts making up the fact of domination
are too complex or controversial for political philosophy to acknowledge. The fact of
domination can no more be dismissed as beyond the scope of political philosophy
than the fact of oppression or the fact of reasonable pluralism, which similarly
presuppose complex and controversial empirical issues, to say nothing of assumptions about moral psychology. Wall continues:

> Rawls claims that it is beyond the scope of political philosophy to "consider in any
> detail the kinds of arrangements required to insure the fair value of the political
> liberties." My claim is that, for the same reasons, it is beyond the scope of political
> philosophy to determine whether the instrumental link we are now considering is
> tight or loose. This claim would need to be substantiated by comparative historical
> and sociological analysis; and it is surely a claim about which citizens could
> reasonably disagree.
>
> (Wall 2006, 267 n. 41)

The analogy Wall suggests is not apt. For one thing, writing as a political philosopher, Rawls does state the *kinds* – though not the minute details – of arrangements
he thinks necessary to secure fair value. For another, Rawls's reasons for not
elaborating institutional details for realizing fair value are not transferable by a mere
wave of the hand to the question whether the fair value of political liberty is itself a
demand of justice in a constitutional democracy.

The only place Rawls suggests the fact of domination is reasonably contestable,
and thus not a truth of commonsense political sociology, is in a footnote in *The Law
of Peoples*:

[S]ome writers maintain that full democratic and liberal rights are necessary to prevent violations of human rights. This is stated as an empirical fact supported by historical experience. *I do not argue against this contention, and indeed it may be true.*

(*LP* 75 n. 16; emphasis added)

The tone suggests that fair-valued liberal political equality is not a necessary security for human rights, and that the fact of domination is merely one that Rawls entertains as a possibility having some historical support. The context of the remark shows that this is not what Rawls intended to convey. He is merely exploring the conceptual possibility of a tolerable, non-liberal society. Given this, the kind of decent consultation hierarchy he describes as a possible specification of a decent non-liberal society is simply stipulated to be such that "its rulers do not allow themselves to be corrupted ... by favoring the rich" (*LP* 75). The exercise is counterfactual, and is perfectly consistent with also holding it to be a commonsense truth that self-restraint on the part of persons in power is never an adequate check.

The fact of domination cannot be refuted simply by being denied, and it cannot be dismissed merely on the ground that it can be illuminated by historical and social scientific considerations.[8] Nor can it be discounted as mere hyperbole: what Rawls says about the fact of domination is less hyperbolic than some of his claims about the fact of oppression: for example, "a continuing shared adherence to one comprehensive doctrine can be maintained only by the oppressive use of state power, with all its official crimes and the inevitable brutalities and cruelties, followed by the corruption of religion, philosophy, and science" (*JF* 34). *All* of its official crimes, brutalities, and cruelties? Corruption of science? "This is as true of the liberalism of rightness as fairness, as it is of the Christianity of Aquinas or Luther" (*JF* 188). The liberalisms of Kant and Mill are comprehensive doctrines, no less than messianic religious fundamentalism. Why need assuring continuing shared allegiance to the Categorical Imperative or the Harm Principle lead to official brutality and corrupt science? Rawls's sometime Harvard colleague and *Dissent* editor Michael Walzer places the thought in the context of revolutionary change:

No vanguard victory is possible without radical coercion. Given that law, it is best to insist, if one can, and as early as one can, upon the superfluity of the vanguard. The best revolutions are made by social groups capable of articulating their own collective consciousness and defending themselves against the initiatives of radical intellectuals.

(Walzer 1979, 43)

---

[8] Political theorist Robert Dahl (whom Rawls cites on the elements of democratic governance) says "a relationship, even if a complex one, undoubtedly exists between the extent of political equality possible in a society and the distribution of income, wealth, status, and control over organizational resources" (1956, 81). Dahl again: "from Aristotle onward political theorists have recognized that the functioning of democratic processes will be impaired if citizens are vastly unequal in economic means or in other crucial resources" (1989, 167).

Rawls was no doubt conscious all the while of the terrible – and deliberately terrifying – excesses of the English, French, Russian, and Chinese revolutions, as much as of those of the continental Wars of Religion. Rawls was convinced that modern, reasonably liberal conditions could not allow any single, homogeneous group to find itself alone in a position simply to articulate and enact its consciousness.

We can compare the fact of domination with two facts the later Rawls did name: the fact of reasonable pluralism and the fact of oppression. The two latter facts, in combination, required major adjustments in Rawls's account of stability; but the fact of reasonable pluralism and the fact of oppression do not by themselves require any modification of the principles chosen in the original position. Rather, they require an overhaul of the guidelines of reasoning by which public discussion in a society well-ordered by liberal principles of justice is to be conducted – in particular, public political justification is required, rather than any ultimate appeal to truth as couched in a comprehensive religious, moral, or philosophical view.

In contrast, the fact of domination directly affects the content of the principles of justice chosen in the original position. It demands the fair-value guarantee that is already present in the 1971 version of the theory, and it forces a matter of distributive justice into a lexically prior position in the theory. Recall Rawls's statement of the "more general conception of justice" from which the two principles derive:

> All social values – liberty and opportunity, income and wealth, and the social bases of self-respect, are to be distributed equally unless an unequal distribution of any, or all, of these values is to everyone's advantage.

(TJ 54)

The political liberties are unlike all other values in that there is no possibility of an unequal division enhancing the influence of the less influential. The very idea is self-contradictory unless one supposes that the less influential will gain more influence via the greater influence of a powerful champion. But this is a description of demagoguery, not democracy.

There are still deeper grounds for the fair-value guarantee. Fair-valued political equality is essential to the "adequate development and full exercise" (*JF* 114) of the moral powers of free and equal citizens, especially to the sense of justice upon which stability depends. Stability for the right reasons is not achievable in a society in which private economic power dominates politics. In the next chapter, I will set the stage for exploring further ramifications of the fact of domination in Rawls's system.

4

The Four-Stage Sequence

The two principles of justice tentatively selected in Part One of the original position procedure are abstract. Because the parties are choosing "the foundation charter for their society" (*TJ* 10), the need for an institutional framework to focus and clarify the demands of justice "is evident" (*TJ* 171). Rawls accomplishes this – still in Part One – via a four-stage sequence. The three stages subsequent to the original position are suggested by three kinds of question the citizen will have to face. The first has to do with the justice of legislation – a matter as to which reasonable minds may differ. The second has to do with the justice of the procedures in place to resolve questions about the justice of legislation. And third, the citizen must ask which pieces of legislation are sufficiently just to be binding on her personally. The latter three stages of the four-stage sequence do not strictly correspond to these three questions, but they do suggest the need for a sequential approach.

At the constitutional stage, certain but not all institutions of the basic structure – those that are necessary to implement the two principles – are chosen. The constitutional stage is where the governmental structure is chosen, at least in broad outline. The choice is made by delegates having the benefit of additional knowledge of their particular society. At the next stage, the legislative stage, the veil of ignorance is lifted further to enable legislators to deal intelligently with the myriad practical decisions faced there, many of them having a bearing on the economy. The final stage is something of a residual stage. The veil of ignorance is fully lifted and the legislative decisions made at the previous stage are effectuated. I call it the administrative/judicial stage because it encompasses judicial review of legislation to assure that it is constitutionally sound, as well as execution of legislation and the behavior of persons in their role as citizens.

Rawls's former student and interpreter Thomas Pogge has suggested that the latter stages of the four-stage sequence, with the incremental lifting of the veil of ignorance, may be an "unnecessary shuffle" (Pogge 1989, 144 n. 42).[1] Why can the parties

---

[1] Rawls uses this very phrase in stating Hume's view of the social contract theory (*LHPP* 170).

in the original position not compare, in hypothetical form, all the proposals needing to be compared? This is a reasonable point, but I think the four-stage division does help isolate and clarify a range of issues; in particular, it is necessary to reinforce the plausibility of Rawls's claim that – although "the political process is at best one of imperfect procedural justice" (*TJ* 173) – resulting economic inequalities can be assessed as instances of pure procedural justice (*TJ* 76–77, 478). Imperfect procedural justice is the category of cases in which there exists an independent standard that a procedure tries to achieve but is not guaranteed to succeed. Rawls's example is a criminal trial, whose procedures are intended to minimize mistaken guilty verdicts, which may nonetheless result. Rawls's well-known example of the cutting of a cake into fair shares is a case of perfect procedural justice. Make the cutter of the cake take the last slice, and then (assuming no slips) the independent criterion of fair shares, that is, equal shares, is sure to be met.

Pure procedural justice means the inapplicability of any independent standard at all. If the procedure is carried out, there is no external standpoint or criterion from which the justice of the result can be questioned. If the sequence operates as it should, then certain decisions made at later stages can be defended as just simply by appeal to the justice of the process by which they were reached, given that the procedures ultimately flow from the two principles chosen in the original position. Rawls's effort to reduce the question of distributive justice to a matter of pure procedural justice is the element that endeared A *Theory of Justice* to Hayek. This idea is also the core of Robert Nozick's "entitlement theory" of distributive justice: if what everyone owns complies with a principle of just acquisition and with a principle of just transfer, there is no reason in justice to disturb the pattern, no matter how unequal. Set up a fair procedure, and let's have no bellyaching about the outcome. Nozick, Hayek, and Rawls disagree about what principles are needed to assure a fair procedure, but all three share the ambition of stating general principles that leave no room for further complaint about the distributive justice of the result, however unequal it might be. Of course, Rawls considers the range of and patterns of inequality allowed under a candidate principle, such as the difference principle, as relevant to the question whether that principle is one the parties in the original position will choose. But if the principles are satisfactory in the abstract, and are implementable, then questions like "Am I getting my due, my just share?" are ultimately to be treated as a matter of pure procedural justice (*TJ* 267, 478). The burdens of judgment assure that mistakes of application will be made, just as they assure that mistaken perceptions of injustice will occur. But the principles of justice will already have made allowance for the burdens of judgment.

The four-stage sequence was "suggested," Rawls says, by the example of the U.S. Constitution (*TJ* 172 n. 1), and he asserts that the two principles themselves can pro tanto be vindicated by being shown to "define a workable political conception, and [to be] a reasonable approximation to and extension of our considered judgments" (*TJ* 171). Taken together but otherwise in isolation, these remarks could be read as an endorsement of the at least near-justice of the status quo in the United States, circa 1971. Rawls goes on to caution that the four-stage sequence "is a part of moral theory" and not part of "an account of the working of actual constitutions" (*TJ* 173), but this kind of distancing was not enough to dispel the impression many have gotten that the whole apparatus was intended as a "transcendental deduction" of the status quo in Western constitutional democracies.

Because fair value is a constitutional essential, the constitution itself ought to secure it, so far as possible. A reminder: we are still working in Part One of the original position procedure. In Part Two of the original-position procedure, the constitution's provision to protect fair value and other constitutional essentials will have to be reassessed, to determine whether the solution works conspicuously enough to address the stability problem. The stability problem grew out of the "assurance problem" that *Theory* already acknowledged in Part One of the original position procedure (*TJ* 237–238), but it is complicated by the revelation to the parties of the special psychologies. As I described in the Introduction, Rawls's writings from the early 1980s to the mid-1990s were concentrated on correcting an inconsistency in the theory as presented in 1971. The 1971 theory relied on a comprehensive liberal philosophy to fashion and transmit the sense of justice needed to stabilize a well-ordered society. In the early 1980s, Rawls realized that the stability of a liberal society could not be achieved in this way. The adjustments Rawls made to correct this defect effectively meant assigning the constitutional convention an additional task: that of fashioning institutions answering the need to assure stability in conditions of reasonable pluralism. And the convention itself is subject to a related constraint: the discipline of public reason – that is, the requirement that the constitutional design be justifiable by appeal to a political, rather than a comprehensive, conception of justice.

The constitutional stage is also where the later Rawls chose to put matters of regime choice on the agenda. Rawls does not otherwise explain why he decided to add this task to the agenda of the constitutional convention. Perhaps it seemed to Rawls already obvious that, at some point, the issue had to be addressed. But it is also likely that Rawls believed that it was at this stage of the four-stage sequence that the break with capitalism in both its laissez-faire and welfare-state manifestations had to be made, if it was going to be made. His dismay at being misunderstood as an apologist for capitalism was likely to have put him on the lookout for a propitious point of entry to make the break in clear terms that left no chance of misunderstanding.

Rawls had intimated in the 1982 paper, "Social Unity and Primary Goods," that the historic question of the choice between what he there terms "private property democracy" and "democratic socialism" might be settleable in the original position. In the article, Rawls was concerned with defending the claim that the index of primary goods used in *Theory* avoids problems of interpersonal comparison that beset utilitarianism. He set out the primary goods as a list of five:

(a) First, the basic liberties as given by a list ...;
(b) Second, freedom of movement and choice of occupation ...;
(c) Third, powers and prerogatives of office and positions of responsibility,
    particularly those in the main political and economic institutions;
(d) Fourthly, income and wealth; and
(e) Finally, the social bases of self-respect. (CP 362–363)

This list prefaced the following remark:

> On the assumption that the question of private property democracy versus demo-
> cratic socialism involves the weighting of primary goods under (c), (d), and (e) *using*
> *income and wealth alone in the difference principle presumably cannot resolve this*
> *historic question.*
>
> (CP 363; emphasis added)

Interpreting this isolated and somewhat opaque passage requires care. It shows that
Rawls was already mindful of the possibility of, and need to, address the property
question with reference to the two principles. There is no indication that Rawls is
thinking here beyond Part One of the original position procedure, so the complications introduced by the special psychologies, and the ways they aggravate the
problem of stability, are not in immediate contemplation. The passage indicates also
that Rawls believed it could, at most, only be assumed that first-principle values
would not decide the issue.

His key point, then, is that the question of regime choice, if it has to be decided
under the difference principle, will not be decidable if the index of primary goods is
restricted to income and wealth – what he here and elsewhere calls the "objective"
primary goods (*TJ* 466). The implication is that under a wider index of primary
goods, which would include "powers and prerogatives of office and positions of
responsibility, particularly those in the main political and economic institutions;
income and wealth; and the social bases of self-respect" (CP 362), the "historic
question" might very well be decidable. Alternatively, Rawls might be read as
suggesting that the decision will favor the regime form that satisfies the demands
of stability without needing to "subjectivize" the index of primary goods. It will be
illuminating, as we will see in Chapter 6, to compare what Rawls says here with his
discussion in *Theory* §82 of the priority principles and the desirability of dealing with
the "excusable envy" aspect of the problem of stability before the legislative stage is
reached (*TJ* 478–479).

By 1993, Rawls made it clear, in remarks in *Political Liberalism*, that he does not
intend for the principles of justice chosen in the original position already to require
socialism in the sense of a right to be involved in industrial management. This was
in response Rodney Peffer's (2014 [1990]) analysis of "Marx's implicit theory of
distributive justice," which was preliminary to the "modified version of Rawls' theory
of social justice" that Peffer put forward as an "adequate Marxist moral and social

theory" (2014 [1990], 13–15). Peffer had proposed replacing Rawls's two principles of justice as fairness with the following, lexically ordered set of four:

(1) Everyone's basic security and subsistence rights are to be met . . . .
(2) There is to be a maximum system of equal basic liberties, including . . . the right to hold (personal) property . . . .
(3) There is to be
  (a) equal opportunity to obtain social positions and offices, and
  (b) *an equal right to participate in all social decision-making processes within institutions of which one is a part.*
(4) Social and economic inequalities are justified if and only if they benefit the least advantaged, consistent with the justice savings principle, but are not to exceed levels that will seriously undermine equal worth of liberty or the good of self respect. (Peffer 2014 [1990], 14; emphasis added)

Acknowledging Peffer, Rawls says that "important aspects of the principles [of justice as fairness] are left out in the statement as given [at *PL* 5–6]. In particular, the first principle covering the equal basic rights and liberties may easily be preceded by a lexically prior principle requiring that citizens' basic needs be met . . . . Certainly any such principle must be assumed in applying the first principle" (*PL* 7). What is significant for the present purpose is what Rawls says in a footnote:

> For the statement of such a principle, as well as an instructive fuller statement in four parts of the two principles, with important revisions, see Rodney Peffer's *Marxism, Morality, and Social Justice* . . . p. 14. I should agree with most of Peffer's statement, but not with his 3(b), which appears to require a socialist form of economic organization. The difficulty here is not socialism as such; but I should not include its being required *in the first principles* of political justice.
>
> (*PL* 7–8 n. 7; emphasis added)

Curiously, when Rawls subsequently reiterates his endorsement of Peffer's first principle, in the *Restatement*, he does not repeat this discussion (*JF* 44 n. 7). Peffer's principle 3(b) does not address ownership of the means of production; and the parentheses in the term "right to hold (personal) property" in Peffer's second principle seems to be designedly non-committal. The parentheses mirror language in the first edition of *Theory* that Rawls, without explanation, removed in the second (compare *TJ* 1st ed. 61 with *TJ* 53).[2] What 3(b) states is "an equal right to participate in all social decision-making processes within institutions of which one is a part,"

---

2 Frank Michelman (1973, 975) noticed "the textual irresolution . . . concerning the inclusion of property rights in the lexically preferred basic liberties" and took it this way: "The qualifier '(personal)' is, in context, evidently meant to exclude at least the means of production and so recognize that socialist schemes may be just" (973 n. 31). The removal of the parentheses could be taken as Rawls's way of resolutely emphasizing this point, and even as an acknowledgement that non-socialist schemes may be unjust.

which, taken in isolation, seems to sweep beyond the basic structure and into the background culture. Nonetheless, Rawls read it, and disclaimed it, as requiring a "socialist form of economic organization." Rawls continues:

> These principles I see (as I did in *Theory*) as setting out fundamental values in terms of which, depending on the traditions and circumstances of the society in question, one can consider whether socialism *in some form* is justified.
>
> (*PL* 8 n. 7; emphasis added)

Socialism is not a fundamental value but, given further knowledge, it may be justified. The further factors, "traditions and circumstances of the society in question," as we shall see in a moment, are revealed at the constitutional stage, to the delegates to a "constitutional convention." As to the different "forms" of socialism that might be considered, Rawls did not specify. Nor did he specify the significance of such forms being found to be "justified." It might mean "eligible," or it might mean "required." That Rawls's meaning is the latter, that is that it might be required, is indicated by what he says in the 1975 article, "Fairness to Goodness":

> Marx would question the stability of a well-ordered society in the absence of some form of socialism ... in any case, the principles of justice do not exclude certain forms of socialism *and would in fact require them* if the stability of a well-ordered society could be achieved in no other way.
>
> (*CP* 276–277; emphasis added)

The questions of what forms of socialism are eligible, and what forms might be required in order to stabilize a well-ordered society, are not mentioned; and disappointingly, nothing more is said about how an argument, premised on the demands of stability, might go. Recall that stability-testing resumes in Part Two of the original position procedure, where the special psychologies are taken into account, in addition to the Part One strains of commitment. Completeness requires that the four-stage sequence initiated in Part One be confirmed in Part Two. I will return to this pivotal matter after looking in detail at the stages of the four-stage sequence. But note that already it is clear that the disjunctive proposition, "justice as fairness requires either property-owning democracy or liberal democratic socialism for its realization" – though not itself a principle of justice – is a theorem of Rawls's theory.

THE CONSTITUTIONAL-STAGE: KNOWLEDGE AND TASK

At the constitutional stage, the representative equal citizen evaluates alternatives put to her not behind the full veil of ignorance that characterizes the original position, but in light of certain additional knowledge. The two principles are known, of course, but delegates to the constitutional convention also know "general facts about their society, that is, its natural circumstances and resources, its level of economic advance and political culture, and so on" (*TJ* 172–173), "general knowledge of how political and social institutions work" (*PL* 336), and all this in addition to the "principles of social theory" understood in the original position, from which the two principles were derived, and the reasoning by which they were derived, including the general reflections that motivated the veil of ignorance. Among the general facts of their society that delegates learn, presumably, is what the available means of production are in their society and which of those means occupy the commanding heights of the economy.

The task facing the delegates to the constitutional convention is described this way:

> Given their theoretical knowledge and the appropriate general facts about their society, they are to choose the most effective just constitution, the constitution that satisfies the principles of justice and is best calculated to lead to just and effective legislation.
>
> (*TJ* 173)

Notice that the "most effective" and "best calculated to lead to just and effective legislation" is what must be the representative's choice, even if the alternatives have appeal. Since "the ideal of perfect procedural justice cannot be realized," the choice problem is "to select from among the procedural arrangements that are both just and feasible those which are most likely to lead to a just and effective legal order" (*TJ* 173); and,

> To solve this problem intelligently requires a knowledge of the beliefs and interests that men in the system are liable to have and of the political tactics that they will find it rational to use given their circumstances. The delegates are assumed, then, to know these things.
>
> (*TJ* 174)

The delegates thus have on hand not only the knowledge that led them to insist on the fair value guarantee but also further knowledge about their political culture. Since this process is unfolding in Part One of the original position procedure, the parties do not yet have to confront the special psychologies and the distinctive problem of stability they create. They still do not know "their own social position, their place in the distribution of natural attributes, or their conception of the good" (*TJ* 172), but – given the additional knowledge of their political culture – can make informed estimates of the relative likelihood of alternative outcomes.

Although it has a limited agenda, the constitutional convention is under a wide-ranging mandate:

> The aim of constitutional design is to make sure, if possible, that the self-interest of social classes does not so distort the political settlement that it is made outside the permitted limits.
>
> (*TJ* 318)

In other words, the "constituent power" of the people is set the task of choosing the institutional design that best assures that the "ordinary power" exercised legislatively and administratively is unbiased by the class interests and self-interests that it will confront.

THE CONSTITUTIONAL STAGE: THE RULE OF DECISION

Rawls is not as explicit as he might be about the rule of decision in the constitutional convention (*TJ* 314). A rule of unanimity seems the only eligible one, but this has to be inferred. In his review of *Theory*, Rawls's Harvard colleague Frank Michelman says, "the principle of unanimity ... governs the original position and, *presumably*, the constitutional stage" (1973, 994 n. 98; emphasis added). Rawls cited Michelman's review approvingly, and did not register any reservation about this particular assertion (*PL* 339 n. 47). Unanimity has to be presumed because the conspicuous alternative, majority rule, is explicitly adopted constitutionally to govern at the legislative stage to accommodate the burden of additional information while assuring the most extensive right of participation (although other devices might be open to him as well (Gutmann 2003, 187–192)). The unanimity requirement may have seemed to Rawls as too obvious to require mention, but if the text is read with a certain emphasis, the unanimity rule can be heard.

> A just constitution is defined as a constitution that would be *agreed upon* by rational delegates in a constitutional convention who are guided by the two principles of justice. When we justify a constitution, we present considerations to show that it *would be adopted* under these conditions.
>
> (*TJ* 314; emphases added)

Other passages support this reading. For example, employing Michelman's interpolations,

> Now since even rational legislators would often reach different conclusions, there is a necessity for a vote under ideal conditions. The restrictions on information [*applicable at the legislative stage; i.e., the ideal legislator is supposed to be ignorant of his particular situation in society*] will not guarantee agreement [*as in the prior stages*], since the tendencies of the general social facts will often be ambiguous and difficult to assess. (*TJ* 314; bracketed italicized text is from Michelman 1973, 994–995 n. 98).

As the interpolations merely serve to emphasize, this passage cannot naturally be construed without understanding majority rule, with a voting procedure employing it, as not coming in until the legislative stage, which means that the unanimity criterion carries over from the original position to the constitutional stage.

Although it is fairly clear that this was Rawls's *Theory* view, it can be doubted whether he stuck to it, or could stick to it. Rawls introduces the expression "constitutional consensus" in *Political Liberalism*, but cautions that it is "not deep" and "not wide" and is "narrow in scope, not including the basic structure but only the political procedures of democratic government" and "the content of certain political basic rights and liberties" (*PL* 159, 161). He is not as explicit here as elsewhere about whether that "content" will include what is demanded to assure fair value in advance of the "regulated rivalry" that is to ensue.

Rawls writes: "[I]t is too much to expect complete agreement on all political questions. The practicable aim is to *narrow disagreement* at least regarding the more divisive controversies, and in particular those that involve *constitutional essentials*" (*JF* 28; emphasis added). Were one to leave off at this point, one might have gotten the impression that Rawls believed consensus as to constitutional essentials is both impracticable and unnecessary. But Rawls continues:

> for what is of greatest urgency is *consensus* on those essentials, for example:
> (1) the fundamental principles that specify the *general* structure of government and the political process; the powers of the legislature, executive, and the judiciary; the limits of majority rule; and
> (2) the equal basic rights and liberties of citizenship that legislative majorities must respect, such as the right to vote and to participate in politics, freedom of thought and association, liberty of conscience, as well as the protections of the rule of law.
>
> (*JF* 28; emphases added)

Rawls is careful to acknowledge that consensus as to constitutional essentials is both practicable and basic to public justification, and at the same time that the consensus will form around general principles and "the main outlines" (*JF* 49) rather than programmatic details.

> The point is that if a political conception of justice covers the constitutional essentials, it is already of enormous importance even if it has little to say about many economic and social issues that legislative bodies must consider. To resolve these it is often necessary to go outside that conception and the political values its principles express, and to invoke values and considerations it does not include. But so long as there is *firm agreement on the constitutional essentials*, the hope is that political and social cooperation between free and equal citizens can be maintained.
>
> (*JF* 28; emphasis added)

Free and equal citizens express their reciprocal respect for one another by publicly justifying to one another the positions they take when they disagree. But "[p]ublic justification proceeds from some consensus" (*JF* 27) – a consensus as to the constitutional essentials. It is the fact that citizens as free and equal affirm the same constitutional essentials that "distinguishes public justification from mere agreement" (*JF* 29). Mere agreement merely splits the difference – public justification involves an appeal to the consensus underlying the difference. It is only within the boundaries set by the constitutional essentials that bargains may be struck and compromises reached.

THE CONSTITUTIONAL STAGE: FAIR VALUE

"What is essential is that the constitution should establish equal rights to engage in public affairs and that measures be taken to maintain the fair value of these liberties" (*TJ* 200; cf. *TJ* 197; *PL* 357–362; and see Daniels 1975). It must

> meet the urgent political requirement to fix, once and for all, the content of certain political basic rights and liberties, and to assign them a special priority. Doing this takes those guarantees off the political agenda and puts them beyond the calculus of social interests, thereby establishing clearly and firmly the rules of political contest.
>
> (*PL* 161; cf. *JF* 194)

One would naturally expect that it is at the constitutional convention (and not later) that, for Rawls, the problem of fair value must be resolved – if necessary, by crafting not only the legislative process but also other parts of the basic structure (even if not all of the basic structure is involved).

> The liberties protected by the principle of [political] participation lose much of their value whenever those who have greater private means are permitted to use their advantages to control the course of public debate. For *eventually* these inequalities will enable those better situated to exercise a larger influence over the development of legislation. *In due time* they are likely to acquire a preponderant weight in settling social questions, at least in regard to those matters upon which they normally agree, which is to say in regard to those things that support their favored circumstances.
>
> (*TJ* 198; emphases added)

Rawls has insisted on the fair-value guarantee largely because of the tendency of unequal social and economic advantages to translate themselves into political advantages – I have termed this *the fact of domination*. Even though Rawls does not give it a name, "[t]he idea is familiar," as Harry Brighouse (1997, 157) drily summarizes. The following chapter will explore the ramifications of this concern.

THE CONSTITUTIONAL STAGE: "WIDE" VERSUS "NARROW" DISTRIBUTIVE JUSTICE

The significance of fair value as a first-principle matter is of particular importance because Rawls holds that the second-principle guarantees of fair equal opportunity – insofar as it is unrelated to equality of political liberty – and the difference principle are not matters for constitutional decision. As I detail in Chapter 6, the reasons Rawls gives for deferring second-principle guarantees to the legislative stage would also help determine the issue between socialism and property-owning democracy at the constitutional stage. In *Theory*, he proposes a "division of labor" (*TJ* 174) between the constitutional convention and the process of ordinary (majoritarian) legislation that "roughly corresponds to the two parts of the basic structure" (*TJ* 174), by which he means those two parts corresponding to the two principles.

> The first principle of equal liberty is the primary standard for the constitutional convention. Its main requirements are that the fundamental liberties of the person and liberty of conscience and freedom of thought be protected and that the political process as a whole be a just procedure . . . . The second principle comes into play at the stage of the legislature. It dictates that social and economic policies be aimed at maximizing the long-term expectations of the least advantaged under conditions of fair equality of opportunity, subject to the equal liberties being maintained. At this point *the full range of general economic and social facts* is brought to bear. The second part of the basic structure contains the distinctions and hierarchies of political, economic, and social forms which are necessary for efficient and mutually beneficial cooperation. Thus the priority of the first principle of justice to the second is reflected in the priority of the constitutional convention to the legislative stage.
>
> (*TJ* 174–175; emphasis added)

It would have been helpful had Rawls had indicated more precisely what additional "general economic and social facts" come in to fill out the "full range" at the legislative stage. Bear in mind that, at the constitutional stage, the delegates are already in command of "general" facts about their society's "level of economic advance and political culture" (*TJ* 173). This is a crucial point, to which I later return.

In the *Restatement*, Rawls remarks that "we can expect *more* agreement on constitutional essentials than on issues of *distributive justice in the narrow sense*" (*JF* 48; emphases added). By "more agreement" I take him to mean "a readier consensus" rather than "a larger plurality in agreement." By "in the *narrow* sense" or "*narrower* sense" he means "in the second-principle sense." The implicit reference to a "wide sense" acknowledges that certain matters of distributive justice – primarily the guarantees needed to assure the fair value of political liberties – are to be decided as first-principle matters (see *JF* 42, 43, 61). He further writes, "Differences about the most appropriate principles of distributive justice in the narrower sense, and the ideals that underlie them, can be adjudicated, though not always properly, within the existing political framework" (*JF* 49). This implies that it is only narrow-sense distributive justice, which already presupposes fair value, that is deferred to the third and fourth stages. Elsewhere, Rawls writes: "What is at issue, then, is the most appropriate principle of distributive justice (in the narrow sense); and whether the difference principle or the principle of restricted utility is more appropriate" (*JF* 122). The context here is the choice in Part One of the original position between the difference principle and the restricted-utility principle, to fill out the second half of the second principle. Other than in these cited passages, I have been unable to locate anywhere in Rawls's work a distinction between narrower and wider senses of distributive justice. It is impossible to avoid concluding, however, that distributive justice in the wide sense is a concern of both the first and second principles, and therefore a matter to be considered both at the constitutional convention and in subsequent legislation – not to mention judicial review.

THE FIVE IDEAL REGIME TYPES

Rawls has been criticized for framing his discussion in terms of ideal-types, and for imposing the short list of ideal types he chose (e.g., Weithman 2013). I think both the methodology and the selection of candidates can be defended (cf. Thomas 2016, 291 ff). These choices are consistent, anyway, with his broader methodology and substantive commitments. The history of political philosophy and the focal points of recent dispute are reasonable to consult in deciding how to frame the inquiry. Looking at these two sources, the only dubious choice is the inclusion of property-owning democracy, which, as I showed in Chapter 2, has a far shorter pedigree. In that respect, Rawls's list might be criticized as over-inclusive.

One could even conjecture that property-owning democracy operates only as a stalking-horse for socialism, to avoid pitting socialism against welfare-state capitalism directly. *In a head-to-head contest between liberal democratic socialism and welfare-state capitalism, Rawls has socialism the winner* – about this there can be no doubt.[3] But welfare-state capitalism is eliminated at the constitutional stage not because it comes off poorly in comparison with socialism. The comparison is not made. Rather, welfare-state capitalism is eliminated because, for reasons that I enumerated earlier, it cannot realize justice as fairness even in favorable circumstances. Liberal democratic socialism can, as Rawls states consistently, over several decades (*TJ* 248; *CP* 277; *JF* 138–139).

If, on the other hand, the list is under-inclusive, the burden of producing a case for including some other ideal type has yet to be taken up. Is there a blanket objection to the very idea of ideal types? If so, it is not obvious what it is, or how political philosophy would proceed without them.

In any case, Rawls is clear that the fair-value guarantee is a component of the first principle and that it falls to the constitutional convention to decide how to realize it.

> The first [but not the second] principle applies at the stage of the constitutional convention, and whether the constitutional essentials are assured is more or less visible on the face of the constitution and in its political arrangements and the way these work in practice.
>
> (*JF* 48)

This in itself suggests that Rawls did not consider *any pair* of the five ideal types of regime to diverge only with respect to second-principle subjects. The constitutional

---

[3] There can be no doubt either that in the original position Rawls also would decisively prefer the two principles over what could be termed *Neoliberalism*, which is just like the two principles, but without a guarantee of the fair value of equal political liberty.

convention judges each solely on the basis of its suitability to the task of assuring "constitutional essentials," under the assumption that it could be "effectively and workably maintained" (*JF* 137).

As already noted, two of the five ideal types – laissez-faire capitalism and one-party socialism – would be rejected out of hand, under the assumption that what does not at least aim to realize the two principles will not reliably succeed in doing so (*JF* 137). Welfare-state capitalism survives the rough first cut as a possible implementation of the two principles because it is defined as committed to honoring the bundle of formally equal political rights and liberties featured in the first principle. Under welfare-state capitalism, productive assets are privately owned, and the state's involvement in the economy is restricted to two roles: assuring the functioning of free markets and assuring an adequate safety net for citizens who do not fare well in the market. Rawls rejects welfare-state capitalism because it does not seek to assure the fair value of the political liberties, and is not serious enough about fair equality of opportunity. There is a further reason: welfare-state capitalism allows unbounded inequalities of wealth and, even if it were generous in guaranteeing a minimum income, it would not honor the idea of reciprocity. Ownership of central means of production, along with everything else, is up for grabs in the competitive free-for-all, and winners can be allowed to hoard or dispose of their winnings as they see fit. Losers in the economy would come to be regarded not as equal participants in a common enterprise, but as dependents (*JF* 137–138; cf. Thomas 2016, 286ff.).

The two surviving ideal types, property-owning democracy and liberal socialism, both aim to fulfill the two principles of justice. Both types of regime are taken to be constitutional democracies in which the basic liberties, fair-valued equal political liberties, and fair equality of opportunity are guaranteed, and some principle of reciprocity for the division of the social surplus, such as (but not necessarily) the difference principle, is in place. As I showed in Chapter 2, the key difference between the two regime types is that the legislature of a property-owning democracy has the option of allowing private ownership of the means of production. The legislature of a liberal democratic socialist regime is denied this option. One must ask: Is the exercise, and even the availability, of a legislative option to allow private ownership of the means of production consistent with maintaining the fair-value guarantee and with satisfying other demands, such as publicity, reciprocity, and stability? As I will indicate in a moment, Rawls stated that he had misgivings.

It is important to recall that the delegates will know general facts about their society's resources and level of economic development. This means that they will know that their society is not a feudal or a caste society, but is a developed industrial one. They will certainly also know what means of production are available, and which of them are so central and pervasive as to stand on the commanding heights of their economy. A question of clarification arises: Are the delegates confronted with an existing allocation of productive means, or not? If they are, then the choice facing them is whether or not to accept the status quo as a presumptively just baseline. If the delegates are not faced with an existing allocation, then of course there is no de facto baseline. Although Rawls is not explicit, surely he must have intended that the delegates not be bound in any way by a preexisting allocation. If there is a preexisting *unjust* allocation, the issue is one of non-ideal theory and the problem is one of transition (*PL* 17–18). The delegates, then, will write on a clean slate, but they must do so with regard to their responsibility to assure that their decisions whether or not to permit private ownership of the key means of production is in keeping with their duty to choose the best constitution.

The task of the theory of justice is to locate principles by which "fundamental social and economic inequalities" can be "made legitimate and consistent with the idea of free and equal citizenship in society seen as a fair system of cooperation" (*JF* 40). This is, in the wide sense, a problem of distributive justice. So, of course, the "main problem of distributive justice is the choice of a social system" (*TJ* 242), as Rawls says. This means that the task of a theory of justice is not complete until the choice of a social system is determined or the impossibility of making that determination has been shown. The issue between the two remaining ideal types is not "indeterminate" or one of "quasi-pure procedural justice" (*TJ* 176) if one or the other is likelier, given the information available to the constitutional convention, to achieve and maintain a stable, just regime.

THE THIRD, LEGISLATIVE STAGE

Matters of governance not settled at the constitutional stage are referred to the next, legislative stage. The legislative stage is governed by the two principles arrived at in the original position and the constitutional essentials settled at the constitutional stage. But the rule of decision at the legislative stage is not unanimity, but majority rule. Others have made the case that majoritarian rule has certain epistemic virtues or is inherently fairer than its alternatives. Rawls is content to remark that the "traditional" procedure of "majority rule duly circumscribed" (*TJ* 172) has the virtue of "a certain naturalness; for if minority rule is allowed, there is no obvious criterion to select which one is to decide" (*TJ* 313; cf. Dahl 1956).

The constitutional and legislative stages are not considered in strict sequence. At the legislative stage,

> [T]he justice of laws and policies is to be assessed . . . . Proposed bills are judged from the position of a representative legislator who, as always, does not know the particulars about himself. Statutes must satisfy not only the principles of justice but whatever limits are laid down in the constitution. *By moving back and forth between the stages of the constitutional convention and the legislature, the best constitution is found.*

(*TJ* 174; emphasis added)

The legislature of a constitutional democracy is the arena of "normal politics" (*PL* 405), in which legislators represent individuals that are fully aware of what they have to gain.[4] Rawls acknowledges that "[c]itizens and legislators may properly vote their more comprehensive views when constitutional essentials and basic justice are not at stake; they need not justify by public reason why they vote as they do" (*PL* 235, see also *PL* 252). That is what normal or ordinary politics is. Yet Rawls, in virtually the same breath, assigns to the legislature alone the task of devising "an orderly public financing of elections and constraints on private funding that achieves the fair value of the political liberties, or at least significantly moves the political process in that direction" (*PL* 235 n. 22). Although constrained by public reason, the temptation of incumbents to further entrench, rather than to revamp, the process by which they themselves attained office is too obvious to require further comment. *A constitution is defective to the extent that it needlessly consigns to majoritarian legislation alone the design and maintenance of fair-value protections.* No plausible reading of Rawls could represent him as rejecting the proposition stated in the preceding sentence, which is pregnant with further consequences.

THE FOURTH, AND FINAL, ADMINISTRATIVE/JUDICIAL STAGE

I described this as a residual stage to draw attention to its hybrid character. One department of the fourth stage is quotidian, encompassing the executive functions needed to make a government work. The other, judicial, department decides disputes and thus – if only reactively – oversees the justice of the institutions of government and nongovernmental institutions, insofar as they are legally regulated or have a bearing on constitutional essentials and basic liberties. The central player in the latter department is a supreme judiciary, which Rawls describes as "the exemplar of public reason" (*PL* 231).[5] As just noted, Rawls does not assign to the legislature the chief responsibility of protecting fair value. At one point, he expresses an apparent skepticism about the effectiveness of constitutionally entrenching basic rights.

> [I]n the *long run a strong majority* of the electorate can eventually make the constitution conform to its political will. This is simply a fact about political power as such. There is no way around this fact, not even by *entrenchment clauses* that try to fix the basic democratic guarantees.

> (*PL* 233; emphases added)

---

[4] Rawls describes an "exchange" branch to decide on public expenditures where no issue of justice is presented, and background justice is in place. Rawls gives a qualified endorsement of the Wicksell "unanimity criterion" (*TJ* 249–251), and allows representatives to vote their interests – implying that ideal legislators will not. Rawls said no more about this, and it is reasonable to conclude that he came to accept the account of the ideal legislative process given in the text, above. The constitution that is settled on so constrains ordinary majoritarian legislation that pure procedural justice, as to distributive issues, is assured.

[5] Bernard Williams remarked on the peculiarly moralistic American view of "the practice of politics," which rests on a "division of labor ... between the 'politics' of Congress and the principled arguments of the Supreme Court ... a Manichean dualism of soul and body, high-mindedness and the pork barrel" (Williams 2005, 12).

But this is not skepticism. By implication, entrenchment clauses might withstand less-than-strong majorities, or withstand strong majorities over the short term. So Rawls does not despair of them at all; and he acknowledges that a supreme judiciary

> is to prevent [the "higher" law] from being eroded by the legislation of transient majorities, or more likely, by organized and well-situated narrow interests skilled at getting their way.

> *(PL 233)*

How is the judiciary to do this? Direct appeals to higher law will surely seem more objectionably antidemocratic than judicial application of textual or structurally implicit rights. The choice of the personnel who compose the supreme judiciary can be expected to become a flash point of dissension unless the court at least gives lip-service to the principle that the judge's role is to apply the law, not to legislate.

Rawls mentions the possibility of unamendable entrenchment clauses, such as certain basic rights inscribed in the German constitution: "It places those rights beyond amendment, even by the people and the German supreme court, and in enforcing those rights can be said to be undemocratic. Entrenchment has that consequence" *(PL 234)*. This kind of "super"-entrenchment, although pro tanto antidemocratic, does not per se disqualify such provisions as inconsistent with "the values of a reasonable political conception of justice" *(PL 234–235)*. The "constituent power" of the people may indeed curtail its very own "ordinary power" of legislation *(PL 231)*.

5

The Circumstances of Politics

In *Justice as Fairness: A Restatement* (§11.3), Rawls lists five "very general facts of political society and human psychology" as "especially important" (*JF* 33). These are: (1) the fact of reasonable pluralism; (2) the fact of oppression; (3) the fact that a stable democracy must have the willing support of "at least a substantial majority of its politically active citizens" (*JF* 34); and (4) the public political culture of a stable constitutional democracy "normally contains, at least implicitly, certain fundamental ideas from which it is possible to work up a political conception of justice" (*JF* 35). Underlying and explaining these four – and particularly the first two – are certain further facts, which Rawls summarizes as the burdens of judgment: such things as difficulties in agreeing on the relevance and weight of evidence, conceptual vagueness and indeterminacy, divergence of experiential backgrounds, normative differences, and the like. All point to a fifth fact, that "many of our most important political judgments involving the basic political values" (*JF* 36) are unlikely to command a consensus of reasonable inquirers.

Rawls marks the importance of some, but not all, of these listed facts by giving them names. And the list is hardly compendious, for, as noted more than once already, Rawls invokes other general facts that are equal in importance to those on this list, in one way or another. One of them, for which I have suggested the label "the fact of domination," sets the background for this chapter. The fact of domination is one that Rawls showed early but increasing concern about, although the increase was less evident than the more conspicuous attention Rawls gave later in his career to the first-listed fact, that of reasonable pluralism. I will argue that the confluence of the two concerns – reasonable pluralism and domination – was at least partly responsible for Rawls's late-career explicitness about the injustice inherent in welfare-state capitalism.

The parties in Part One of the original position have no "strong will to dominate and exercise power over others" (*JF* 87). They "do not try to gain relative to one another" (*TJ* 125) – that is, they do not try to advantage the groups they represent over other groups. Those for whom the choosers choose, on the other hand, are known in Part

Two to be disposed and possibly determined to try to dominate their peers. The original position and its veil of ignorance are designed to free the choice of principles from the distorting effects that can arise if a chooser knows the specific traits, natural advantages, interests, goals, or conception of the good of those for whose benefit the choice of principles is made. "The only particular facts which the parties know is that their society is subject to the circumstances of justice and whatever this implies" (*TJ* 119; cf. *JF* 15–16). The circumstances of justice are simply the "normal conditions under which human cooperation is both possible and necessary" (*TJ* 109).

ANXIETY IN THE CIRCUMSTANCES OF JUSTICE

The circumstances of justice are of two kinds: one "objective," the other "subjective." The objective circumstances include the fact that people have to share a certain territory, that they are of approximately equal strength and ability, all are vulnerable, and each is liable to be overcome by the combined might of others. Conditions of material scarcity exist such that cooperation is possible and advantageous even though it cannot yield a material dividend capable of satisfying all desires. The subjective circumstances have to do with the members of society. They have similar but competing interests that make cooperation both desirable and possible. They have their own conceptions of the good life. Most notable here, however, are their common limitations:

> Their knowledge is necessarily incomplete, their powers of reasoning, memory, and attention are always limited, and their judgment is likely to be distorted by anxiety, bias, and a preoccupation with their own affairs. Some of the defects spring from moral faults, from selfishness and negligence; but to a large degree, they are simply part of men's natural situation.
>
> (*TJ* 110)

Those who do the choosing, however, have no natural situation. They have no moral faults – nor, for that matter, any moral virtues. The choosers are a theoretical device, a construction, and they have only the powers and limitations that the theory of justice turns out to require.

In addition to what the circumstances of justice already entail, the choosers also know whatever they need to know of a general nature in order to choose principles of justice:

> There are no limitations on general information, that is, on general laws and theories, since conceptions of justice must be adjusted to the characteristics of the systems of social cooperation which they are to regulate, and there is no reason to rule out these facts.
>
> (*TJ* 119)[1]

---

[1]   The later Rawls limits the scope of general knowledge somewhat by adding the qualifier "whenever uncontroversial" (*JF* 90, 190). The qualification is in line with his standing desire to seek as wide an agreement as possible, but it perhaps also reflects his growing concern not to limit unnecessarily the prospects for maintaining an "overlapping consensus" of reasonable, but competing, comprehensive conceptions of the good.

The need to choose principles capable of stabilizing a well-ordered society is instanced to illustrate the importance of allowing the choosers to have the widest possible access to general facts. "It is, for example, a consideration against a conception of justice that, in view of the laws of moral psychology, men would not acquire a desire to act upon it" (*TJ* 119). The reference here to "the laws of moral psychology" should be taken in the sense of "laws of psychology with respect to the moral" rather than to a moral psychology presupposing a particular comprehensive conception of morality. Over time, Rawls grew increasingly concerned not to be understood to be advancing a "comprehensive" Kantian liberalism, on the one hand, or to be relying on an empirical theory of moral psychology on the other.

It may be that Rawls accepted Kant's view that "radical evil" – that is, a desire to dominate others – is simply a metaphysical fact about human beings (see *BI* passim). But Rawls has not said that it is a fact of moral psychology that people inevitably tend to try to dominate one another. In describing the subjective circumstances of justice he has only referred in a nonspecific way to "moral faults," but Rawls has also, more concretely, pointed to an epistemological weakness: not only do people not know everything; "their judgment is likely to be distorted by *anxiety*, bias, and a preoccupation with their own affairs" (*TJ* 110; emphasis added). As noted earlier, in Chapter 1, Rawls regards it as a "general psychological fact" that anxiety is a source of "strong or inordinate desires for more primary goods ... greater income and wealth and prerogatives of position ... to be wealthy (to have more wealth than others)" (*CP* 277). These desires are natural, in a certain sense, and they threaten the stability of any scheme of social cooperation. So, even before the special psychologies are revealed in Part Two, the parties know that it is their task to choose principles that will reliably allay the anxieties that underlie the destabilizing psychological need to possess *comparatively* greater income, wealth, and positional prerogatives – not for its own sake, but defensively.

THE LIMITED SPACE OF THE POLITICAL

Whether or not people would otherwise naturally desire to dominate others, they are naturally anxious about being dominated. Their anxieties already cloud their judgment, but the anxiety about being dominated naturally generates a desire to become *indomitable* (cf. *LHPP* 49–50). But one person's fulfillment of this desire coordinately gives others greater grounds for anxiety on their parts. For what gives the other a position of greater indomitability also gives the other a greater ability to dominate, unless all are secure in the knowledge that all possess, and are reliably controlled by, a sense of justice – that is, a firm disposition to apply and adhere to commonly agreed principles of justice. These principles can only be realized by the establishment of a coercive apparatus – gently and rarely to be applied – that is the political expression of society's determination to live cooperatively. Coercion, for Rawls, is a fact of political life.

In a variety of contexts, Rawls acknowledges it as a general fact that disparate economic power inevitably conveys disparate political power. This is the fact of domination. He invokes the fact of domination, for example, in arguing that a Lockean "ideal historical process view" is to be rejected as incompatible with the maintenance of "pure procedural justice" over time (*JF* 53). It is a fact to be reckoned with at the constitutional stage, where a democratic political process has to be set in motion. Rawls describes the fact of domination as one that has afflicted all constitutional democracies; we do not need to know which society we inhabit to know this general fact. The fact of domination is already in contemplation in Part One of the argument for the two principles: it is not merely a matter of the special psychologies – envy, spite, the *will* to dominate – that are brought into view in Part Two. The fact of domination is a source of unrelenting pressures acting upon the shape and trajectory of political institutions; and it must be reckoned with in the fashioning of principles of justice even before these principles are queried in Part Two from the standpoint of their stability in the face of the special psychologies.

The fact of domination already raises the question of how, at the constitutional stage, to protect the fair value of political liberty and, in that respect, to assure that the criterion of reciprocity is publicly met. In other words, it raises the question of what type of constitution most plainly and publicly views "all [citizens as] having an equal share in the corporate political power of society" (*JF* 191). Constitutional measures to prevent economic inequality from ever rising to a level sufficient to undermine the political process seem entirely apt, but Rawls avoids confronting the challenge that way. Instead, he writes, "[c]ompensating steps must, then, be taken to preserve the fair value for all the political liberties. A variety of devices can be used. For example, in a society *allowing* private ownership of the means of production. ..." (*TJ* 198; emphasis added).[2] This brisk movement avoids the question whether a stable guarantee of fair value, that is open and evident to public view, is consistent with allowing private ownership of productive means in the first place. Instead, Rawls appears ready to assume that the tendency of private ownership of productive means to undermine stability and fair value can be compensated for by certain devices, such as subsidies for political parties and political discussion and coordinate limits on private political spending. Following Krouse and McPherson (1988, 86), I will call reliance on these devices an *"insulation strategy."*[3]

---

[2]   To guarantee fair equality of opportunity, a "free market system must be set within a framework of political and legal institutions that adjust the long-run *trend* of economic forces so as to *prevent* excessive concentrations of property and wealth, especially those *likely to lead to* political domination" (*JF* 44; emphases added). Notable here is the ambivalence between prevention and adjustment. Contrast Rawls's repeated insistence that "political power is *always* coercive power," and therefore illegitimate unless it is "*at the same time* the power of free and equal citizens as a *collective* body" (*JF* 40; emphases added).

[3]   Martin O'Neill (2014, 93) argues that "fair equality of opportunity and the fair value of the political liberties could plausibly be achieved under a variety of different socioeconomic

Rawls does not mention liberal socialism as a device to guarantee fair value. This is especially noteworthy, for at this so very crucial juncture in *A Theory of Justice* Rawls begins one of the most remarkable paragraphs in his extensive body of work.

> Historically one of the main defects of constitutional government has been the failure to insure the fair value of political liberty. The necessary *corrective steps* have not been taken, indeed, *they never seem to have been seriously entertained*. Disparities in the distribution of property and wealth that far exceed what is compatible with political equality have generally been tolerated by the legal system. Public resources have not been devoted to maintaining the institutions required for the fair value of political liberty.

> (*TJ* 198–199, emphases added)

This fact about the political culture is available to the constitutional convention on its own, whether or not packaged with an explanation of why it is a fact. Rawls does not here – or anywhere else – take this fact as calling into question his confidence that he has accurately identified the fundamental, organizing ideas that are "deeply imbedded" in our "not unambiguous" public political culture (*JF* 25). It is these ideas – and not any drawable solely from a comprehensive moral/political doctrine, even the true one – that he intends to "work up" into a theory of political justice. But this is consistent with the method of reflective equilibrium, which in its application to the design of the original position entitles us to discard philosophically dubious convictions, such as the conviction that political institutions must be shaped by pre-political conceptions of desert, or of property. Our public political culture may indeed seem not to have taken fair value seriously; but it does not follow that the best theory of justice for such a culture will not take it seriously either.

Compare chattel slavery. Perhaps the best theory of American constitutional law forbade slavery, as Frederick Douglass believed. Whether or not that is so, surely the best theory of justice for the United States, circa 1860, forbade slavery despite the fact that slavery was so deeply entrenched that Congress had adopted rules forbidding debate on the subject. Rawls remarked that "the difference principle is not often expressly endorsed; indeed, it may prove to have little support in our public political culture at the present time" (*JF* 132–133). But Rawls nonetheless proceeded to argue that the difference principle is part of the most plausible theory of *our* political conception of justice. In parallel fashion, it is reasonable to construe Rawls as

regimes." This overlooks the fact that for Rawls fair value is a constitutional essential, and that parties to a constitutional convention are not to take unnecessary gambles. Allen Thomas (2014, 123), emphasizing the importance of cultivating a republican ethos, recognizes that fair value is a constitutional essential, but he concludes that property-owning democracy is the required type of regime. Samuel Freeman (2007a 105–198; 2007b 133–135, 224–226) acknowledges that fair value as a first-principle concern decides against welfare state capitalism and in favor of property-owning democracy. He, like Thomas, does not acknowledge that liberal socialism must be preferred over property-owning democracy on similar grounds.

implicitly rejecting any suggestion that the idea of fair value equivalently lacks support in the public political culture. His critique of the decision in *Buckley v. Valeo* faults the U.S. Supreme Court for being oblivious to a principle deeply rooted in America's public political culture, from which, via congressional passage and presidential signature, the Election Act Amendment of 1974 had emerged (*PL* 359, 361–363).

As an aside, I note that Rawls was anyway mistaken to say the difference principle lacks support, for it is repeatedly invoked, under different names, to justify tax cuts for the wealthy. The "trickle-down" and "rising tide that raises all boats" similes that were the standard talking points of the Reagan and Thatcher governments are the close cousins – if not the monozygotic siblings – of the difference principle in the sense of a general conception. What Rawls says about "precepts of justice" is apropos here, "the contrast between conceptions of justice does not show up at the level of common sense norms but rather the relative and changing emphasis that these norms receive" (*TJ* 270). The status quo Rawls opposes does not deny the trickle-down, raise-all-boats precept; to the contrary, it embraces it as a general conception rather than in the subordinate position it is assigned in justice as fairness. What the political rhetoric shows is not a lack of endorsement or support in the political culture, but the instability of the principle of priority that subordinates the difference principle to the first principle of equal basic liberty, and to the principle of fair equality of opportunity. In a well-ordered society, this priority would not only be plain to all but would be stable. The argument for the stability of the priority principles, given in Part Two of the original position procedure, is the subject of Chapters 6 and 7.

The constructivist method Rawls propounds is importantly motivated by the possibility of discovery. As he elsewhere says, "There are facts about justice that may be discovered, as there are possibilities before anyone goes through a construction, say the possibilities that certain principles would be agreed to in the original position" (*PL* 125). But why have the corrective steps needed to assure fair value never been taken seriously, despite fair value's latency in our public political culture? Rawls continues:

> Essentially the fault lies in the fact that the democratic political process is at best a regulated rivalry; it does not even in theory have the desirable properties that price theory ascribes to truly competitive markets.

(*TJ* 199)

It is an axiom of price theory that competition for a certain good or service stimulates further production or provision and, over time, competition will lead to lower prices. In a perfectly competitive market, demand for more beer leads dependably to more and cheaper beer. But political influence is different. Rawls is adverting to the fact that increasing demand for political influence will never make political influence more affordable – rather, the reverse is the case. He continues:

Moreover, the effects of injustices in the political system are much more grave and long lasting than market imperfections. Political power *rapidly* accumulates and becomes unequal; and making use of the coercive apparatus of the state and its law, those who gain the advantage can often assure themselves of a favored position. Thus inequities in the economic and social system may *soon* undermine whatever political equality might have existed under fortunate historical conditions.

(TJ 199; emphases added)

An arms-race of ever-greater spending for political influence is the theoretical and practical result, which coordinately prices the less wealthy out of the market altogether. Just as the "fact of oppression" so central to political liberalism "seems evident ... from the history of democratic states [and] the development of thought and culture in the context of free institutions" (*JF* 84; cf. *JF* 34 n. 25); the fact of domination is sufficiently clear to count among the circumstances of justice known in the original position, Part One. What might be done about it?

> Universal suffrage is an insufficient counterpoise; for when parties and elections are financed not by public funds but by private contributions, the political forum is so constrained by the wishes of the dominant interests that the basic measures needed to establish just constitutional rule are seldom properly presented.

(TJ 199)

Rawls here is not merely repeating that formal equality does not itself guarantee fair equality. He is also suggesting that any corrective will have to be sturdy enough to withstand the distorting influence of unequal wealth before the political process unfolds, for its influence may affect public deliberation on a topic even before it has begun. If that is the case, though, should we not worry that the legislative design and implementation of these measures will itself be warped by the influence they are intended to control? Or that they might already be too late – especially if only "compensatory"?[4] Might the inequalities of wealth themselves have to be addressed before attempts are made to dampen their influence or compensate for them post facto? Rawls has assumed that the "strains of commitment" that property-owning democracy and liberal socialism confront are manageable; the occasion seems ripe to inquire further. But, concluding the paragraph, Rawls abruptly dismisses the matter:

> These questions, however, belong to political sociology. I mention them here as a way of emphasizing that our discussion is part of the theory of justice and must not be mistaken for a theory of the political system. We are in the way of describing an ideal arrangement, comparison with which defines a standard for judging actual institutions, and indicates what must be maintained to justify departures from it.

(TJ 199)

---

4   "[I]njustice exists because basic agreements are made too late" (*CP* 225; cf. *LHPP* 17).

It is unclear what questions are being assigned to political sociologists for further study.[5] Such results, whatever they turn out to be, are presumably unavailable until we have passed from the constitutional stage and are into the legislative or the administrative/judicial stage. But Rawls does not take back the historical claim with which this remarkable paragraph begins. What has been achieved?

> By way of summing up the account of the principle of participation, we can say that a just constitution sets up a form of fair rivalry for political office and authority. By presenting conceptions of the public good and policies designed to promote social ends, rival parties seek the citizens' approval in accordance with just procedural rules against a background of freedom of thought and assembly in which the fair value of political liberty is assured.

(TJ 199)

A fair rivalry for office and authority presupposes a basic structure in which fair value is already assured. But Rawls does not consistently formulate the problem that way. Instead, it is more often stated in terms of "compensating steps" whose design presents a problem in "political sociology."

This ambivalence may manifest the evolution of Rawls's conception of the knowledge and the point of view to be taken by representatives at the legislative stage. Obviously, if legislators are expected to be choosing behind a thickish veil of ignorance, a legislatively crafted insulation strategy might be as robust as any constitutionally embedded measure would be. If this is the case, then delegates to the constitutional convention can assume that an actual legislator – as a "representative legislator" – will not "know the particulars about himself" *(TJ* 174), or "the particulars of his own condition" *(TJ* 175), or "any knowledge that is likely to give rise to bias and distortion and to set men against one another" *(TJ* 176). After all, the task of constitutional design is "to choose the most effective just constitution" that is, "the one that is best calculated to lead to just and effective legislation" *(TJ* 173). This is to be determined by judging which constitution is likeliest to arrange it so actual legislators will approximate the ideal of the representative legislator.

---

[5]   Christian Schemmel gives an important reminder:

> In his discussion of different socio-economic regimes Rawls abstracts from all questions of "political sociology" concerning the different interests that regimes may engender over time, which may threaten, or enhance, their stability. Yet, it is clear that such an abstraction can only be preliminary. It would make little sense to embark on a thorough discussion of the institutional content demanded by Rawlsian principles without double-checking, as far as this is possible, whether the institutions in question are, or would be, reasonably stable and therefore apt to ensure social justice over time.

> (Schemmel 2015, 397)

> Note also that the double-checking takes place both in Part One and Part Two of the original position procedure, as I explain more fully in later chapters.

Rawls only later acknowledged that the strictures of public reason, which approximate the effects of a thickish veil of ignorance, do not place an epistemological barrier between actual legislators and their constituents.[6] True, as to constitutional essentials and matters of basic justice, actual legislators are supposed to put aside such knowledge, and to deliberate and vote within the confines of public reason. But this is akin to expecting that a bell in their heads can be unrung. Because the fact of domination is pervasive, the constitution best calculated to counter it will not rely on a corrective insulation strategy that is to be devised and maintained by legislators who know whose interests they represent. There are limits to what justice can leave to legislators to work out. As Rawls elsewhere asserts,

> our considered judgments with their fixed points – such as the condemned institutions of slavery and serfdom ... the subjection of the working classes ... and the unlimited accumulation of vast fortunes, together with ... the evil of the pleasures of exercising domination – stand in the background as substantive checks showing the illusory character of any allegedly purely procedural ideas of legitimacy and political justice.

(PL 431)

The question that has to be confronted, and not only for completeness's sake, is whether a pure procedural distributive justice is stably achievable in a constitutional regime that tolerates private ownership of a society's central productive means. It is a question that has to be continued in Part Two of the original position procedure. The two principles of justice of fairness can only be established if they are realizable institutionally in a society in which the special psychologies are in play. It will emerge that taking on the special psychologies, in Part Two, forces decisions at the constitutional stage that, in Part One, already appear unsafe to refer to majoritarian legislation.

---

[6] In the *Restatement*, Rawls writes that "we strive for publicly based justifications regarding the constitutional essentials and basic questions of distributive justice" (JF 91 n.13), but the reader is left to guess how "basic" and "non-basic" questions of distributive justice are to be distinguished and – more crucially – by whom the distinction is authoritatively to be made. As to "non-basic" questions of distributive justice, the legislature decides, but legislation based "solely on political values covered by the political conception of justice [is] neither attainable nor desirable" (JF 91 n.13).

6

Rescuing the Difference Principle

I concluded the previous chapter with an extended discussion of that remarkable passage in A *Theory of Justice* in which Rawls acknowledges that the corrective measures needed to assure the first-principle guarantee of the fair value of political liberty have never been taken seriously in the modern history of democratic government (*TJ* 198–199). This passage had been preceded by Rawls's tentative suggestion that legislative measures to insulate money and politics could sufficiently protect fair value, and that private ownership of the central means of production – and the additional inequalities of economic and political power that are known to accrue therefrom – does not itself dangerously undermine those very measures (*TJ* 198). The question that would naturally occur to one – that is, the question whether the failure of democratic governments to take fair value seriously might itself be the artifact of the unequal ownership of capital – was not raised. But Rawls later does acknowledge this very possibility, in the context of inequality's effect on stability.

Concern with the "problem of stability" runs throughout Rawls's theory: "[T]he scheme of social cooperation must be stable: it must be more or less regularly complied with and its basic rules willingly acted upon; and when infractions occur, stabilizing forces should exist that prevent further violations and tend to restore the arrangement" (*TJ* 6). Concern with stability features more prominently in Part Two of the original position procedure, where the parties have to confront the circumstance – excluded from their view in Part One – that the citizens they represent in fact do take an interest in each other's interests, for these citizens are moved by the special psychologies that involve envy, spite, the will to power, and inordinate attitudes toward risk.

A well-ordered society is one that "endures over time," which entails that it is stabilized *by* its conception of justice:

> [T]hat is, when institutions are just (as defined by this conception) those taking part
> in these arrangements acquire the corresponding sense of justice and desire to do

their part in maintaining them. *One conception of justice is more stable than another if the sense of justice that it tends to generate is stronger and more likely to override disruptive inclinations and if the institutions it allows foster weaker impulses and temptations to act unjustly.* The stability of a conception depends upon a balance of motives: The sense of justice that it cultivates and the aims that it encourages must normally win out against propensities toward injustice. . . . Other things equal, the *persons in the original position will adopt the more stable scheme* of principles.

(TJ 398; emphases added; see also TJ 436)

The stability problem in Part Two is a cumulative as well as a continued worry. The principles of justice tentatively picked in Part One are known to, and are designed to, conflict with and to hold in check what a rational, self-interested person will at least sometimes want to do. There is thus an assurance problem, because self-interested persons will not want to make sacrifices that benefit them only on the condition that others make similar sacrifices unless there is good reason to suppose that others are in fact making those sacrifices. There is a strains-of-commitment problem because the parties in Part One realize that, even given the needed assurances, there is a limit to the sacrifices persons can commit themselves to making. And there is a burdens-of-judgment problem because various epistemological barriers will sometimes cause both real and apparent deviations from compliance with what justice requires, even under the perfect-compliance assumption of ideal theory.

RELATIVE STABILITY: THE TWO FUNDAMENTAL COMPARISONS

Rawls never rejects a conception of any sort on the ground that it is absolutely unstable. But there are two instances – really, the sole examples – of his weighing a pair of conceptions in terms of their relative stability. These occur in the "two fundamental comparisons" in Part One of the original position procedure. Although *Theory* divides the argument for the two principles of justice into Part One and Part Two, *Theory* does not make a division, within Part One, into two fundamental comparisons. The division is a change "in how the argument for [the two] principles from the original position is organized" (*JF* xvi). It is introduced, in the *Restatement*, in order to respond to certain misunderstandings about the crucial argument against utilitarianism. The argument does not rest

> as K.J. Arrow and J.C. Harsanyi and others have not unreasonably thought . . . on a great aversion to uncertainty viewed as a psychological attitude. That would be a very weak argument. Rather, the appropriate reasons rest on such ideas as *publicity* and *reciprocity*.

(JF xvii; emphasis added)

Stability, publicity, and reciprocity are the key ideas. The first fundamental comparison pits the two principles of justice as fairness against (average) utilitarianism.

The second fundamental comparison, however, pits the two principles against a mixed conception called the principle of restricted utility. Restricted utility adopts the first principle of equal liberty and its priority, but replaces the difference principle with (again, average) utilitarianism. Rawls, recall, had admitted in the introduction to the paperback edition of *Political Liberalism* that restricted utilitarianism was a reasonable liberal conception of justice, albeit less reasonable, he opined, than justice as fairness. But Rawls, there, provided no reason to prefer justice as fairness to restricted utility. In the *Restatement*, Rawls provides new reasons, organized as a novel argument, to rescue the difference principle – and justice as fairness itself – from objections that in 1996 he seemed unable to counter.

The first fundamental comparison relies – though less extensively than the second fundamental comparison – on stability, publicity, and reciprocity. The first comparison is conducted under the aegis of the maximin criterion of decision under uncertainty: choose the alternative that has the best outcome in its worst case. In this first comparison, the three conditions for using the maximin principle of choice are all (to a degree) present: (a) there is significant uncertainty about the probability of outcomes under both conceptions, (b) under one of the conceptions there is a highly satisfactory guaranteeable level, and (c) under the other there is no satisfactory guaranteeable level. Justice as fairness is the conception that guarantees a highly satisfactory outcome, and so it is the rational choice. Insofar as *Theory* is conceived as a contractarian refutation of utilitarianism, the first fundamental comparison in the *Restatement* clarifies and sharpens the argument for *Theory*'s major result: the two principles "as a unit" are rationally preferred to the principle of average utility, if the latter is considered "as the sole principle of justice" (*JF* 119).

FIRST FUNDAMENTAL COMPARISON: "STRESSING THE SECOND CONDITION"

I will not recapitulate the first fundamental comparison in its complex entirety. What is relevant to my purpose is a separate section (*JF* §33) of the first fundamental comparison, in which Rawls deliberately lays stress on the condition that justice as fairness assures a highly satisfactory guaranteeable level (*JF* 115–119). This is presented as a distinct argument for justice as fairness, and it is in effect and essentially an argument that justice as fairness makes for a more stable regime than utilitarianism even if we set aside the fact that utilitarianism allows – even demands – very bad outcomes for some, wherever average utility is improved. Justice as fairness is still rational to prefer because

> those [two] principles are more effective than the principle of (average) utility in guaranteeing the equal basic liberties and therefore in meeting *three essential requirements for a stable constitutional regime.*

(*JF* 115; emphasis added)

We could equally take the "therefore" in the converse direction: justice as fairness better meets these three stability requirements and *therefore* is more effective in guaranteeing equal basic liberty. In essence, this is a relative-stability argument, focused not on individual liberty directly but on "the nature of the public political culture" (*JF* 119) necessary to secure liberty.

The Reconciliation Requirement

I will separately restate the requirements of stability, with an eye toward making later application of them in the way Rawls, I believe, anticipated they must be.

> The first requirement, given the fact of reasonable pluralism, is to fix, once and for all, the basic rights and liberties, and to assign them a special priority. Doing this takes these guarantees off the political agenda of political parties; it puts them beyond the calculus of social interests, thus securing clearly and firmly the terms of social cooperation on a footing of mutual respect.
>
> (*JF* 115)

Justice as fairness does this, but utilitarianism does not. Even a rule-utilitarian formulation that purports to establish basic rights "leaves the status and content of those freedoms still unsettled" (*JF* 115). Of course, justice as fairness does not wholly determine the "status and content" of any particular basic liberty – beyond its "central range of application" – either, but the priority of the package of basic liberties is absolute. Utilitarianism, by contrast, exposes the basic liberties both singly and as a package "to the shifting circumstances of time and place, and by greatly raising the stakes of political controversy, it greatly increases the insecurity and hostility of public life" (*JF* 115). Rawls suggests this example:

> Consider the unwillingness to take off the political agenda such questions as which faiths are to have liberty of conscience, or which groups are to have the right to vote. Such an unwillingness perpetuates the deep divisions latent in a society marked by the fact of reasonable pluralism. It may betray a readiness to revive old antagonisms in the hope of gaining a more favorable position should circumstances prove propitious later on. By contrast, securing these basic liberties and affirming their priority more effectively does the *work of reconciliation* among citizens and promises mutual recognition on a footing of equality.
>
> (*JF* 115; emphasis added)

Rawls does not do so, but we can call this first stability requirement the *reconciliation requirement*. A regime is less stable to the extent that its political agenda is open to such a degree that deeply divisive fissures are often implicated in the people's exercise of the ordinary power of legislation. It can be objected here that Rawls is presupposing some effective institutional means of defining and enforcing the political agenda. Without such means, it would appear that all justice as fairness has to offer is lip service to the idea of not bringing certain things up for a vote. Rawls's answer is to be found in his discussion of the four-stage sequence and in his remarks on judicial review.

The Publicity Condition

The second stability requirement is termed *the publicity condition*, and Rawls often invokes a "publicity principle" and the related idea of "public reason" in various contexts.

> The second requirement of a stable constitutional regime is that its political conception should specify not only a shared but if possible a *clear* basis of public reason, and one that can be seen to be sufficiently *reliable* in its own terms.
>
> (*JF* 116; emphases added)

The publicity condition encompasses two ideas: clarity and reliability. They are distinct but related notions. Despite its calculative pretensions, utilitarianism as a principle of justice does not show well, for

> if the elaborate theoretical calculations involved in applying the principle of utility are publicly viewed as decisive, the highly speculative nature and great complexity of those estimations are bound to make the application of the principle highly uncertain. To see this, consider the difficulties of applying it to the basic structure.
>
> (*JF* 116)

Rawls is adverting to technical problems, such as interpersonal comparisons of utilities, which he discusses more thoroughly in *Theory* (*TJ* 282–285). To the extent that utilitarianism has to assign individual utilities to categories of liberties that justice as fairness regards as pearls beyond price, it is instantly involved in these kinds of additional difficulty. But to make the comparative notions precise, it is necessary to rely on ethical and moral judgments that will themselves invite controversy. For example, one way of increasing satisfaction is to cultivate preferences for what is in plentiful supply. ("Let them eat cake.") Another is to accentuate compensating benefits: Should those denied the right to vote be considered better rather than worse off, for being relieved of burdensome expectations that amount almost to a duty? Despite its fishiness, this kind of argument is at least invited by the utility principle.

> [T]he principle of utility may prove to be politically unworkable, for people are likely to be highly suspicious of one another's arguments. The information these complex arguments presuppose is often hard if not impossible to obtain, and frequently there are grave problems in reaching an objective and agreed upon assessment. Moreover, even though we think our arguments sincere and not self-serving when we present them, we must consider what it is reasonable to expect others to think who stand to lose should our reasoning prevail. Arguments

supporting political judgments should, if possible, be not only sound, but such that they can publicly be seen to be sound.

(JF 116)

Rawls grants that some of the political reasoning allowed and necessary under justice as fairness will also be received with suspicion. But a firm comparative judgment is warranted nonetheless: "[T]he two principles (with an index of primary goods *defined in terms of the objective features* of people's social situation) seem superior to the principle of utility" (*JF* 116; emphasis added). The parenthetical caveat must be borne in mind.

The Express Reciprocity Criterion

The third required condition for a stable constitutional democracy "is that its basic institutions should encourage the cooperative virtues of political life" (*JF* 116). These cooperative virtues form a compendium that includes "reasonableness and a sense of fairness, . . . a spirit of compromise and a readiness to meet others halfway" (*JF* 116), and "a disposition to honor the duty of public civility," that is, to "appeal to political values in cases involving constitutional essentials" and in divisive cases bordering thereon (*JF* 117). In other words, public civility is a disposition to preface comments with the clause "We all agree . . ." rather than with "What you don't see . . . ." Justice as fairness promotes and maintains these virtues more effectively than utilitarianism does because "the two principles of justice *express an idea of reciprocity* that is lacking in the principle of utility" (*TJ* 117; emphasis added).

Rawls footnotes the argument with an illustrative analogy. A commercial franchiser, like Dunkin' Donuts, has to decide whether to offer its franchisees contracts with a variable percentage for the division of revenue or a single, flat percentage. The first strategy allows the franchisor to take a higher percentage of the profits initially from the better-situated and, later, from the better-performing franchisees, while the second fixes a single percentage across all franchisees.

> [G]iven the very great initial uncertainty the franchiser faces, the great uncertainty in cooperative relations between franchiser and franchisee that the first strategy would perpetuate, and the continuing suspicion and distrust which that uncertainty would cause, the second strategy is superior . . . . [I]t is more rational to try to create a climate of fair cooperation based on clear and fixed terms that strike all parties as reasonable than to try for adjustable fine-tuned contracts that might enable the franchiser to increase profits as particular opportunities arise. There is some evidence that in fact successful franchisers follow the second strategy.

(JF 119 n. 39)

The cooperative enterprise of brand-building, Rawls is suggesting, is more stably pursued by clear, reasonably fair, fixed terms rather than terms that are subject to opportunistic fine-tuning. Rawls might have gone a step farther. The point carries equally well if a third strategy were available, just like the first but providing not a higher take for the franchiser from the better-performing franchisees, but a higher "keep" for the less-promising and, later, the less-well-performing franchisees. This third strategy is appealing insofar as it puts productive resources into the hands of the needier franchisees "at the beginning of each period, so to speak," but it, like strategy one is less stable than strategy two, the fixed percentage.

SECOND FUNDAMENTAL COMPARISON: PUBLICITY,
RECIPROCITY, STABILITY

As Rawls acknowledges, the first fundamental comparison does not complete the argument for the two principles of justice as fairness. Wrapping up the argument requires a further comparison, the "second fundamental comparison," which pits justice as fairness against what he calls a "mixed conception" or, more precisely, the "principle of restricted utility" (*JF* 120; cf. *TJ* 107). The idea of restricted utility is simple. It takes on all of justice as fairness except the difference principle. In other words, restricted utility admits the first principle of equal liberty, and the principle of fair equal opportunity, which is the first part of the second principle. But restricted utility rejects the difference principle and replaces it with the principle of utility subject to a guaranteed social minimum. The "restriction" in restricted utility is the priority of the principles borrowed from justice as fairness, and the additional restriction of a social minimum.

So defined, restricted utility looks to be a formidable competitor to justice as fairness. Restricted utility is designed to incorporate all the components of justice as fairness – including its guarantee of the fair value of political liberty (*JF* 120) – except for the difference principle. Recall that the difference principle as a "general conception" has to yield to a prior first principle of equal liberty once society achieves even a moderate degree of material abundance. So, the difference principle is no more acceptable as a *general* conception than is average utilitarianism. Recall also that justice as fairness also recognizes the need for a social minimum, as Rawls concedes in his response to Rodney Peffer, discussed in Chapter 4. A rational party, in the original position, is now faced with a choice between two residual, lexically posterior principles of distribution: one is the difference principle, and the other is utilitarianism with a guaranteed social minimum set at a "fully satisfactory" level.

What is there to choose? Rawls confesses that the argument for justice as fairness over restricted utility is not as compelling, and "the outcome is certainly less clear and decisive" (*JF* 133). In the first fundamental comparison, the conditions for applying the maximin criterion were well enough satisfied. That is no longer the case in the second fundamental comparison. Restricted utility now is stipulated to have a fully satisfactory worst outcome too. Maximin is therefore inapplicable.

Under restricted utility, once equal liberty, fair equal opportunity, and a social minimum are in place, material inequalities are justified if, but only if, they raise the average index of primary goods. Some might not benefit, but they have their equal liberties, their fair equal opportunities, and a fully satisfactory social minimum. They cannot complain to the parties that represent them that they are envious: the parties are in Part One of the original position procedure, and so "interests in the interests of others" are concealed behind the veil of ignorance. The difference principle gives them a ground of complaint: no one is to benefit unless all do. But does reason require a principle that supports their complaint?

Rawls argues that reason does indeed decisively favor the difference principle in this contest too. Leaving probability arguments aside, and accepting that both principles avoid terrible outcomes,

> We assume that there are two groups in society, the more and the less advantaged; and then we try to show that both would favor the difference principle over that of restricted utility. In effect, we argue that the second condition of the maximin rule is fully satisfied, or nearly enough so to provide an independent argument for the two principles.
>
> (*JF* 120)

Full satisfaction of the second condition means that the guaranteeable level of one of the two alternatives is so high that

> it must be rational for the parties as trustees not to be much concerned for what might be gained above what can be gained (for those they represent) by adopting the alternative whose worst outcome is better than the worst outcomes of all the other alternatives.
>
> (*JF* 98)

In other words, Rawls will show that whatever the guaranteeable level – whatever "the best worst outcome" (*JF* 98) – under restricted utility is stipulated to be, the guaranteeable level under the difference principle is not only higher but sufficiently higher that it is irrational for the parties to gamble for gains above that. No matter how much the highest payoff may be under restricted utility, reason requires sticking with the higher guaranteeable level provided by the difference principle.

Now, I set aside the possible objection that Rawls is, in effect, appealing to maximin even as he concedes that two of the three conditions for its application are unsatisfied. I am concerned not with the strategy itself, but with what Rawls says by way of carrying it out. Rawls may, in fact, mischaracterize the strategy itself, but I leave that aside as well. His intended argument depends on an appeal to stability under the strains of commitment, in the light of ideas of publicity and reciprocity. Justice as fairness is chosen in the second fundamental comparison of Part One of the original position procedure, the argument goes, because it can be seen to do a better job than restricted utility in withstanding these strains. To facilitate exposition, I will stick fairly closely to the headings Rawls uses.

Grounds of Publicity

The characterization of these grounds is consistent with what was said in making the first fundamental comparison, but with the addition of an acknowledgment that the publicity condition assigns "an educational role" to conceptions of justice. But this is to be contrasted to a merely ideological role. "The hope is that a well-ordered society in which the full publicity condition is satisfied ... is a society without ideology (understood in Marx's sense of false consciousness)" (*JF* 121). The content that is common to both justice as fairness and restricted utility provides a footing for this educational but non-ideological role. The question becomes: Which of the distributive principles – the difference principle or average utility – better complements and completes the educational task?

Grounds of Reciprocity

The idea of reciprocity is developed further here, beyond its role in the first fundamental comparison. One refinement is to define reciprocity with reference to a *starting point of equality*. Another is to draw attention to the importance of selecting a *natural focal point*, if there is one, that picks out a salient reference point from which to halt departures from the starting point of equality.

> Since the parties in the original position are symmetrically situated and know (from the common content of the two alternatives) that the [distributive] principle adopted will apply to citizens as free and equal, they take equal division of income and wealth ... as the starting point. They ask: are there good reasons for departing from equal division, and if so, which inequalities arising in what ways are acceptable?
>
> (*JF* 123)

In brief, reciprocity requires (a) a starting point of equal division, (b) good reasons to depart from equal division, and (c) a reference point for determining whether the degree and manner of departure are justified.

The parties recognize that "requirements of social organization and economic efficiency" (*JF* 123) can provide good reason to depart from the starting point of equal division. Rationally, the parties also accept departures from a starting point of equal division that are to the benefit of all. The point at which a departure that is beneficial in terms of average utility ceases to benefit all is a "natural focal point" (*JF* 123) for settlement between the now conflicting claims of equality and average utility. Rawls credits economist Thomas Schelling with the idea that a prominent focal point can make coordination possible, in circumstances in which individuals would otherwise have to guess what others will do. In the passage Rawls cites, Schelling says:

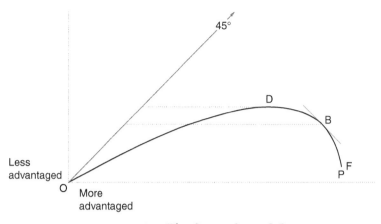

FIGURE 6.1. The Output Curve O-P

People *can* often concert their intentions or expectations if each knows the other is trying to do the same. Most situations ... provide some clue for coordinating behavior, some focal point for each person's expectation of what the other expects him to be expected to do .... A prime characteristic of most of these "solutions" to the problems, that is of the clues or coordinators or focal points, is some kind of prominence or conspicuousness.

(1960, 57)

The D point (see Figure 6.1) is both unique and unambiguous: the "idea of reciprocity" reflected in the difference principle insists on this point as the limit. Restricted utility knows no limit, other than what is already imposed by the common content.

Grounds of Stability

The idea of stability is also developed further here, building on what Rawls says about it in making the first fundamental comparison. The innovations are several. One is the idea of self-enforcing institutions: "[I]n order to be stable, a political conception of justice must generate its own support and the institutions to which it leads must be *self-enforcing*, at least under reasonably favorable conditions" (*JF* 125; emphasis added). Another is the idea of a conflict zone or segment. Stability must withstand temptations that citizens can be expected to feel, to renegotiate the basic terms of the social settlement once their own positions and prospects are plain to them.

In the well-ordered society of justice as fairness it seems that those most likely to be discontent are the more advantaged; and hence they are more likely to violate the terms of cooperation, or to urge renegotiation. For the further they can shift the distribution of income and wealth into the *conflict segment*..., the more they benefit. Then why aren't they continually urging renegotiations? (*JF* 125; emphasis added; and see *JF* 62, figure 1)

The conflict segment is a zone in which the better-off might plausibly and even sincerely claim that a greater average of social utility is achieved even though some citizens are not as well-off. The conflict segment is the portion D-F of the output curve O-P past its peak at the point designated D to the "feudal point," F, where the less-advantaged continue to lose despite no further gain to the more-advantaged. The principle of restricted utility permits and even encourages the better-off to advance such claims. But gains in this segment come at the expense of some sub-group or another. The already less-well-off might mistake these claims as attempts on the part of the better-off to leverage their advantaged position to renegotiate the terms of the social settlement generally. Moreover, even assuming good faith all around, multiple groups might similarly make sincere claims as ways to increase the social sum, always at some other group's expense. As Schelling says, prominence can make coordination possible:

> But it is a prominence that depends on time and place and who the people are. Ordinary folk lost on a plane circular area may naturally go to the center to meet each other; but only one versed in mathematics would "naturally" expect to meet his partner in the center of gravity of an irregularly shaped area.

> (Schelling 1960, 57–58)

The conflict segment to which Rawls draws our attention resembles in a certain way the irregularly shaped area in Schelling's example. Ordinary people cannot find B, the Bentham point, without expert assistance, and the experts will disagree about where that point falls. Better, then, for us to avoid getting lost by not entering areas where there is no natural focal point for us to reunite. In addition to prominence, "[e]qually essential is some kind of uniqueness," Schelling (1960, 58) says: not only is uniqueness itself a kind of prominence, "uniqueness avoids ambiguousness." A house is prominent in the rural Great Plains, but not so in a residential subdivision. The better-off, and those wanting to join them, can grasp that the balance of reasons favors "a culture that inhibits the wastes of endless self- and group-interested bargaining" (*JF* 126) within the conflict segment. Here, my purpose is simply to inventory the ideas Rawls is using in conceptualizing stability. The purpose is not to explicate or defend the detailed use Rawls makes of Schelling's ideas in the second fundamental comparison.

The parties in the original position recognize that stability cannot as well endure the stresses that restricted utility allows, and moreover,

> since the difference principle expresses an agreement not to enter the conflict segment, and since the more-advantaged ... are better placed to enter it, their publicly affirming that principle conveys to the less advantaged their acceptance of an appropriate idea of reciprocity in the clearest possible way.

> (*JF* 126)

This is the third of the refining ideas about stability introduced in the second fundamental comparison: the idea of a *clearest public affirmation* of general acceptance of reciprocity. In a footnote, Rawls credits E. F. McClennan with the point and an instructive discussion. It is worth quoting a more focused remark McClennan makes in the passage Rawls cites approvingly,

> [I]n the context of deliberation and debate over alternative proposals, virtually any distributive proposal carries with it a problem of ambiguity concerning the intention of the proposer. But a proposal that accords less, or at least no more, to oneself than to others would seem to offer the best hope that the signal will not be destabilizing.
>
> (McClennan 1989, 23)

Now, the difference principle does not always realize this "best hope," since it notoriously allows anyone to propose that others accept a lesser relative gain, with the assurance that the resulting share realizes for all a gain in absolute terms. But it is nonetheless true that the least destabilizing distributive signals are ones sent by proposals that leave others at least as well off as the proposer. The significance of this point will become plainer in Chapter 8, in which the mechanics of property-owning democracy are examined through the lens of stability.

Counting Up the Grounds

Rawls proceeds with further point-by-point comparisons. Restricted utility, Rawls says, is less determinate than the difference principle. Determinacy is of course related to publicity and to clarity.

> [W]here in the conflict segment is the Bentham point [where the sum of utilities is at its maximum]; or indeed any other point specified by a utility principle . . .? We require a workable public interpersonal measure to identify it . . . that should be, if possible, recognized by all as reasonably reliable. This is one consideration that led us to introduce the idea of *primary goods based on objective features of people's circumstances*. The difficulties with the principle of utility on this count are substantial. Uncertainty is likely to increase disputes and mistrust for much the same reason that unclear and ambiguous principles do.
>
> (JF 126–127; emphasis added)

Rawls does not note the similar uncertainty involved in locating the "D point" that is crucial in applying the difference principle. The D point is the point at which the OP curve is at its maximum on the y axis, and it signifies that any further gains to the more advantaged, measured on the x axis, will correspond to losses realized by the less-advantaged. (It is of course irrelevant that the D point might be easier to spot visually from the back of the classroom once it has been drawn on the blackboard.) Moreover, Rawls elsewhere acknowledges that restricted utility could easily elude part of his objection by adopting the objective primary goods index as its measure of utility (*TJ* (1st ed.) 175; cf. McClennan 1989, 28). Again, my task here is not to assess the soundness of Rawls's argument. Rather, it is to collect the conceptual tools and argumentative lemmas that Rawls employs. I note again the emphasis Rawls places on the advantage in terms of determinacy and publicity of the objective conception of the primary goods.

Reciprocity and Strains of Commitment

In two respects, restricted utility involves greater "psychological strains that may lead to instability" (*JF* 127). These are the strains of commitment: for, "to make an agreement in good faith, [the parties] must be reasonably confident that the person each represents will be able to honor it" (*JF* 128) when that person surveys her actual social position and life prospects, insofar as the basic structure of society determines them. Bear in mind that these strains are strictly separate from the special psychologies of envy, spite, greed, and so forth. We have not reached Part Two of the original position procedure.

Restricted utility, in effect, asks some to accept worse prospects for themselves on the ground that the average citizen is better off. This is, Rawls says, an appeal to disinterested benevolence, a sympathy that, as moralists over the ages have remarked, is not the strongest or most reliable human motive. By contrast, the difference principle, in effect, asks some to accept an only relatively lower position on the ground that they are better off in terms of their own interests. By drawing on a more dependable and stronger motive, the difference principle does not add to the strains of commitment the less-advantaged must bear. But what of the more-advantaged? They are, in effect, asked to take less in absolute terms on the ground that their taking more would diminish the nonetheless adequate position of the less advantaged. But Rawls reckons that this is a lesser strain or, if it is not lesser, that it is likely owing to the circumstance that the economically more-advantaged hold greater political power and authority. But this is already a reason not to allow proposals within the conflict segment, which restricted utility invites; and Rawls warns, "[i]t may be that the inequalities permitted by the difference principle are already too great for stability" (*JF* 127). This is a reminder of the comparative form of the argument: justice as fairness has not been shown to be stable – that will require not only an exploration of possible institutional realizations but also the further stability-testing of Part Two of the original position procedure.

Another, and final, comparison has reference to the role the social minimum must play in applying the principle of restricted utility. How is that minimum level set? How low can it go before the least-advantaged cease to be able to affirm the principles of justice? Suppose the minimum is specified as whatever is needed to live a decent life. Those who come to depend on the minimum might manifest the strains in two ways: first, by oppositional activity (and attitudes tending thereto); and second, by withdrawal. The strains that can be foreseen might not be such as to lead to manifestations of the first kind, to bitterness, a sense of oppression, and violent rebellion, but will they not lead the least-advantaged "to grow distant from political society and retreat into [their own] social world . . . feel[ing] left out, withdrawn and cynical" (*JF* 128)? Rawls does not suggest the applicability of Marx's term "alienation" here, but Rawls's discussion in the *Lectures* of one aspect of Marx's concept of alienation is apt:

> Human beings are a distinctive natural kind – or species – in the sense that they collectively produce and reproduce the conditions of their social life over time . . . . [E]ventually, a social form develops that is more or less adequate to their nature as rational and active beings who, as it were, create, working with the forces of nature, the conditions of their complete social self-realization. The activity by which this collective self-expression is accomplished is species-activity; that is, the cooperative work of many generations . . . of the species over its history. To be alienated from species activity is first of all not to comprehend or to understand this process; and second, it is *not to participate in this activity in a self-realizing way.*
>
> (*LHPP* 363; emphasis added)

What Rawls refers to as the second of the two ways we can react, when we cease to affirm the public conception of justice as our own, is of a piece with the manifestation of an aspect of Marxian alienation. The human individual does not feel that she is part of the enterprise, but is simply caught up in it.

Rawls might be read as saying that to be alienated is a to suffer a violation; for he says that a social minimum that "suffices to prevent the strains of commitment from being violated in the first way . . . seems inadequate to ensure that the strains of commitment are not violated in the second way" (*JF* 120). We should read "violated" as "exceeded," of course, to avoid needlessly personifying the strains; but, in a sense, those who must live in a coercive regime governed by principles they cannot freely affirm *are* being oppressed, and thus are entitled to feel that they are. So, the distinction between the first and second ways of manifesting excessiveness of strains is not airtight. Both are destabilizing.

By contrast, under justice as fairness, the social minimum does not derive from an essentially humanitarian notion of decency. Rather, "the social minimum, whatever it may provide beyond essential human needs, must derive from an idea of reciprocity appropriate to political society" (*JF* 130) conceived as a fair system of productive cooperation over time.

"We hope that even the situation of the least advantaged does not prevent them from being drawn into *the public world* and seeing themselves as full members of it" (*JF* 130; emphasis added). The idea of a public world is integral to realizing the ideas of reconciliation, publicity, reciprocity, and stability. Restricted utility does not derive its social minimum from an idea of reciprocity, and therefore its message, whether or not intended as such, is an invitation to the least-advantaged to view themselves as casualties, dependents, or mere beneficiaries rather than participants in a public world.

Reflection on the Part One Argument for Justice as Fairness

Rawls concludes the two fundamental comparisons with the cautious reminder that while the argument aspires to the rigor of "moral geometry," it has remained "highly intuitive" (*JF* 133). Not to be misunderstood, Rawls adds that one aim of the original position procedure is *explicitness*, to "keep track of our assumptions" so that we always "know which ones we have to justify" (*JF* 133). Reasoning cannot be rigorous without the assistance of assumptions that seem reasonable but cannot be supported by anything else that is not, for all we can tell, merely a reiteration of what has already been assumed.

> In political philosophy, as elsewhere, we must rely on judgment as to what considerations are more and less significant, and when in practice to close the list of reasons. Even when judgment is unanimous we may not be able to articulate our reasons any further.
>
> (*JF* 134)

Rawls is less emphatic than he is entitled to be. Each of the grounds falling under publicity, reciprocity, and stability favor the difference principle over restricted utility. Since the difference principle dominates its rival in each of these comparisons, the argument seems to be complete. It is one of the general "counting principles" (*LP* 88; *TJ* (1st ed.) 411–415) of rationality that if a choice A is superior to choice B in all relevant respects *x*, *y*, and *z*, then a rational chooser must choose A.[1] But of course, as Rawls points out, the list of relevant considerations is potentially endless. What I want to emphasize is that if judgment tells us that a consideration belongs in the closed list, then it must be applied, in a consistent fashion, wherever it is relevant. When we return to the choice between liberal socialism and property-owning democracy, in Chapter 10, this framework will prove to be decisive.

---

[1]   In the third lecture on Hobbes, Rawls calls this the "Principle of the Dominant Alternative" (*LHPP* 60).

7

The Special Psychologies

The special psychologies introduce a new kind of difficulty. It is not merely that citizens are uncertain whether others are doing their part, or whether the sacrifices justice requires are worth it, or what justice requires, or whether the laws under a just constitution have missed the mark. These are already problems in Part One. In Part Two, what is new is the sidelong glance one citizen casts at another, taking an interest in what the other has. Less-well-off citizens might want better-off citizens not to have what those better-off citizens justly have. Similarly, better-off citizens might not want less well-off citizens to rise to their level, as the less-well-off might do by acquiring what those lesser-off justly could acquire. These are the problems of envy and spite. The envious person is not consoled by the thought that if things were more equal, she would have less. She is willing to take less on the condition that others are brought down to or nearer to her level. The spiteful person is not content to have what he has: he must have more than others, and he would rather give up some of what he has than to allow others to rise to or to approach his level.

The reasons Rawls gives for ignoring the special psychologies in Part One are straightforward. One is that envy and spite are usually disdained as unworthy emotions, and thus as unsuitable factors to include in a procedure for identifying principles of justice. The other is that to include them would be complicating theoretically. People are envious in degrees, for example, and the degree of sacrifice that a less-advantaged person might be willing to make to bring a more-advantaged person down a peg in one dimension can vary from the degree of willingness in another dimension. Just as in the case of risk averseness generally, it is far simpler to "normalize" and stipulate that the parties represent persons who have no unusual averseness to risks, including the risks of having relatively less than or relatively no more than certain others, or others generally. Rawls's strategy is thus to set all this aside in Part One, to derive the principles, and then, in Part Two, inquire whether there is any positive reason to think that the special psychologies would destabilize a

well-ordered society in which those principles serve as the public basis of justification (*TJ* 123–125, 464–465).

Rawls chooses envy as representative of the special psychologies and, in *Theory*,
considers envy in the greatest detail:

> [J]ealousy and grudgingness are reverse, so to speak, to envy. A person who is better
> off may wish those less fortunate than he to stay in their place. He is jealous of his
> superior position and begrudges them the greater advantages that would put them
> on a level with himself. And should this propensity extend to denying them benefits
> that he does not need and cannot use himself, then he is moved by spite. These
> inclinations are collectively harmful in the way that envy is, since the grudging and
> spiteful man is willing to give up something to maintain the distance between
> himself and others.
>
> (*TJ* 467-468)

The Part Two "problem of envy" is, in essence, a problem of stability. Stability is
already a concern, of course, in Part One. "Free-rider egoism" tempts citizens to
shirk and to defect from what the rules require, and one's awareness of this tendency
in oneself feeds suspicions about others (*TJ* 295–296). Rawls eschews the Hobbesian
solution that relies on a powerful sovereign to detect, punish, and thus to deter, and
develops instead a conception of a sense of justice that is sufficiently strong to
counterbalance these tendencies.

> Just arrangements may not be in equilibrium ... because acting fairly is not in
> general each man's best reply to the just conduct of his associates. To assure stability
> men must have a sense of justice or a concern for those [if any] who would be
> disadvantaged by their defection, preferably both. When these sentiments are
> sufficiently strong to overrule the temptations to violate the rules, just schemes
> are stable. Meeting one's duties and obligations is now regarded by each person as
> the correct answer to the actions of others. His rational plan of life regulated by his
> sense of justice leads to this conclusion .... Of course, some infractions will
> presumably occur, but when they do feelings of guilt arising from friendship and
> mutual trust and the sense of justice tend to restore the arrangement.
>
> (*TJ* 435)

Rawls's immediate focus in *Theory* is on the question whether utilitarianism or
justice as fairness would be the more stable of the two conceptions. "[A] decision in
the original position depends on a comparison: other things being equal, the
preferred conception of justice is the most stable one" (*TJ* 436). The winner will
win because it is "perspicuous to our reason, congruent with our good, and rooted
not in abnegation but in affirmation of the self" (*TJ* 436). And that conception is
justice as fairness, chiefly because it, unlike utilitarianism, satisfies the "reciprocity
principle" and does so with "manifest intent": if I am better off than you, it is not by
any violation of your basic equal liberty, and it is because, and only because, we are
both better off for it than we would otherwise be. Utilitarianism, by contrast, is

willing to justify the condition of the worse-off by reference to a "vague and amorphous" (*TJ* 439) aggregate whose size and composition need not leave, or be intended to leave, the worse-off any better off, and indeed might have been gotten by using the worse-off as a mere means.

Driving Part Two, Rawls's motive is not so much to continue the comparison of justice as fairness with utilitarianism in terms of relative stability as it is to check to see whether the two principles are stable considered by themselves. The case for justice as fairness is not secured simply by showing that it is likely to be more stable than utilitarianism: it is necessary to show that it is likely to be stable, period. Rawls notes, "the reason why envy poses a problem [is] the fact that the inequalities sanctioned by the difference principle may be so great as to arouse envy to a socially dangerous extent" (*TJ* 466). A "socially dangerous extent" means a "destabilizing extent."

VARIETIES OF ENVY

Rawls takes care to distinguish between envy and similar but distinct emotions and attitudes. For the sake of clarity, envy is defined in terms of the "objective primary goods, [i.e.,] liberty and opportunity, income and wealth" – leaving aside the social bases of self-respect. Envy, then, "we may think of as the propensity to view with hostility the greater good of others even though their being more fortunate than we are does not detract from our advantages" (*TJ* 466). (If the subjective primary good of self-respect were included, it would be unwieldy to use this definition, for reasons I will mention shortly.) So defined, "envy is not a moral feeling" (*TJ* 467). It is unlike resentment, which is a negative emotion that can be explained as, and only as, a reaction to real or perceived injustice. What is resented is the conduct or condition of others that detracts from our having our due. In contrast, in the case of envy, "it is sufficient to say that the better situation of others catches our attention. We are downcast by their good fortune and no longer value as highly what we have; and this sense of hurt and loss arouses our rancor and hostility" (*TJ* 467). Given the burdens of judgment, we might misperceive our situation as one warranting resentment, but wholly aside from that, "we are willing to deprive [the better-off] of their greater benefits even if it is necessary to give up something of ours" with no other compensating benefit. Rawls has narrowed his topic to "general envy," where what has caught the envious person's eye is the generally "greater wealth and opportunity" of the better-off rather than that "particular" envy that is "typical of rivalry and competition" where the envious "covet the very same thing" the better-off have (*TJ* 466). The envious in the general-envy sense would rather both lose if she cannot be a winner. We, the envious, are willing to sacrifice what we have if only we can bring the more-fortunate down far enough. The corrosiveness of envy does not stop there, for the better-off, knowing that their position is envied, take costly precautions.

Being reminded of all this, we may feel grateful that Rawls arranged Part One of the original position procedure to exclude envy and similar traits from consideration. "Many conservative writers have contended that the tendency to equality in modern social movements is the expression of envy" (*TJ* 471). The exclusion forestalls the objection. But why readmit envy at all? Certain negative, unreasonable human traits – cruelty, for example – do not get a hearing in Part Two, despite the fact that they, like envy, might disturb a just social equilibrium. Here, Rawls introduces a distinction between "excusable" envy and other kinds. Only excusable envy has to be considered. What is it, if it is not resentment by another name?

> We are normally expected to forbear from the actions to which [envious feelings] prompt us and to take the steps necessary to rid ourselves of them. Yet sometimes the circumstances evoking envy are so compelling that given human beings as they are no one can reasonably be asked to overcome his rancorous feelings. A person's lesser position as measured by the index of objective primary goods may be so great as to wound his self-respect; and given his situation, we may sympathize with his sense of loss. *Indeed, we can resent being made envious, for society may permit such large disparities in these goods that under existing social conditions these differences cannot help but cause a loss of self-esteem.* For those suffering this hurt, envious feelings are *not irrational; the satisfaction of their rancor would make them better off.* When envy is a reaction to the loss of self-respect in circumstances where it would be unreasonable to expect someone to feel differently, I shall say that it is *excusable.* Since self-respect is the main primary good, the parties would not agree, I shall assume, to count this sort of subjective loss as irrelevant. Therefore the question is whether a basic structure which satisfies the principles of justice is likely to arouse so much excusable envy that the choice of principles should be reconsidered.
>
> (*TJ* 468; emphases added)

Is excusable envy then a "moral feeling" after all? Or is Rawls subtly disclosing an unappreciated ground for genuine resentment? One may genuinely resent being needlessly caused to feel, to keen enough a degree, any unpleasant emotion whatever. For example, suppose that Gershon, the school handyman, is a Holocaust survivor, and Senior, a student, amuses himself by whistling the Horst Wessel Lied within Gershon's hearing.[1] Senior has a right of free expression, of course. But Gershon's dislike of being reminded of something he would rather forget is a moral emotion, whether we want to call it resentment or not. If "envy proper" – in contrast to merely "benign" envy and to "emulative" envy – is by definition "a form of rancor that tends to harm both its object and its subject" (*TJ* 467), then excusable envy does not appear to fit that definition. Nor does it seem to count as a vice, if the vices are defined as "broadly based traits that are not wanted ... since they are to everyone's detriment" (*TJ* 468). Satisfying the rancor of the excusably envious person, much

---

[1]   The example is loosely modeled on Tobias Wolff's story, "Class Picture," in his collection *Old School* (Vintage 2003).

like satisfying the indignation of the resentful person, is not necessarily to her detriment.[2] Likewise, an excusably envious person's success in repressing her rancor is not necessarily to her benefit, for it can easily lead to submissive withdrawal and disengagement, which are inconsistent with a secure sense of self-worth.

ENVY AND INEQUALITY

With these distinctions in hand, Rawls is prepared to consider "whether the likelihood of excusable general envy" (*TJ* 468) requires reconsideration and amendment of the two principles of justice as fairness. Before proceeding, he takes on yet another assumption, "that the main psychological root of the liability to envy is a lack of self-confidence in our own worth combined with a sense of impotence" (*TJ* 469). Rawls's strategy is to show that a society that is well ordered by the two principles deprives the roots of envy of sustenance. Envy will not grow to destabilizing proportions. Conditions that would "encourage hostile outbreaks of envy" (*TJ* 469) are mitigated because, for one thing, "in the public forum each person is treated with the respect due to a sovereign equal" (*TJ* 470). Secondly, "Although in theory the difference principle permits indefinitely large inequalities in return for small gains to the less favored, the spread of income and wealth should not be excessive in practice, given the requisite background institutions" (*TJ* 470). The background institutions referred to here assure the fair value of political liberty and equal opportunity. This point is later emphasized in the *Restatement*, along with an effervescent tendency of the OP curve to rise quickly to its peak (*JF* 67; and see figure 6.1 on page 99, supra). Rawls, in *Theory*, adds:

> Moreover the plurality of associations in a well-ordered society, each with its secure internal life, tends to reduce the visibility, or at least the painful visibility, of variations in men's prospects. For we tend to compare our circumstances with others in the same or a similar group as ourselves …. The various associations in

---

[2] Consider someone like Robin S. Dillon's Carissa. Carissa is ashamed of herself because she is dogged by persistent, unwanted feelings of resentment toward her better-off neighbors, whom she knows have not wronged or affronted her in any way.

> Her resentment is mistaken that [*sic*] those who own nicer homes have wronged her and affronted her dignity. But her sense that she has been wronged and her dignity undermined is not mistaken; in a way, she has been set up: encouraged by social institutions to predicate her sense of worth on bases that social institutions conspire to insure cannot be hers. Her resentment is misdirected but not wholly unwarranted – it arises from evidence processing functions and makes sense of the world as her explicit beliefs do not. And the conflict between belief and emotion accurately reflects conflicting social messages about worth.
>
> (Dillon 1997, 238)

Carissa's envy is not merely excusable; it is the inescapable by-product of her resentment of social structures that diminish her self-regard by subjecting her to these kinds of psychological stress. Jeffrey Green 2013 defends "reasonable envy" of the superrich as a ground for attending preeminently to distribution rather than production.

society tend to divide it into so many *noncomparing groups*, the discrepancies between these divisions not attracting the kind of attention which unsettles the lives of those less well placed.

(TJ 470; emphasis added)

The anesthetizing effect of the "noncomparing groups" is not invoked in the *Restatement*, but it may explain some of the features of the "decent consultation hierarchy" described in *Law of Peoples*. In *Law of Peoples*, decent societies are admitted to the Society of Well-Ordered Peoples even though citizens are not sovereign equals in the political forum. Their members' sense of self-worth is sufficiently ratified by their membership in one or another noncomparing group, one has to assume.

CIRCUMSTANCES OF POLITICS BRING IN EXCUSABLE
PARTICULAR ENVY

Convinced that general excusable envy does not require revising the two principles, Rawls turns to the problem of particular excusable envy, which is "endemic to human life; being associated with rivalry, it may exist in any society" (*TJ* 471). The specific questions for political justice are "how pervasive are the rancor and jealousy aroused by the quest for office and position, and whether it is likely to distort the justice of institutions" (*TJ* 471). Here, without further discussion, Rawls immediately concludes with only this brief and baffling remark:

> It is difficult to settle this matter in the absence of the more detailed knowledge of *the social forms available at the legislative stage*. But there seems to be no reason why the hazards of particular envy should be worse in a society regulated by justice as fairness than by any other conception.

(TJ 471; emphasis added)

What are the "social forms" that more is to be known about? This reference is presumably an adumbration of the choice between property-owning democracy and liberal socialism, which Rawls takes up later, in the *Restatement*. No other reading offers itself, for there is no other choice of social *forms* – as opposed to the routine application of the people's ordinary power to particular problems – that Rawls ever speaks of as available at the legislative stage. He has, in *Theory*, spoken of a "division of labor" that assigns the application of the second principle, comprising the principle of fair equal opportunity and the difference principle, to the legislative stage (*TJ* 174–175). The implication is that some selection among "social forms" will have been made at the constitutional stage, and that the question of whether a destabilizing degree of particular political envy will be left in play at the legislative stage will depend on that selection.

It is the limited space of the political, and the nature of democracy as a regulated rivalry, that make the problem one of what Rawls calls *particular* envy. In a political contest, the loser is not better off for losing. What the winner wins is "the very same thing" (*TJ* 466) that the loser wanted. But, aggravatingly, and complicatingly, the fact of domination means that general economic envy and particular political envy are freely inter-translatable. The less-well-off who feel general excusable envy of the better-off suffer particular envy of the electoral victories of the candidates of the better-off over the champions (if any) of the less-well-off. Cognizant of this, the better-off now jealously guard their political and economic advantages, not only for the sake of having what others lack but also to protect both their particular, political advantages and the general economic advantages with which they are combined.

Since the space of politics is limited, the political successes of the wealthy operate automatically, regardless of spiteful intention, to handicap the opportunity of the less-advantaged to exert equal political influence. But the grudging and spiteful person will also deny the less-advantaged other goods, such as access to education and health care, even though they have no direct tendency to undermine political dominance.[3] The fact of domination that motivates Rawls's insistence on the fair-value guarantee means that the destabilizing tendencies of, respectively, general and particular envy cannot be addressed separately, but require a combined solution. It also means that the problem of stability cannot be deferred to the legislative stage for resolution. What is needed – to address the worries Rawls himself voices – is a prior specification of the constitutional essentials that can assure that majoritarian legislation does not tend to arouse hostile envious reactions (which might be manifested as, or lead to, apathetic resignation), and does not tend to express spiteful entrenchment of economic advantage.

THE STABILITY OF THE PRIORITY PRINCIPLES

After stability-testing the two principles, Rawls separately addresses the stability of the priority principles. Justice as fairness asserts not only the first and second principles of justice; it also asserts the lexical priority of the first principle of equal basic liberty to the second principle, and, within the second principle, the lexical priority of fair equal opportunity to the difference principle. Lexical priority means that trade-offs that sacrifice a prior principle even in the slightest degree to gain an advantage, no matter how great, in terms of a posterior principle, are absolutely disallowed. Unsurprisingly, the rigidity of the priority principles is tempered by their being carefully conditioned on the achievement of some sufficient level of individual and social economic development. But even supposing these conditions are met, the special psychologies can apply additional stresses to what the priority principles otherwise already have to bear.

---

[3] Daniel Brudney (2014, 459) points out that "lack of respect is not the only problematic social attitude. Another is lack of concern .... [H]istory has made us assume that to be treated as second-class is to be the object of disrespect. Yet to be the object of indifference can also count as second-class treatment."

Rawls reviews the Part One grounds for the priority principles. In the second-edition reworking of the argument, Rawls credits Mill with the idea that, as general economic development progresses, people's "higher-order interests and fundamental aims" (*TJ* 476 n. 13) become increasingly important to them, psychologically. Assume a sufficient general and individual level of economic security is achieved: the higher-order aims now become decisive. To secure the higher-order interests of those whom they represent, the parties in the original position assign a priority to the liberty to pursue these aims. The parties are not willing to trade a lesser liberty for greater wealth (*TJ* 474–475). Since they do not regard social institutions as constituting a fixed, unamendable natural order, the parties now also recognize that they have a *highest*-order interest: namely, a "highest-order interest in how their other interests, including even their fundamental ones, are shaped and regulated by social institutions" (*TJ* 475).

The invocation of Mill in the second edition is somewhat surprising, in light of the later Rawls's determination to recast justice as fairness as a "freestanding" conception not beholden to the "comprehensive liberalisms of Kant and Mill" (*PL* 78). Referring to "the first part of the last paragraph of §3 of ch. 1 of bk. II" of Mill's *Principles of Political Economy*, Rawls says, "If we read this passage to imply the notion of a hierarchy of interests, which leads to a lexical ordering, the view I express in the text is essentially Mill's" (*TJ* 476 n. 13). This is what Mill had said:

> If a conjecture may be hazarded, the decision [– between "individual agency in its best form, or Socialism in its best form" as "the ultimate form of human society" –] will probably depend mainly on one consideration, viz. which of the two systems is consistent with the greatest amount of human liberty and spontaneity. After the means of subsistence are assured, the next in strength of the personal wants of human beings is liberty; and (unlike the physical wants, which as civilization advances become more moderate and more amenable to control) it increases instead of diminishing in intensity, as the intelligence and the moral faculties are more developed. The perfection both of social arrangements and of practical morality would be, to secure to all persons complete independence and freedom of action, subject to no restriction but that of not doing injury to others: and the education which taught or the social institutions which required them *to exchange the control of their own actions for any amount of comfort or affluence, or to renounce liberty for the sake of equality,* would deprive them of one of the most elevated characteristics of human nature.
>
> (Mill 2006 vol. 2, 208–209; emphasis added)

Rawls adds that Mill's "contention here fits the passage in *Utilitarianism*" that was earlier cited for the proposition that Mill and others made use of the idea of lexical, or "lexicographical," ordering of principles (*TJ* 37–38 n. 23). But Rawls evidently was consulting Mill on the question of socialism, for that is the context of the passage cited. (Mill immediately goes on to say, "It remains to be discovered how far the preservation of this characteristic would be found compatible with the

Communistic organization of society. No doubt this, like all the other objections to the Socialist schemes, is vastly exaggerated" [2006 vol. 2, 209; cf. Arneson 1979].) Moreover, the passage conveys Mill's belief that what the choice turns on is whether socialism, or its "individual agency" competitor, is better at stably securing the priority of liberty. This, as I will show, was Rawls's view as well.

The priority principles reflect the parties' appreciation of a hierarchy existing within the domain of their own interests. The highest-order interest is reflected in the priority of political liberty and its fair value. The higher-order interests are reflected in the equal priority of the other fundamental liberty interests. "The realization of these interests may necessitate certain social conditions and degree of fulfillment of needs and material wants . . .. But once the required social conditions and level of satisfaction of needs and material wants is attained, as they are in a well-ordered society under favorable circumstances, the higher-order interests are regulative from then on" (*TJ* 476). Such is what Part One has prioritized. Can the special psychologies of Part Two undo this?

Social status now matters. Might it come about, if "everyone wants a greater proportionate share" of the objective primary goods, that "society might conceivably become more and more occupied with raising productivity" and that in turn "these objectives might become so dominant as to undermine the precedence of liberty" (*TJ* 477)? Rawls thinks that in a just society this will not happen, but "it does not follow that in a just society everyone is unconcerned with matters of status," that is, with relative social and economic position. What is the brake, then, to prevent this concern from becoming widespread enough to cause a slide back to, say, the "general conception," in which every inequality, even in basic liberties, is justifiable if it lifts the least-advantaged? This is how Rawls answers:

> The account of self-respect as perhaps the main primary good has stressed the great significance of how we think others value us. But in a well-ordered society the need for status is met by the public recognition of just institutions, together with the full and diverse internal life of the free communities of interest that the equal liberties allow. The basis of self-respect in a just society is not then one's income share but the publicly affirmed distribution of fundamental rights and liberties . . .. When it is the position of equal citizenship that answers the need for status, the precedence of the equal liberties becomes all the more necessary. Having chosen a conception of justice that seeks to eliminate the significance of relative economic and social advantages as supports for men's self-confidence, it is essential that the priority of liberty be firmly maintained.
>
> (*TJ* 477–478)

So, this is the solution: in a well-ordered society, citizens' sense of self-worth is tied to their equality as citizens, not to their position in the social order defined by other measures, such as wealth and income – or, one might add, ethnicity, race, sex, and so forth. No one is tempted, for example, to accept political inferiority in an undemocratic, technocratic system in return for the promise, even the assurance, of her getting a relatively greater share of social wealth. This trade is irrational because political equality is the measure of self-worth in a just society.

> No one is inclined to look beyond the constitutional affirmation of equality for further political ways of securing his status. Nor, on the other hand, are men disposed to acknowledge a less than equal liberty. For one thing, doing this would put them at a disadvantage and weaken their political position. It would also have the effect of publicly establishing their inferiority.
>
> *(TJ 477)*

So, the priority principles pass the Part Two stability test, too. To summarize, what follows is one of Rawls's most perspicuous, and most concise, statements of his theory of distributive justice for a democratic society:

> In a well-ordered society then self-respect is secured by the public affirmation of the status of equal citizenship for all; the distribution of material means is left to take care of itself in accordance with pure procedural justice regulated by just background institutions which narrow the range of inequalities so that excusable envy does not arise.
>
> *(TJ 478)*

The advantages of a theory that achieves stability in this way are evident. (I set aside the appeal it has to those who, like Nozick and Hayek, are attracted to the idea of rendering distributive justice as a "pure procedural" matter, "left to take care of itself" once the institutions of equal citizenship are in place.) By putting relative economic position aside, as a measure of self-worth, one avoids the "great misfortune" of the project of securing self-worth becoming a zero-sum game, in which "each man's gain is another's loss" (*TJ* 478). "The best solution" to the problem of stability "is to support the primary good of self-respect as far as possible by the assignment of the basic liberties *that can indeed be made equal*, defining the same status for all" (*TJ* 478; emphasis added). To insist on equality where it is not attainable, while trivializing equality that is attainable, is indeed to invite "great misfortune."

Is this solution too neat? Rawls suspects it may be. Human nature being what it is, "[t]o some extent men's sense of their own self-worth may hinge upon their institutional position and their income share." With the appropriate background institutions in place, we might be entitled to assume that "these inclinations" to tie self-worth to status "should not be excessive" (*TJ* 478). But there is an alternative, theoretical response that does not leave so much to speculation:

> [W]e can if necessary include self-respect in the primary goods, the index of which defines expectations. Then in applications of the difference principle, this index can allow for the effects of excusable envy; the expectations of the less advantaged are lower the more severe these effects. Whether some adjustment for self-respect has to be made is best decided from *the standpoint of the legislative stage* where the parties have more information and the principle of political determination applies.
>
> *(TJ 479; emphasis added)*

The "principle of political determination" means, simply, majority rule. It is disconcerting to try to imagine how a majoritarian legislature could process the highly abstract question whether the Rawlsian index of primary goods ought to remain strictly objective or should, in light of the fresh information disclosed at that stage, be expanded to encompass the subjective matter of self-respect. Rawls immediately backs away:

> Admittedly this problem is an unwelcome complication. *Since simplicity itself is desirable in a public conception of justice, the conditions that elicit excusable envy should if possible be avoided.* I have mentioned this point not to settle it, but only to note that when necessary the expectations of the less advantaged can be understood so as to include the primary good of self-respect.

> (*TJ* 479; emphasis added)

This is a crucial passage because it identifies the preferred solution to the problem of excusable envy as one that better avoids legislative-stage temptations to revisit the question whether to keep the index of primary goods objective.

It is awkward having to imagine how the less-advantaged can maintain their sense of self-respect even as their representatives in a legislature are pressing, perhaps without success, to include their lack of it in an index of primary goods. Rawls is evidently uncomfortable with the dilemma that would create. The legislative stage is being called upon, again – provisionally and, I suggest, aporetically – to grapple with issues that ought to be taken off the agenda, once and for all, before the regulated rivalry of ordinary politics begins.

One more thought has also to be dismissed. Why not simply direct the envious to the consolations available in their respective "noncomparing groups," such as one's church, social club, neighborhood bar, or bowling league? That preserves simplicity: the index of primary goods remains objective, and background institutions have already assured that there is a diverse array of associations available to every citizen, including even the worst-off, in which her self-worth can be validated. During the era of Dickens and Engels, for example, the Salvation Army emerged to perform the office of noncomparing self-worth validator of last resort, by providing "soup, soap, and salvation." The consolations available in a well-ordered society, however, rest atop a social safety net, so the relevant noncomparing associations need not be conceived merely as private relief agencies.

Rawls acknowledges that "societies have other ways of affirming self-respect and coping with envy and other disruptive inclinations" (*TJ* 479). Feudal and caste societies assign everyone to a noncomparing group that is understood to be her natural and inevitable social matrix. The self-worth of each is ratified not by citizenship, but by station in the noncomparing caste or status group to which she is assigned. The partitioning of the social world in this way might be endorsed by a dominant religious or folk-sociological dogma. Envy is dampened because sidelong glances reach no further than to co-members of one's own noncomparing group.

(The contented Betas, Gammas, and Deltas of Aldous Huxley's *Brave New World* come to mind.) This kind of stability of course does not reinforce the priority principles. But the examples are irrelevant. A well-ordered society – a liberal one, anyway – is ordered by principles that are based on general facts, and the publicity condition assumed in *Theory* requires that the parties choose principles with reference to the same general facts. "Thus when the belief in a fixed natural order sanctioning a hierarchical society is abandoned, assuming here that this belief is not a true one, a tendency is set up in the direction of the two principles of justice in serial order" (*TJ* 480). Rawls does not conceive this tendency as an inevitability, however.

STABILITY OF A CONCEPTION AND STABILITY OF INSTITUTIONS

It is important to bear in mind that although the stability Rawls is concerned with is spoken of as a property of a "conception of justice," questions about the stability of a conception are inevitably questions also about the institutions needed and available to realize that conception. The institutional contribution is not merely a homeostatic resilience, but a robust tendency to stay *just*: "stability means that however institutions change, they still remain just or approximately so" (*TJ* 401). As I will emphasize in the next chapter, one factor – perhaps the preeminent factor – determining what are the "tolerable bounds" of injustice is the principle of publicity, which demands that all citizens know that all are committed to justice as their highest regulative end (*TJ* 476). The constitutional design itself has a preeminent role both in educating citizens and in conveying publicly the assurance that a consensus, political conception of justice is indeed stably established.

At one point in the *Restatement*, Rawls says that "stability as defined here is a property of a conception of justice, and not a property of a scheme of institutions. The latter is a different though not unrelated topic" (*JF* 181 n. 1). This suggests that Rawls saw the question of stability, abstractly framed, as not one directly applicable to the discussion of ideal types of regime – assuming that an ideal regime type is more like a "scheme of institutions" than a "conception of justice." But Rawls otherwise consistently treats the question of stability as one that directly involves the security of "the institutions of a constitutional regime" (*JF* 183). Indeed, the stability question cannot be compartmentalized.

> [T]he soundness of a theory of justice is shown as much in its consequences as in the prima facie acceptability of its premises. Indeed, these cannot be usefully separated and therefore the discussion of institutional questions ... which may seem at first unphilosophical, is in fact unavoidable.

(*TJ* 81)

Rawls never states or suggests that the relegation of the choice between the two surviving regime types to the legislative stage is final, in the sense that it is not to be reviewed in Part Two of the argument from the original position, where the special psychologies of envy, grudgingness, and spite must be reckoned with as well. A passage that I have already quoted deserves repeating.

> The parties will surely prefer conceptions of justice *the realization of which* does not arouse these propensities. We are normally expected to forbear from the actions to which they prompt us and to take the steps necessary to rid ourselves of them. Yet sometimes the circumstances evoking envy are so compelling that given human beings as they are no one can reasonably be asked to overcome his rancorous feelings. A person's lesser position as measured by the index of primary goods may be so great as to wound his self-respect; and given his situation, we may sympathize with his sense of loss. Indeed, we can resent being made envious, for society may permit such large disparities in these goods that ... these differences cannot help but cause a loss of self-esteem. For those suffering this hurt, envious feelings are not irrational; the satisfaction of their rancor would make them better off . . .. Since self-respect is the main primary good, the parties would not agree, I shall assume, to count this sort of subjective loss as irrelevant. *Therefore the question is whether a basic structure which satisfies the principles of justice is likely to arouse so much excusable envy that the choice of principles should be reconsidered.*
>
> (*TJ* 468; emphases added)

The question is therefore equally pertinent to the choice between the two candidate regime types: property-owning democracy and liberal socialism. Which is less likely to arouse excusable envy – that is, to arouse a moral emotion that is as potent and as legitimate as outright resentment?

8

Socialism and Stability

Rawls hinted from time to time that he realized that justice as fairness might require socialism. He spoke more clearly when correcting the suggestion that the original position procedure already requires "associational" socialism as a principle of justice. In *Political Liberalism*, he disapproved Rodney Peffer's proposed revision, discussed earlier in Chapter 4, that effectively would elevate a syndicalist variety of socialism to the status of a principle of justice of intermediate priority, subordinate to the first principle of equal basic liberty but prior to the difference principle. What Rawls repeatedly adumbrates is that socialism might be required as the institutional realization of justice as fairness, rather than as one of the principles. The style is what Burton Dreben would have called guarded, muffled, and cramped. But the message is plainly there.

Its first appearance is in the 1975 paper, "Fairness to Goodness," where Rawls answers the charge that the account of primary goods in *Theory* is unfairly biased in favor of those who turn out to hold individualistic conceptions of the good. In the course of the argument, Rawls gives his first indication that *their relative stability* is the key determination to be made in choosing between liberal socialism and property-owning democracy. In defense of the claim in *Theory* that a desire for primary goods will motivate any rational person, Rawls relies on the sociological proposition that "the primary goods are socially strategic. This means that if these goods are justly distributed as the principles of justice require . . . then other injustices are unlikely to occur" (CP 276). This is the flip side of the fact of domination. The fact of domination calls forth an insistence on the fair value of political liberty precisely because political liberty is assumed to be useful in protecting one's equal corner in the limited space of the political. There is nothing especially individualistic about being motivated not to be a victim of injustice. Rawls continues:

> The supposition is that, given a just distribution of primary goods, individuals and associations can protect themselves against the remaining institutional forms of injustice. Both Marx and Mill could, I believe, accept this assumption.

> (CP 276)

It is noteworthy that Rawls here imagines himself to be conferring with Marx and Mill on a question as to which it made sense to think both took an interest in.

> Marx stressed the control of the means of production, the sources of income and wealth, whereas Mill emphasized the importance of liberties and opportunities. Of course, Marx would question the stability of a well-ordered society in the absence of some form of socialism, but this is not to deny that, given a well-ordered society, primary goods are strategic ... and, in any case, the principles of justice do not exclude certain forms of socialism *and would in fact require them* if the stability of a well-ordered society could be achieved in no other way.
>
> (CP 277; emphasis added)

Rawls's conception of the problem of stability draws into view the close tie between the strategic value of wealth and the strategic value of political power – what I have been calling the fact of domination. This passage shows that Rawls already sees the question of socialism as relevant to the seemingly unrelated question of stabilizing a well-ordered society – so much so that he imagines Marx voicing an opinion on the stability of a well-ordered society!

In the *Restatement*, published a quarter of a century later, Rawls returns to this same theme. He acknowledges that his description of property-owning democracy as an ideal regime type raises the possibility that it "generates political and economic forces that make it depart all too widely from its ideal institutional description" (*JF* 178). Therefore, he says, we have to ask ourselves whether – given the assumptions we have found it reasonable to make – a liberal socialist regime would stand the better chance of stably realizing justice as fairness. "Should it do so, then *the case for liberal socialism is made*" (*JF* 178; emphasis added). In the rest of this chapter, I review the groundwork of the stability case for socialism that Rawls has in view. To do this, it is necessary to locate the "historic question" carefully within Rawls's structure of argument.

OVERVIEW: FOUR STAGES IN TWO PARTS

"Awful and artificial" is how one might describe the architectonic of Rawls's theory of justice. As Rawls was fond of pointing out, those words, at one time, would have been complimentary. "Impressive and rational," is what they meant in the mouth of Charles II, complimenting Christopher Wren's design for St. Paul's Cathedral in London (*LHMP* 52; *LHPP* 169). ("Amusing, awful, and artificial" is the phrase sometimes reported – but "amusing" too meant something else: "amazing," allegedly, rather than "funny.") Some have taken the architectural simile as far as to suggest that the structure of Rawls's theory is baroque, or rococo, rather than gothic. It is spacious and it is complicated, that much is agreed.

There is one particular complication that does more than anything else to make Rawls's socialism hard to discern. Or, rather, it is not one complication, but the coincidence of two complications. The first complication is that the argument for justice as fairness has to be presented in two parts, which were described in Chapter 6. In Part One of the original-position procedure, the parties ignore the special psychologies that citizens will be prey to. In Part Two, the veil of ignorance is lifted significantly but not entirely, so that the parties in the original position now know that there are special psychologies, of envy, greed, spite, and unusual attitudes toward risk, needing to be taken into account. Otherwise, the veil remains as before. The parties are still unaware of any traits or circumstances that would tempt or enable them to pick principles specially to favor those whom they represent; but, so far, they are also ignorant of the situation of the society whose basic structure is to be governed, ignorant of its resources, its level of economic development, its political history and culture.

The second complication also involves lifting the veil of ignorance, but now in successive stages: this is the four-stage sequence (JF 48; TJ 172–176; PL 397–398), which was discussed in Chapter 4. The transition from the original position to the second, constitutional stage reveals to the parties the general facts about the society – the people – whose basic structure is to be regulated by the principles of justice. The general facts are those that pertain to the "natural circumstances and resources . . . level of economic advance and political culture, and so on" (TJ 172–173) – but not so detailed as to include, for example, "information about the prevalence of various diseases and their severity, the frequency of accidents and their causes," (JF 173) which is not made known until the legislative stage. Rawls changed his stated position of what else is known at the legislative stage, or rather, of the viewpoint taken by the representative legislator, as I outlined earlier in Chapter 4.

The two liftings of the veil are not sequential or simultaneous, but are uncoordinated. Rawls's discussions of the four-stage sequence mostly occur in the context of Part One. It is in this context that Rawls proposes a division of labor: the first principle of equal basic liberty is to be achieved by "constitutional essentials" determined at the constitutional stage. But fair equality of opportunity and the difference principle are not constitutional essentials, and so are to be provided for legislatively. The constitutional stage of course has as its primary task that of settling upon a form of government, which, it will turn out, must be a majoritarian representative democracy with judicial review. The stability-testing undertaken in Part Two is not integrated into this sequence, but will still need to be performed on any result arrived at in Part One. Reflective equilibrium requires that the four-stage sequence be rehearsed again, in Part Two, to complete the process of checking for stability.

Despite the division of labor between the stages, there are certain matters of distributive justice, or matters having a bearing on distributive justice, that Rawls does assign to the constitutional stage. The fair value of political liberty is a constitutional essential, and provision for it must be made at the constitutional stage – and that provision must withstand further scrutiny in Part Two, where the special psychologies are known. A provision for fair value that seems adequate if we ignore excusable envy may turn out to be inadequate once excusable envy and its counterpart, (in)excusable spite, are taken into account. And, of course, the choice of an ideal regime type is added to the constitutional-stage agenda in the *Restatement*. Regimes that do not take fair value and reciprocity seriously are ruled out, and so three of the five regime types that history has offered us are excluded: laissez-faire capitalism, command-economy socialism, and welfare-state capitalism.

The decision between the surviving regime-types – property-owning democracy and liberal socialism – could be deferred, Rawls says, to the legislative stage. But he does not mean this to be final. For one thing, this deferral itself has to be reviewed in Part Two, where (again) excusable envy and (in)excusable spite, greed, and extreme risk aversion and risk seeking come into play. For another thing, the question whether a certain matter is to be dealt with as a constitutional essential or an item on the legislative agenda is also open, under the method of reflective equilibrium. To repeat what was quoted in Chapter 4: "By moving back and forth between the stages of the constitutional convention and the legislature, the best constitution is found (*TJ* 174).

To summarize, briefly: Rawls is not willing to assign the choice between liberal socialism and its property-owning democracy competitor to legislative decision unless, after Part Two, it is safe to say that a well-ordered society can stably endure having the question of public ownership of the means of production always up for legislative reconsideration. In the remainder of this chapter, I will show (1) that Rawls himself doubted that this is safe to say, and (2) that Rawls himself had collected sufficient reasons to conclude that the stability of a well-ordered society requires that common ownership of the commanding heights of the economy be constitutionally guaranteed. Rawls did not set forth the reasons in the emphatic form we call argument. For that, his socialism has to be seen as "guarded," and "muffled" – reticent, but nonetheless real.

FROM COMPREHENSIVE TO POLITICAL STABILITY

Before going further in constructing the stability argument for socialism, I ask you to recall that Rawls's conception of stability was undergoing a major revision. This fact makes it somewhat more cumbersome to present the argument, but on the other hand it makes the argument all the more compelling. In the essays collected in *Political Liberalism*, which first appeared in 1993, Rawls repudiates the solution to the problem of stability that he advanced in *Theory*. Rawls withdraws justice as fairness insofar as it could be taken as stating a comprehensive moral view (viz., one addressing all values, ideals, and human relationships) and recasts it as a "political conception" of justice.[1] The change was motivated in large part by Rawls's realization of "the fact of reasonable pluralism," that is, that in a well-ordered liberal society a multitude of diverse but

---

[1]   Paul Weithman corrects Rawls's way of expressing himself: what Rawls realized was that *Theory* assumed a *partially* comprehensive (not a fully comprehensive) view (Weithman 2010, 80–81; cf. *PL* 13). Rawls hints in *Theory* that he might go on at some future time to propound a more comprehensive view – "more or less an entire ethical system ... including principles for all the virtues and not only for justice" (*TJ* 15) – but he never does so.

equally reasonable conceptions of the good life (not all of them liberal, some of them "salvation religions" [*PL* xliii]) will over time sprout and thrive. In such circumstances, a perpetual consensus on the principles of justice cannot be assured if it rests on a comprehensive conception of the good, for some citizens will reasonably disagree with that rationale. Moreover, "the fact of oppression" tells us that a consensus comprehensive conception cannot be recovered or maintained unless by objectionably coercive exercises of state force. Therefore, Rawls felt it necessary to explain how a society governed by the two principles (or close analogues of them) might not only be stable but stable "for the right reasons" (*PL* xxxix).

By the expression "stable for the right reasons," Rawls means stable neither by way of an uneasy modus vivendi among groups wedded to irreconcilable comprehensive doctrines, nor by way of coerced unanimity upon any one such doctrine. Rather, his project was to outline a "freestanding" political conception that each citizen could freely affirm from within his or her own comprehensive doctrine, and that at the same time assures that "inevitable deviations from justice are effectively corrected or held within tolerable bounds by forces within the system" (*TJ* 45), like a sailboat righting itself on its keel. (Sailing was one of Rawls's pastimes.)

STABILITY AND THE CONSTITUTIONAL CONVENTION

In *Political Liberalism*, in the essay "The Basic Liberties and Their Priority," Rawls also elaborates his understanding of the task to be accomplished at the constitutional stage. The essay intends to fill "serious gaps" left by *Theory*, one of which concerns us here:

> [W]hen the principles of justice are applied at the constitutional, legislative, and judicial stages, no satisfactory criterion is given for how the basic liberties are to be further specified and adjusted to one another as social circumstances are made known.
>
> (*PL* 290)

The criterion cannot involve an appeal to a comprehensive political conception. Moreover, because a shared, consensus comprehensive conception of justice cannot be either relied on or appealed to anymore, citizens will be anxious to have assurance that majoritarian political power is not being used in service of a comprehensive conception with which they reasonably disagree. With this additional concern now in play, the guarantee of the fair value of political liberty assumes added importance. Rawls envisages a just society as a deliberative democracy in which citizenship is "a relation of free and equal citizens who exercise ultimate political power as a collective body" (*PL* xiv; *JF* 150; cf. Cohen 2003b, 333–334). Its stability consists in there being a reliable passage from a "constitutional consensus" as to basic rights and liberties and "political procedures of democratic government" (*PL* 158–159) to a supportive "overlapping consensus" of the variety of comprehensive views that society will inevitably seed. The transition is made possible by *public*

reason, "a reasonable public basis of justification on fundamental political questions" (*PL* xxi). For a deliberative democracy to be legitimated by public reason it is
essential that the principle of participation and the political liberties deriving from it
be jealously guarded against "the curse of money" (*LP* 139) – a vivid reference to
what Thomas Piketty (2014, 514) is later to call "the drift toward oligarchy" and I have
called the fact of domination. But fair value is to be guarded in the "right way," of
course: not by oppressive force and not by indoctrination into any particular
comprehensive doctrine. Providing the needed insulation in the right way is made
more challenging because diverse, competing comprehensive doctrines, as well as
rivalrous political positions arising from diverse private economic and social interests, have to be held together across generations.

> Since the ideal of public reason contains a form of public political deliberation ...
> public financing of elections ... fair equality of opportunity ... [and] a decent
> distribution of income [assuring] fair access to the political process ... are necessary
> for this deliberation to be possible and fruitful. In the absence of [fair access to the
> political process] those with wealth and income tend to dominate those with less
> and increasingly to control political power in their own favor . . .. Without [these or]
> similar arrangements, reasonable political liberalisms hold that these excessive
> inequalities tend to develop. This is an application of common sense political
> sociology.

> (*PL* lvii–lix; reordered)

This passage confirms several things. First, it states that what I have called the fact of
domination, the tendency of unequal wealth to lead to political and social subordination, is for Rawls a commonsense truth, as well as a matter of general knowledge.
Second, it makes plain that political legitimacy cannot be achieved without
adequate measures in place to prevent such inequalities from developing.[2] Third,
it supplements the insulation devices mentioned previously with an acknowledgment that a "decent distribution" of income *is a prerequisite to* meaningful democratic politics.

If the commonsense, political-sociological fact of domination is known no later
than the constitutional stage, and if it is also revealed there (if not earlier) that
measures to correct for disparities in fair value "never seem to have been seriously

---

[2] Rawls is aware of the difficulty. Once the political game has started, it is too late to set fair
ground rules.

> [This] is why it is so difficult to pass laws reforming elections and establishing public
> financing. In this instance it is obvious that the party that can raise the most money will
> have less desire for reforms of this kind, and if it is in power, can block reform efforts. If
> both parties in a two-party system are corrupt and can raise large funds, such efforts at
> reform may be practically impossible without major political change via, say, a third party.
> (*LHPP* 18)

> Rawls was drawn to the idea of a third-party solution in the United States, as I discuss in
> Chapter 12.

entertained" in constitutional democracies, then a sturdy, entrenched structural safeguard or safeguards must be a "constitutional essential."

MIRRORING THE ORIGINAL POSITION

Just as he insists that judicial review is constitutionally required as a structural safeguard to assure formal equality of political liberty, Rawls acknowledges the need to assure fair value structurally:

> The guarantee of fair value for the political liberties is included in the first principle of justice because it is essential in order to establish just legislation and also to make sure that the fair political process specified by the constitution is open to everyone on a basis of rough equality. The idea is to incorporate into the basic structure of society an effective political procedure which *mirrors* in that structure the fair representation of persons achieved by the original position.

(PL 330; emphasis added)

Rawls says no more about this idea of arranging the basic structure to mirror the original position. The original position is a powerful but abstract conception. What points of contact might he have had in mind?[3] If one took the mirroring idea seriously, one might suggest that fair value be guarded against the fact of domination by institutionalizing ownership within the basic structure so as to reproduce as closely as possible ownership as it is represented in the original position. But, of course, in the original position, all primary goods are, in effect, viewed by the parties as jointly owned, for all are regarded as products of cooperative social enterprise. Even the valuable exercise of individual talents (though not the talents themselves) are regarded as a common asset.[4] The question of how to divide the product of a joint enterprise is, as Mill pointed out, entirely distinct from the question how the means of production are to be held (Mill 2006 [1852], 201–202). If society is a fair system of cooperation, how can the property that is essential to everyone's productive activity not ultimately be the property of all cooperating members? And given the fact of domination, how can essential productive capital justly be allowed to be distributed unequally merely to push total wealth further beyond what a decent society needs, even on the (contestable) ground that greater social output is achievable only by offering incentives?

Or rather, to serve as the mirror, did Rawls instead have in mind insulation devices? It seems unlikely. Public financing of parties and elections mirrors, in a

---

[3] Joshua Cohen (2003b, 344–345) interprets Rawls's mirroring image abstractly. He thinks Rawls ought not to have intended the political structure to mirror "ideal fairness," but, rather, to mirror a "system of ideal deliberation."

[4] Compare: "Capital is a collective product, and only by the united action of many members, nay, in the last resort, only by the united effort of all members of society, can it be set in motion. Capital is, therefore, not a personal, it is a social power" (Marx and Engels 1978 [1848] 485).

certain sense, an important feature of the veil of ignorance. No public official or political party or candidate "knows" with any particularity who is the source of financial support: it comes from every taxpayer and thus from none in particular. But the similarity ends abruptly there. In the original position, no party could know who in particular would benefit by one choice or another. In politics, decision-makers are keenly aware of whose interests will be furthered and whose interests overridden or set back by one choice or another.

I return to the subject of insulation devices in the next chapter. But it is already clear that assuring fair value by political processes that mirror the original position has a bearing on "the property question" of ownership of the means of production. It is also clear that the processes assuring fair value must satisfy the demands of stability. The mirror must reflect publicly and objectively, and it must return to its proper shape whenever it is distorted. And, of course, it must not shatter under the strains of commitment or the stresses of the special psychologies.

PROPERTY REGIMES IN THE CONSTITUTIONAL CONVENTION

The application of the first principle in the constitutional convention "means that the political liberties ... *enter essentially into the specification of a just political procedure*" (*PL* 336; emphasis added). Thus, "the constitution is seen as a just political procedure which *incorporates* the equal political liberties and *seeks* to assure their fair value so that the processes of political decision are open to all on a roughly equal basis" (*PL* 337; emphases added). Formal political equality is incorporated; but is fair value, and the rough equality of wealth it entails, likewise incorporated, or is it rather a goal to be attained by the procedure?

> The emphasis is first on the constitution as specifying a just and workable political procedure so far without any explicit constitutional restrictions on what the legislative outcome may be. Although the delegates have a notion of just and effective legislation, the second principle of justice, which is part of the content of this notion, is not incorporated into the constitution itself. Indeed, the history of successful constitutions suggests that principles to regulate economic and social inequalities, and other distributive principles, are generally not suitable as constitutional restrictions. Rather, just legislation seems to be best achieved by assuring fairness in representation and by other constitutional devices.
>
> (*PL* 337)

The "initial emphasis" is to devise a process that achieves two things. One is to give great scope to the "principle of representation," that is, to allow the constituent power of the people – their common expression of their individual moral power form and to act upon a sense of justice – to flow freely into and through the channels of ordinary power. Another is to assure as far as possible that matters of distributive justice can be publicly regarded as matters of pure procedural justice.

Rawls's reference here to the "history of successful constitutions" is opaque. He offers no examples and refers to no sources. He cannot be referring to constitutions that fail to take fair value seriously as "successful"; what he means is that, to be taken seriously, fair value should be assured by some mechanism other than judicial review, unless the judiciary can apply a standard more concrete than that of fair value itself. Rawls quickly adds that this "initial emphasis is not, of course, final" (*PL* 337). What about promoting fair value indirectly, by a substantive constitutional restriction of ownership of the means of production? The five ideal regime types to be canvassed in the *Restatement* have yet to be formulated, but the question of ownership can still be posed in terms of abstract forms:

> Thus, the basic liberties of liberty of conscience and freedom of association are properly protected by explicit constitutional restrictions. These restrictions publicly express on the constitution's face, as it were, the conception of social cooperation held by equal citizens in a well-ordered society . . . . [A]ll legal rights and liberties other than the basic liberties as protected by the various constitutional provisions (including the guarantee of the fair value of the political liberties) are to be specified at the legislative stage . . . . This implies, for example, that *the question of private property in the means of production or their social ownership* [is] not settled at the level of the first principles of justice, but depends upon the traditions and social institutions of a country and its particular problems and historical circumstances.
>
> (*PL* 338; emphasis added)

Like too many other passages in Rawls, this one combines obscurity of argument with opacity of reference to create an interpretive puzzler. Rawls promises to fill gaps, but gap-filling is a process that should leave fewer, rather than more, openings. Is fair value one of, or other than, those basic liberties protected by "various constitutional provisions" though not by "explicit constitutional restrictions"? What is the status of fair value? Is it to be provided for in the constitution, or left to the legislature to sort out? Rawls must mean the former – as I have argued – but the location of the parenthetical reference is ambiguous.

Even more frustrating is what Rawls says following the "this implies": Is the socialism question, which is not settled "at the level of the first principles of justice" then to be settled at the constitutional stage, with reference to "the traditions and social institutions of a country and its particular problems and historical circumstances"? Or is it to be deferred to the legislative stage, where "particular problems" revealed for the first time there – like the prevalence of illness and incidence of accidents – come into view? Rawls had stated, earlier in the essay, that the "merits of [socialist] and other conceptions of property are decided at *later stages* when much more about a society's circumstances and historical traditions is available" (*PL* 298; emphasis added). But this is precisely the information revealed at the constitutional stage.

Rawls's discomfort is evident as he shrugs off another challenge, parts of which I quoted earlier, in Chapter 1:

Moreover, even if by some convincing philosophical argument – at least convincing to us and a few likeminded others – we could trace the right of private or social ownership back to first principles or to basic rights, there is a good reason for working out a conception of justice which does not do this. For ... the aim of justice as fairness as a political conception is to resolve the impasse in the democratic tradition as to the way in which social institutions are to be arranged .... Philosophical argument alone is most unlikely to convince either side that the other is correct on a question like that of private or social property in the means of production. It seems more fruitful to look for bases of agreement implicit in the public political culture and therefore in its underlying conceptions of the person and of social cooperation.

(*PL* 339)

This might be taken merely as Rawls's reiteration of his earlier demurral to Rodney Peffer's proposal to, in effect, build socialism into the principles of justice, combined with a reminder that justice as fairness is to be understood now as a political rather than a comprehensive conception of justice. But there is more. Principles belonging to a political conception like justice as fairness

enable us to account for many if not most of our fundamental rights and liberties, and they provide a way to decide the remaining questions of justice at *the legislative stage*. With the two principles of justice on hand, we have a *possible court of appeal* for settling the question of property as it arises in the light of current and foreseeable social circumstances.

(*PL* 339; emphases added)

Rawls's meaning must be that, as far as Part One goes, the "question of property" is to be left to the legislative stage. This is confirmed later, in the *Restatement*, where Rawls stipulates that "further specification of the rights to property is to be made at the legislative stage, *assuming the basic rights and liberties are maintained*" (*JF* 114; emphasis added). The italicized assumption is always subject to review, in both Part One and Part Two of the original position procedure. In Part Two, the focal question is whether the special psychologies are consistent with the maintenance of the basic rights and liberties and their priority. The stability of a scheme in which "the property question" is kept in play in the legislative arena is to be confronted. And it is here, as Rawls repeatedly indicates, that the case for socialism will be resumed.

9

The Common Content of the Two Regimes

The "property question," that is, the "historic question" of ownership of the means of production, comes down to the choice between liberal socialism and property-owning democracy. It is a decidable question in justice as fairness. Rawls never worked through the necessary steps, but he framed the question in a way that determines an answer, a unique answer, within his system of thought.

In his 1995 "Reply to Habermas," Rawls depicts the constitutional decision whether or not to inscribe the "modern" first-principle liberties – for example, thought and conscience, basic rights of the person and personal property – into a bill of rights as one "on all fours with" the choice between property-owning democracy and liberal socialism (*PL* 416). Whether or not to inscribe the basic liberties in a written constitution, "*thereby* subjecting parliamentary legislation to certain constitutional constraints ... is a matter to be decided by the constituent power of a democratic people ...." The question is one of constitutional design" (*PL* 414–415; emphasis added). The "thereby" must not be misconstrued. In a constitutional democracy, "there is in effect a constitution (not necessarily written) with a bill of rights ... interpreted by the courts as constitutional limits on legislation" (*JF* 145). Necessarily, "certain matters," such as the principle of toleration, are "fixed" and are to be taken off the political agenda "*once and for all* ... [b]y using that phrase citizens express to one another a firm commitment about their common status. They express a certain ideal of democratic citizenship" (*PL* 152 n. 16; emphasis added). The question is whether social ownership of the means of production performs the same expressive function as the principle of toleration. It is a separate and further question whether this "taking off the political agenda once and for all" is to be accomplished by incorporating explicit language to that effect into a written constitution. Bear in mind that for Rawls the constitution is fundamental or higher law that need not be reduced to writing. In fact, Rawls goes so far as to say that the processes that normally suffice for amending a written constitution do not necessarily allow alterations in the fundamental law (*PL* 237–239).[1]

The principle of reciprocity demands that the equality of free citizens as cooperating members of society as a productive enterprise be publicly evident, and the principle of publicity demands that it be the "evident intention" (*JF* 196–197) of the institutions of the basic structure to treat each citizen as a political and social equal.[2] These principles frame the problem of assuring the fair value of political liberty in the circumstances of politics, where the strategic value of political influence already commingles with the strategic value of economic advantage, and the strains of commitment are already being felt.

The demand of publicity is harder to satisfy in Part Two of the original position procedure. Excusable envy and unusual extremes of risk aversion and risk tolerance combine to put additional stress on the index of primary goods. An index restricted to objective primary goods – principally, income and wealth – is to be preferred to a wider index that tries to register, additionally, the degree of self-respect enjoyed by different classes. Even with an objective index of primary goods, the difference principle is already unsuited to furnish a judicially enforceable standard. It is a provable lemma of Part Two of the original position procedure that institutions, and regime types, are disfavored if they permit inequalities that will motivate a persistent call for subjectivizing the index of primary goods. This is a straightforward consequence of the fact that a political contest between the excusably envious and the (in)excusably spiteful is destabilizing.

The issues of capital ownership and assurance of fair value are simultaneously under consideration at the constitutional stage of the four-stage sequence. Because both are properly raised there, they cannot be treated in isolation. The form of reasoning at the constitutional stage, as elsewhere, is holistic. It is accomplished, in part, by applying the "counting principles" that exhaust the content of the concept of rationality (*LP* 88; *TJ* 1st ed. 411–415). In particular, as between two regime types, it will be rational to choose that type, if there is one, which dominates the other on each relevant measure. This, of course, is subject to the ultimate test, that of wide reflective equilibrium.

---

[1] With respect to the repealability of the First Amendment to the U.S. Constitution, Rawls says the Bill of Rights and certain other provisions are

> entrenched in the sense of being validated by long historical practice... They may be amended [by way of correcting weaknesses] but not simply repealed and reversed. Should that happen ... that would be constitutional breakdown, or revolution in the proper sense, and not a valid amendment of the constitution.
>
> (*PL* 239)

[2] Compare: "the original position ... is intended to be fair between individuals conceived as moral persons with a right to equal respect and consideration *in the design of their common institutions*" (*CP* 271; emphasis added).

In this chapter, I compare liberal socialism with property-owning democracy, following as closely as possible the procedure that Rawls uses in the *Restatement* in the first fundamental comparison between justice as fairness and utilitarianism, and in the second fundamental comparison, between the difference principle and the principle of restricted utility. These comparisons belong to Part One of the original position procedure. Part Two introduces the special psychologies, but the points of comparison remain essentially the same. I begin by reviewing the "common content" shared by the two ideal regime-types. In the following chapter, I proceed to the point-by-point comparison. To streamline the discussion, I assume the point of view of the delegates to the constitutional convention in Part Two of the original position procedure. We thus press beyond Rawls's "illustrative and highly tentative" discussion in the *Restatement* by bringing under scrutiny the assumption in place there that each regime can "be effectively and workably maintained" (*JF* 136).

This way of proceeding highlights the difficulties raised when the assumption is relaxed.

> Marx would say that, even accepting the ideal of property-owning democracy, such a regime *generates political and economic forces* that make it depart all too widely from its ideal institutional description. He would say that no regime with private property in the means of production can satisfy the two principles of justice, or even do much to realize the ideals of citizen and society expressed by justice as fairness.
>
> (*JF* 178; emphasis added)

Again, we find Rawls in conversation with Marx, who is now imagined as having a view about realizing justice as fairness, as well as sharing the goal of perfecting the ideal of a constitutional democracy. The political and economic forces in question are of course those that Rawls himself has cataloged. Rawls continues:

> This is a major difficulty and must be faced. But even if it is in good part true, the question is not yet settled. We must ask whether a liberal socialist regime does significantly better in realizing the two principles. Should it do so, then the case for socialism is made from the standpoint of justice as fairness.
>
> (*JF* 178)

Liberal socialism may also generate forces that drive it away from its ideal description. The comparison looks to be ready to proceed,

> [b]ut we must be careful here not to compare the ideal of one conception with the actuality of the other, but rather to compare actuality to actuality, and in our particular historical circumstances.
>
> (*JF* 178)

It is unclear what Rawls means by this caution (and he abruptly turns to a different worry, about what Marx would say about the scope left for workplace democracy). Proverbially, one must not compare apples with oranges. Actual liberal democratic socialist regimes have existed: for example, Great Britain under Attlee.[3] But no property-owning democracy in Rawls's sense, or in James Meade's sense, exists now or has existed. One can compile a long list of attempted but failed socialist democracies, but no country has ever aspired to be, or struggled to become, a property-owning democracy in Rawls's or Meade's sense. No country, in the struggle for property-owning democracy, has veered from democracy into totalitarianism. In *Theory*, by way of illustrating possibilities of institutionalizing justice as fairness, Rawls asks the reader to "assume that the regime is a property-owning democracy since this case is likely to be better known" (*TJ* 242; crediting "the title of ch. V." in Meade 1964 with the term).[4] It is puzzling why Rawls should have said that property-owning democracy was "better known" than socialism, because, as I pointed out in Chapter 2, Rawls cited Meade as his single source, and was evidently oblivious to the vexed history of the term. Martin O'Neill and Thad Williamson are closer to the mark when they point out that "Rawls never followed through on this institutional prospectus [given in *Theory*] by providing a more detailed specification of the architecture of a fully functioning property-owning democracy .... [T]he results of this relative silence are that property-owning democracy is still not well understood as a central idea in Rawls's entire theory of justice" (O'Neill and Williamson 2014, 4).

---

[3] Political philosopher Gerald Gaus writes:

> Rawls can say, without evoking much dissent, that market socialism, which has only been institutionalized by General Tito's repressive Yugoslav state, is within the class of acceptable regimes partly because it *protects* political liberties, whereas a welfare state such as the United Kingdom, which probably protects political rights as well as any regime in history, is unjust because it fails to protect the fair value of political rights.
>
> (Gaus 2011, 528–529)

But Rawls never suggested, nor would he have allowed, that Tito's Yugoslavia respected first-principle political rights, much less their fair value. Nor was he committed to saying so. As for the United Kingdom, there was a patent regression of regard for fair value from that shown under Attlee to that shown under Thatcher. This should register with any Rawlsian as arguing in favor of a constitution that would have impeded that regression.

[4] Privatization in Britain was not yet well advanced until the 1980s. Rawls would have had no reason, in 1971, not to count Britain as a "nearly just" market socialist regime, other than the fact that public ownership of the means of production could not be considered part of the (unwritten) constitution. Krouse and McPherson misleadingly assert:

> Rawls is plainly not committed to the view that any existing system of political economy – property-owning or market socialist – is just. To the contrary, existing property regimes are "riddled with grave injustices." *No example of a market socialist society with political liberties exists.*
>
> (1988, 82–83; emphasis added; quoting *TJ* (1st ed.) 86 [p. 87 is meant]).

In the second edition of *TJ* (1999), Rawls excised the "riddled with grave injustices" language. Perhaps that is why, in praising their work (*JF* 135 n. 2 [2001]), Rawls said nothing to correct Krouse and McPherson, nor to correct the impression that he agreed. Rodney Peffer (2014, 393) points out that, in any case, Rawls at once proceeded to a more hopeful assessment (*TJ* (1st ed.) 87).

Charity requires that property-owning democracy be interpreted in the best light, but it would be frivolous to pretend that it is a more familiar idea than socialism.

So, the comparison Rawls wants to conduct has to be made in terms of general knowledge and historical analogy. Comparing "actuality with actuality" is not a possibility. We have to compare the two ideal-types – as ideal conceptions – with respect to their relative capabilities to stabilize a well-ordered society given the general and particular knowledge available at the constitutional stage. Negative material in the historical dossier on socialism will not be ignored insofar as it indicates potential troubles. We have to ask ourselves whether, given the assumptions we have found it reasonable to make, a liberal democratic socialist regime would stand the better chance of stably realizing justice as fairness; as Rawls says, "Should it do so, then *the case for liberal socialism is made*" (JF 178; emphasis added).

THE COMMON CONTENT

Just as Rawls does in the second fundamental comparison, I prepare an inventory of what the two regime types have in common by stipulation. This will encompass not only stated features but also possible refinements and elaborations, each of which may be, though need not be, pursued under either regime.

Justice as Fairness

The core of the common content of the two regime types is that they are designed to realize justice as fairness:

> Both a property-owning democracy and a liberal socialist regime set up a consti-
> tutional framework for democratic politics, guarantee the basic liberties [including
> a right to private personal property] with the fair value of the political liberties and
> fair equality of opportunity, and regulate economic and social inequalities by a
> principle of mutuality, if not by the difference principle.
>
> (JF 138)

The final clause conveys the later Rawls's intimation that justice as fairness, featuring the difference principle, is but one of a family of reasonable liberal conceptions of justice. I postpone until the following chapter the question of the significance of this change. The term "principle of mutuality" serves here to emphasize that welfare-state capitalism – which, like property-owning democracy, permits "private property in productive assets" – cannot satisfy the "principle of reciprocity" merely by guaranteeing a social minimum. I take the terms "principle of mutuality" and "principle of reciprocity" to be synonymous in the lexicon of Rawls's theory. Liberal socialism and property-owning democracy are both, on this score, distinguished from the principle of restricted utility, which does not concern itself with reciprocity.

But restricted utility at least guarantees fair value, which welfare-state capitalism ignores. This tells us something interesting: that guaranteeing fair value does not, by itself, satisfy the principle of reciprocity. Fitness to satisfy the principle of reciprocity is a further question that is separate from the question of fitness to secure fair value. Liberal socialism and property-owning democracy are similarly committed to both fair value and reciprocity. It is their comparative fitness to stably secure both that is in question. It bears repeating here that the overarching argument for justice fairness presented in the *Restatement* places greater weight on reciprocity and publicity than the 1971 argument with which many readers are more familiar.

Rawls conceives property-owning democracy "as an alternative to capitalism" (*JF* 135–136; citing Elster and Moene 1989 for "discussion of other alternatives").[5] Socialism too, it hardly needs to be said, is an alternative to capitalism. This, then, is the *core* common content shared by the two. Both are constitutional liberal democratic alternatives to capitalism, which are committed to fair valued political equality and a distributive principle of reciprocity.

Redistributive Policies

Much of the remaining, "non-core" common content has to be gleaned by inference from what Rawls says by way of contrasting property-owning democracy with welfare-state capitalism. He never directly compares welfare-state capitalism with liberal socialism, but Rawls all but states that such a comparison would go much the same way. There can be no doubt that in a direct comparison between liberal socialism and any form of capitalism, justice as fairness, and Rawls decisively favor socialism.

To begin: "The background institutions of property-owning democracy work to disperse the ownership of wealth and capital, and thus to prevent a small part of society from controlling the economy, and indirectly, political life as well" (*JF* 139). Here, a means and an end are attributed to property-owning democracy: the means is to disperse wealth, the aim is to prevent concentration of wealth in (presumably private) hands. Nothing yet distinguishes property-owning democracy and liberal socialism. Rawls continues:

> Property-owning democracy avoids this, not by the redistribution of income to those with less at the end of each period, so to speak, but rather by ensuring the widespread ownership of productive assets and human capital (that is, education and trained skills) at the beginning of each period, all this against a background of fair equality of opportunity.

(*JF* 139)

---

[5] None of the contributors to Elster and Moene 1989 mentions property-owning democracy, and the lone reference to Meade is inapposite to the property question.

I will return to the "periodicity" idea later, but evidently a liberal socialist regime will likewise promote education and training, as part of the guarantee of fair equality of opportunity. Also, a liberal socialist regime will likewise, with but the one defining difference, ensure that productive assets are widely available. Access to non-major productive assets may be furnished via private rights of ownership, but of course society's major productive assets will always remain in common ownership. Rawls is not always explicit that the aim of property-owning democracy is widespread private *ownership* of productive means, as contrasted to assured private access, as when he says,

> In a property-owning democracy ... the aim is to realize in the basic institutions the idea of society as a fair system of cooperation between citizens regarded as free and equal. To do this, those institutions must, from the outset, *put in the hands of* citizens generally, and not only of a few, sufficient productive means for them to be fully cooperating members of society on a footing of equality.
>
> (*JF* 140; emphasis added)

One can (permissibly) have one's hands on something one does not own. Likewise, one can have the exclusive right to use and enjoy a thing that one does not own. But I will assume that Rawls means private ownership of productive assets in the whole Hohfeldian "bundle of sticks" sense that includes, importantly, the right to rents and to alienate by sale or gift, subject to the usual modern panoply of regulatory limitations. In Rawls's scheme (as in Mill's), limits on private accumulation over generations take the form of taxes on recipients, leaving individuals nominally in possession of the same "testamentary freedom" they enjoy under capitalism. Nothing stands in the way of a liberal socialist regime allowing for this kind of ownership where non-commanding-heights productive assets are concerned. So, widespread private ownership of non-major productive assets, whether as a means or an end, is available under both property-owning democracy and liberal socialism.

Devices to Assure Fair Value

Justice as fairness guarantees the fair value of the political liberties, meaning that all citizens have a roughly equal chance to affect political outcomes. The reason why this is a requirement of justice, given the fact of domination, was explained in Chapters 3 and 5. In the *Restatement*, Rawls says

> I cannot consider here how this fair value is best realized in political institutions. I simply assume that there are practicable institutional ways of doing this.... Reforms to that end are likely to involve such things as the public funding of elections and restrictions on campaign contributions; the assurance of a more even access to public media; and certain regulations of freedom of speech and of the press (but not restrictions affecting the content of speech) .... In adjusting the basic liberties one aim is to enable legislators and political parties to be independent of

large concentrations of private economic and social power in a private-property democracy, and of government control and bureaucratic power in a liberal socialist regime.

(*JF* 149–150; cf. *PL* 328)

Rawls elsewhere cites other devices. In a property-owning democracy, "the emphasis falls on the steady dispersal over time of the ownership of capital and resources by the law of inheritance and bequest, on fair equality of opportunity secured by provisions for education and training … as well as on institutions that support the fair value of the political liberties" (*CP* 420).[6] Liberal socialism can employ these devices as well. Maintaining fair value in a liberal socialist regime must guard against undue partisan patronage in government employment and contracting – which is contrary to fair equality of opportunity – and high-handed bureaucratic isolation from popular sentiment; but similar challenges face property-owning democracies that have complex economies.

I have used the term "insulation devices" to designate means that are intended to protect the political process from accumulations of wealth and power that are otherwise permitted. Insulation devices, as Rawls notes, are difficult to design in a way that is both fair and effective (*PL* 362–363). Given the fact of domination, those with social and economic advantages can be expected to use them to assure that the insulation is porous. Rawls asks,

> When politicians are beholden to their constituents for essential campaign funds, and a very unequal distribution of wealth obtains in the background culture, with the great wealth being in the control of corporate economic power, is it any wonder that congressional legislation is, in effect, written by lobbyists, and Congress becomes a bargaining chamber in which laws are bought and sold?
>
> (*LP* 24 n. 19)

Legislative safeguards to prevent this are, naturally, going to be among the first items to be bought and sold unless there are prior, constitutional constraints firmly in place. Not only can the well-off be expected to weaken or oppose insulating legislation; nothing prevents their gaining such influence within the judiciary that judicial review undoes rather than reinforces legislative measures to assure fair value. Rawls acknowledges that judicial review "has its dangers: courts may fail in their task and make too many unreasonable decisions not easily corrected" (*JF* 147).

In the worst of cases, the judiciary might declare that the legislature is forbidden to regulate the political process to promote fair value (*PL* 359–363). That is precisely the teaching of a line of U.S. Supreme Court decisions running from *Buckley v. Valeo*, 421 U.S. 1 (1976), to *Citizens United v. Federal Election Commission*, 558

---

[6] Richard Arneson describes some of the perverse incentives that restrictions on inheritance can be expected to engender (1987, 140–141).

U. S. 310 (2010), to *McCutcheon v. Federal Election Commission*, 572 U.S. __ (2014). As legal scholar Timothy Kuhner writes,

> Passing a comprehensive package of campaign finance reforms between 1971 and 1974, Congress aimed to "equalize the relative ability of all citizens to affect the outcome of elections" and slow "the skyrocketing cost of political campaigns[,] thereby ... open[ing] the political system more widely to candidates without access to sources of large amounts of money.

(Kuhner 2011, 419)

Within a remarkably short interval of time, these goals had been declared unconstitutional. Yet even if the Supreme Court were to recognize the fair value of political liberty as a constitutional essential, Rawls would allow it to be balanced against other first-principle rights, such as free speech and press, so long as the "central range of application" of each was secure (cf. *JF* 111–112, 113–114). Moreover, Rawls rightly insists that it is not for the Court to declare "what kinds of electoral arrangements are required ... but to make sure that the arrangements enacted by the legislature accord with the constitution" (*PL* 362) – that is, that legislative arrangements do not unduly burden free speech. Unless fair value and the principle of reciprocity are accorded some more salient protection, they are subject to the vicissitudes of judicial no less than legislative balancing against competing values.

Both regime types face this problem. Given the fact of domination, it is not easy to see how to *assure* rough equality of political influence without giving a credible prior assurance that no individual or class can possess a dominating share of capital resources. Put differently, there is an unsolved assurance problem at the heart of the project of operationalizing justice as fairness. The difference principle does not and is not designed to solve the problem and, owing to the nature of the political, it cannot. Judicial review that reduces to nothing more than balancing fair value against free speech is scant protection.

This is not at all to say that a supreme judiciary can do whatever it wants anyway. Consider, for example, Article V of the U.S. Constitution, which declares that "no state, without its consent, shall be deprived of its equal suffrage in the Senate." The effect of this is highly undemocratic. A Wyoming voter has about sixty-six times the influence of a Californian in the U.S. Senate.[7] The Senate itself has outsized influence with respect to the popularly more representative branch, the House of Representatives. (The Senate alone may confirm or block appointments of officers of the United States, try officers the House has impeached, and ratify treaties.) The process of amending the Constitution (which would otherwise permit a three-fifths supermajority of the states to reform the makeup of the Senate) expressly gives each state a veto over any amendment that would reduce the equal representation of the states in the Senate. The "one person-one vote" principle recognized by the Court

---

[7] "Smaller States Find Outsize Clout Growing in Senate," *New York Times*, March 11, 2013.

in *Wesberry v. Sanders*, 376 U.S. 1 (1964) is inapposite, for it applies only to the House of Representatives. No scholar, politician, or observer of the Court has ever suggested that the Court could cut the Gordian knot by simply voting to abolish the small-state veto over making representation in the Senate more democratic.

Full Employment

There is more common content to be gathered from beyond the *Restatement*. In *Political Liberalism*, Rawls writes:

> [S]tability for the right reasons . . . is always lacking in a purely formal constitutional regime. An indication of institutions required for this stability is the following:
>
> . . .
>
> d. Society as employer of last resort through general or local government, or other social and economic policies. Lacking a sense of long-term security and the opportunity for meaningful work and occupation is not only destructive of citizens' self-respect but of their sense that they are members of society and not just caught up in it. This leads to self-hatred, bitterness, and resentment.
>
> (*PL* lviii–lix; cf. *LP* 50)

This mandates full employment. In effect, if not intention, private employers are deprived of a "disposable industrial reserve army" (Marx 1978 [1867], 423), for which they may create, and upon which they may bestow, jobs according to their pleasure. A full-employment mandate is one that both types of regime can pursue and can be added to their common content.

SUMMING UP

In summary, the common content of property-owning democracy and liberal socialism includes access to all the devices mentioned in this chapter: insulation devices, limits on inheritance and accumulation, full employment, and so forth. The one exception is that, in a property-owning democracy, the constitution allows private ownership of the means of production, subject presumably to some sort of anti-monopoly proviso. Liberal socialism does not permit such ownership. This difference affects how the fair-value problem manifests itself in the two types of regime. The independence of legislators and political parties can be assailed from two different directions. In a property-owning democracy, the most pressing problem is checking the "large concentrations of private economic and social power" that are permitted. In a liberal socialist regime, more pressing is the problem of "government control and bureaucratic power" (*JF* 149–150). Rawls's plausible supposition is that the form of ownership of the means of production on commanding heights of the economy is likely to tip the weight of the problem one way or the other.

Where private capital determines social investment, legislators and political parties – not to mention public officials – are liable to be influenced in myriad small and large ways to make decisions that effectively increase returns to private capital. Recall Rawls's glum observation, noted earlier in Chapter 5, that in constitutional democracies the "necessary corrective steps" to offset the influence of "the more advantaged social and economic interests … have not been taken, indeed, they never seem to have been seriously entertained" (*TJ* 198, reordered). Where social investment is chiefly a matter of deploying publicly owned capital, much decision-making authority will be delegated to agencies of government, staffed by a perhaps coordinated bureaucracy that will in part be motivated by its own interests and conceptions. Either way, maintaining the fair value of political liberty for each citizen looks to be a formidable challenge.

10

The Property Question

In the previous chapter, I explored the "common content" that property-owning democracy and liberal socialism share. I did so to organize the discussion in this chapter so that it has the same overall structure as the first and second fundamental comparisons of Part One, in the *Restatement*'s reorganized and redeployed argument for justice as fairness. I now proceed to compare the two regime types in terms of their relative performance under the same headings, which are, principally, stability, reciprocity, and publicity. But first, a preliminary remark is in order.

The sharpest contrast Rawls draws between socialism and property-owning "systems" is in the language I am about to quote. Bear in mind that Rawls later confesses that in the passage to follow he had not "sufficiently noted" (*JF* 135 n. 2) the distinction between welfare-state capitalism and property-owning democracy, as two quite different species of the genus "property-owning systems." A "property-owning system" is one in which the means of production, on which all depend for the opportunity to exercise all but the most primitive of their productive powers, are privately owned or ownable. In other words, a property-owning system is not simply any system that allows private ownership of something or other. By that definition, every system trivially counts as a property-owning system, even communism. "Communism deprives no man of the power to appropriate the products of society; all that it does is to deprive him of the power to subjugate the labor of others by means of such appropriation" (Marx and Engels 1978 [1848], 486). Also note that Rawls's use of the unqualified term "socialism," in context, is meant to exclude what he will later term "command-economy socialism." Now, the passage:

> It is necessary . . . to recognize that market institutions are common to both private-property and socialist regimes, and to distinguish between the allocative and the distributive function of prices. Since under socialism the means of production and natural resources are publicly owned, the distributive function is greatly restricted, whereas a private-property system uses prices in varying degrees for both purposes.
>
> (*TJ* 242)

The "distributive function" spoken of here is that of "determining the income to be received by individuals in return for what they contribute" (*TJ* 241). Property-owning systems thus appear to be ones in which income from private ownership of productive assets is itself taken to be a "return for what they [the owners] contribute." Rents extracted by private owners in exchange for making productive assets available for deployment are "greatly restricted" under socialism precisely because the major means of production are publicly held.[1] And they are not "entirely" rather than "greatly restricted" because not all means of production are major. Rawls continues:

> Which of these systems *and the many intermediate forms* most fully answers to the requirements of justice cannot, I think, be determined in advance. There is presumably no general answer to this question, since it depends in large part on the traditions, institutions, and social forces of each country, and its particular historical circumstances. The theory of justice does not include these matters. But what it can do is to set out in a schematic way the outlines of a just economic system that admits of *several variations*. The political judgment in any given case will then turn on which variation is most likely to work out best in practice. A conception of justice is a necessary part of any such political assessment, but it is not sufficient.
>
> (*TJ* 242; emphases added)

Rawls does not mean, precisely, that "the theory of justice does not include these matters." What he means is that the two principles of justice do not themselves include them. Recall Rawls's dissent from Rodney Peffer's friendly amendment to

---

[1]   Thad Williamson writes:

> [A]lthough a coherent institutional configuration of property-owning democracy would almost certainly require ... some plainly socialist elements, it could nonetheless be plausibly claimed that property-owning democracy is distinct from democratic socialism as such: most notably, the system sketched above [filling out Rawls's notion of property-owning democracy] *does not involve or require democratic approval of a comprehensive economic plan.*
>
> (2009, 449; emphasis added)

   This is mistaken in two ways. First, as Rawls repeatedly insists, "market institutions are common to both private-property and [liberal democratic] socialist regimes" (*TJ* 242). Rawls speaks of competitive markets in general as operating in "conformity with political decisions reached democratically, [where] the government regulates the economic climate by adjusting certain elements under its control, such as the overall amount of investment, the rate of interest, and the quantity of money, and so on. There is no necessity for comprehensive *direct* planning" (*TJ* 241; emphasis added). Thus, secondly, the defining element of Rawlsian socialism is not "direct" comprehensive planning, but ownership; and comprehensive (*indirect*) planning is already contemplated as necessary to a functioning property-owning democracy. Christian Schemmel also seems to link public ownership of the means of production with direct comprehensive planning, when he refers to "the kind of absolute control over property traditionally associated with ownership rights (*which would thus lead to comprehensive economic planning*)" (2015, 405; emphasis added). Schemmel does correctly note that Joshua Cohen (1989), David Schweikert (2014), and John Roemer (1994) have explained how public ownership of the means of production can proceed without detailed or direct central management, along the lines Rawls had already noted in *Theory.*

the contrary. The theory of justice includes these matters in the sense that it provides guidelines for deciding them at the three later stages of the four-stage sequence. Rawls proceeds to sketch an "ideal scheme" that "makes considerable use of market arrangements" for

> [i]t is only in this way that the problem of distribution can be handled as a case of pure procedural justice. Further, we also gain the advantages of efficiency and protect the important liberty of free choice of occupation.
>
> (*TJ* 242)

The ideal scheme does not, as Rawls later admits, sufficiently distinguish welfare-state capitalism from property-owning democracy. The five regime types resolved in the *Restatement* presumably represent some or all of the "intermediate forms" and "several variations" adverted to in *Theory*. In 1971, Rawls was not ready to pursue the question further.

One consistent theme, from 1971 until Rawls's death in 2002, is the central linkage between handing distributive justice as a case of pure procedural justice and assuring the stability of a well-ordered society (*TJ* 76–77; *JF* 52; see Anderson forthcoming). Distributive justice cannot be a matter of perfect procedural justice because no political or economic process can hope for infallible accuracy in hitting an independently specified target. Distributive justice ultimately cannot be classified as a matter of imperfect procedural justice, either. To treat it so is to invite endless and irresolvable dissension not only about the specification of the appropriate target but also about the appropriateness of various means of hitting it, and the tolerable degree of error in doing so. What is necessary to the stability of a just society is that the question of distributive justice be, and be seen as, a matter of *pure* procedural justice.

This means that the parties agree that once the principles of justice along with their derivation are understood, and are realized in institutions that are open to view, there is no independent standard of justice to which the distribution of the fruits of the productive enterprise could be intelligibly held to. Any complaint about a resulting pattern of holdings must, for stability's sake, be framed as an allegation of a procedural failure. (Or as an objection to the theory as a whole.) Framed as a complaint of failure to follow the procedures defined by a just constitution, an allegation may be correct, or not: call it a case of quasi-pure procedural justice. Framed as a failure to achieve an independently defined share, or pattern of holdings, a complaint cannot be heard, for to hear it would be to undo a well-ordered society's resolve to regard its political conception of justice as the language in which citizens are to press their claims.

THE THREE ESSENTIALS FOR A STABLE CONSTITUTIONAL REGIME

In preparing to make the first fundamental comparison in the *Restatement*, Rawls set out three essential features of principles that are suited properly to stabilize a constitutional regime. First, such a regime must keep highly divisive, irresolvable issues off the public agenda as much as possible. I will call this the "reconciliation requirement." Second, a stable constitutional regime must meet the publicity condition: principles of justice must be stated using clear and reliable criteria and, by the same token, the institutions that are to be measured against those principles must likewise employ clear and reliable criteria, wherever possible, for they are in that sense workable. Three, institutions capable of realizing justice as fairness must be designed in a way that itself expresses allegiance to the principle of reciprocity, that is, the principle that all citizens are regarded as, and should regard themselves as, free and equal members of a cooperative enterprise. Let us compare property-owning democracy and liberal socialism with respect to each of these three essentials.

The Reconciliation Requirement

Liberal socialism removes from the public agenda, once and for all, the divisive issue of whether or not the major, "commanding-heights" means of production shall be common property. Property-owning democracy leaves that issue on the table for majoritarian decision. Laissez-faire capitalism and welfare-state capitalism also remove the issue of private ownership from discussion, but in the opposite way. A capitalist system is a system in which, as Barack Obama has put it, there is "a strong sense of … private capital fulfilling the core … investment needs of [the] country" (Moran 2009). But it is more than that: in a capitalist system, that "strong sense" is rooted not in mere expediency, but in a conception of the basic, off-the-table, individual rights of the private capitalist. For Rawls, capitalist regime types are objectionable, but let us give credit where credit is due. That private ownership of the productive means is a basic right (subject of course to adjustment with respect to other basic rights) is at least settled under capitalism, albeit in the wrong way.

One might object here that liberal socialism leaves a question open too, the question of what capital assets are and what are not among the major productive means at society's disposal. So, as between property-owning democracy and liberal socialism, the objection continues, there is a net wash. In a property-owning democracy, the question whether to allow major productive means to be privately owned and, if so, which ones to allow, is always up for grabs. Under liberal socialism, the question whether or not this or that enterprise or asset is a major or non-major asset is always up for grabs. The reconciliation requirement favors neither of the regimes.

This objection exaggerates the difficulty of settling the extension of the concept of the "commanding heights." As the excerpt from Schumpeter in Chapter 2 illustrates, there can be a consensus as to what the major productive means are even in the midst of controversy as to whether those means should be publicly owned. Banking, insurance, rail, mineral resources, and so forth, were the "natural" candidates for public ownership, in Schumpeter's view, wholly apart from the question of whether to socialize them. Under the British constitution, it was for Parliament to say whether these assets were to be publicly held. That follows from the doctrine of parliamentary supremacy, but that doctrine does not always and everywhere govern. Under the U.S. Constitution, there can be no "taking" of property without just compensation. This is settled, and off the public agenda, even though the questions of what counts as property, what counts as a taking, and what is the measure of just compensation are to be determined case by case. Congress has no power to repeal the "takings" clause or to alter its terms. Whether Congress has that power is off the table. And if a constitution can mark off the range of admissible meanings of "a taking," it could settle the meaning of "commanding heights" in peripheral cases in light of its core meaning.

Suppose the U.S. Constitution were amended to deny Congress the power to privatize the National Parks of the United States, and to require that they be publicly held in perpetuity. Then, controversy might still exist in the "background culture," but reconciliation would have been achieved to the extent that it is achievable at all (cf. Michelman 1973, 1013). Rawls is confident that constitutions (written or other-wise) can entrench certain rights, powers, and disabilities, and he is not friendly to the skeptical suggestion that nothing a constitutional convention could do could take the property question off the public agenda.[2] Whether or not to limit the power of a representative legislature over certain subjects is a question that implicates the "educational role" the publicity condition assigns to the political conception of justice in a well-ordered society (JF 145–148). I take this up in later sections.

The question whether society's productive assets are fairly distributed always has the potential to turn into a very divisive issue. Liberal socialism at least limits the scope of this divisiveness to the distribution of productive assets that are not "major" and thus not already required to be in public hands. Property-owning democracy, as we shall see, keeps this potentially divisive issue always fully alive. The reconciliation requirement appears to favor liberal socialism.

One might object here that taking a divisive issue off the table is one thing, but keeping it off is another. Compare the idea of a constitutional establishment of religion. It may be "settled" what the official religion is, but in a pluralistic, free society, reasonable people will still disagree about religious matters. A stability problem in the background culture is simply duplicated, not relieved, by the attempt to enforce a constitutional settlement. A structure cannot be stabilized – made stable for the right reasons, anyway – by the mere expedient of taking things that are in fact reasonably contentious out of the realm of ordinary politics. Liberal socialism is no more favored than any other forced settlement, as far as the reconciliation requirement goes.[3]

---

[2]   Rawls is friendlier than is generally appreciated to what Phillipe van Parijs calls "social-justice-guided constitutional engineering" (2011, 38 and n. 19).
[3]   Kevin Vallier pressed this objection.

Rawls holds that it was possible for Patrick Henry and James Madison to debate whether to establish the Anglican Church in Virginia "almost entirely by reference to political values alone" (*CP* 602). It is implausible to think that the disestablishment of religion in the resulting Virginia constitution was a mere standoff, or mere imposition. Certainly that is not Rawls's view. Rawls does acknowledge that one might reasonably question whether a property-owning democracy – and, by implication, whether a liberal democratic socialism – needs to be a constitutional rather than a "procedural" democracy in which "there are no constitutional limits on legislation and whatever a majority (or other plurality) enacts is law, provided the appropriate procedures . . . are followed" (*JF* 145). As already noted, Rawls rejects the notion that the theory of justice is indifferent between constitutional and procedural democracy, because indifference

> overlooks the possibility that certain features of a political conception importantly affect the political sociology of the basic institutions that realize it. More exactly, we must consider how that sociology may be affected by the educational role of a political conception of justice.
>
> (*JF* 146)

He goes on to say that "when all three levels of . . . the publicity condition . . . are achieved in a well-ordered society, the political conception has an educational role" (*JF* 146, reordered). I will resume this point in the following section, on publicity. But first let me acknowledge two other objections that fall under the present heading.

I have said that the reconciliation requirement favors liberal democratic socialism because there is a corrosively (and potentially explosively) divisive issue that it takes off the public agenda that property-owning democracy leaves in play. One objection to this is that the difference is *de minimis* at best because liberal democratic socialism still leaves in play too many intimately connected but equally contentious issues. A related objection is that liberal democratic socialism introduces new and different contentious issues that property-owning democracy does not, and hence the comparison is a wash. It would be too quick to dismiss these concerns without further discussion.

Settling ownership of the means of production is not yet to settle how income (or loss) from those assets is to be managed.[4] Is income to be retained or distributed? If distributed, are distributions to be made regularly or on demand? Is it distribution to be joint and equal or joint but unequal to incentivize? Doesn't liberal democratic socialism leave these inflammatory questions on the table? I think Rawls's answer would likely begin with a rehearsal of the case (put in Chapter 2) for singling out the ownership of the means of production as a special one that is distinct from the question of distribution of the social product. Whatever may be the situation of the

---

[4] Jeremy Farris pressed this objection.

more primitive peoples, in modern constitutional democracies there are economic sectors that are strategically important for everyone. This leads almost immediately to the second, more general objection.

This objection is that liberal socialism will instigate controversy about how to operate the means of production (on top of the question how to divide their product) while property-owning democracy will not. The reconciliation requirement therefore does not favor socialism. An answer to this objection has to begin with a reminder that in a property-owning democracy the means of production always may be brought into public ownership. Whether to do so or not, and on what terms, is always subject to the calculus of interests and bargaining that is ordinary politics. But the answer cannot be complete just yet, until the other dimensions and factors of stability are examined. What the reconciliation requirement will ultimately favor turns on the further factors we must now consider.

Publicity Condition: Clear and Reliable Criteria: Workability

Property-owning democracy assures not only that the question whether the major means of production are to be privately owned is always on the public agenda; it also assures that the public agenda is always open to challenges to the distribution of productive assets of all kinds. In the first fundamental comparison, Rawls faulted utilitarianism for lacking clear and reliable criteria for deciding public questions. Applying the utilitarian calculus subjects citizens to heavy informational demands and requires them to follow complex and speculative arguments, which can lead to suspicion that other citizens are not arguing in good faith.

> [E]ven though we think our arguments sincere and not self-serving when we present them, we must consider what it is reasonable to expect others to think who stand to lose should our reasoning prevail. Arguments supporting political judgments should, if possible, be not only sound, but such that they can publicly be seen to be sound.
>
> (JF 116)

Consider the form in which a citizen of a property-owning democracy must put forward a complaint specifically about the distribution of productive assets. In his sympathetic attempt to flesh out Rawls's sketch of this ideal regime-type, Thad Williamson points out that

> a property-owning democracy must concern itself with the distribution of land, holdings in corporations, bond holdings, holdings of real assets (buildings, machinery), and cash savings, as well as, plausibly, intellectual property. Last but not least, [it] must also be concerned with the distribution of human capital, that is, the distribution of ability to earn income through labor (mental or physical).
>
> (2009, 439)

Assume that there is an objective inventory of what the distribution is at a particular time. Unequal distribution of privately held productive assets cannot itself be a ground for complaint if the distribution of objective primary goods satisfies the difference principle, and markets are functioning. The difference principle already requires an adequate social minimum, and justice as fairness already requires full employment. Is the complaint that the market does not provide what the citizen is looking for in terms of productive opportunities? This sounds like a case of an expensive productive taste, and I will come back to it in a moment. Is the complaint then that the inequality in the distribution of productive assets is so great that the fair value of political liberty is threatened? In that case, then, the complaint is not about unequal holdings of productive assets per se, but that the measures to secure fair value are inadequate. Finally, is the complaint that the objective index of primary goods needs to be adjusted to incorporate a subjective element, to register the low esteem in which the productive activities open to the complainant are held? In various connections, Rawls expresses his aversion to subjectivizing the primary goods. "Principles specifying fair distribution must, so far as possible, be stated in terms that allow us publicly to verify whether they are satisfied" (*JF* 78); they must not (as Rawls states in another context) call for "more information than political society can conceivably acquire and sensibly apply" (*LP* 13 n. 3). The complaint must be that the citizen requires, no later than the beginning of the next period, more capital.

Contrast liberal socialism, with respect to the form in which a citizen must put forward a complaint specifically about the distribution of productive assets. The notion of public ownership of the means of production provides a "natural focal point" (*JF* 123): as noted earlier, what these assets are and their dimension are amenable to objective assessment. Public ownership of the means of production is "self-enforcing" (*JF* 125) in the sense that privatization of major productive assets, such as railways, airlines, banks, or mineral resources, is always a conspicuous event that attracts its own opposition, which, if mounted from an entrenched constitutional "veto point" (Stepan and Linz 2011, 844), can resist majoritarian whim and interest-group machination.[5] Residual complaints about the distribution of small-scale productive assets are plausibly regarded as settled, as matters of pure procedural justice, by appeal to the justice of the basic structure overall. Unequal private accumulation of smaller-scale productive capital does not come at the expense of public direction of the major economic institutions, whose effects are the most pervasive.

Property-owning democracy directs its distribution branch "gradually and *continually* to correct the distribution of wealth" (*TJ* 245; emphasis added; see Krouse

---

[5]   Two independent observations of John Dunn's come together here. First, "it is at least as easy to reverse progress towards socialism within a reasonably liberal capitalist democracy as it is to make the progress in the first place" (1984, 72). Second, "socialist politics has a more urgent need than it normally cares to recognize to imbibe the lessons of the political tradition of power-diffusing institutional design [and its] emphasis on constitutionalism" (1984, 81).

and McPherson 1988; Vallier 2014).[6] Efficiency demands that privately held capital assets, both major and minor, be tradable in the market on an ongoing basis, and a property-owning democracy must be on constant guard. This process of correction wanders into range of Robert Nozick's "Wilt Chamberlain" objection, that "to apply the [difference] principle to government must involve *continual* interference with particular individual transactions" (*JF* 52 n. 18). Private purchases and sales of property in productive means do not stay under the umbrella of pure procedural justice, which is why property-owning democracy has to assure gradual but continual corrections in their distribution.

Scrutiny of individual transactions is not up to the task. Imagine a simple case. Owner A agrees to merge with Owner B by selling a significant portion of A's productive assets to B. Owner A retains sufficient productive assets to be happy with the arrangement, and B cannot complain. But now C, who had formerly had affordable access to assets held by A or B by taking the better bid, may be unable to afford the price B can now command. This is the kind of circumstance that Rawls invokes as a conclusive objection to Lockean "historical process" accounts: "[T]he accumulated results of many separate and seemingly fair transactions are likely over an extended period of time to undermine the background conditions required for free and fair agreements" (*JF* 53). Will C be entitled to ownership of supplementary assets at the beginning of the next period (whenever that might be)? Or is C entitled to a judicial injunction against the transaction between A and B? Or is C simply seeking an economic rent? Issues of like these are commonplace in the administration of anti-monopoly and antitrust laws; but what property-owning democracy opens up is a separate question from one about the resulting market power of B. Because, now, there is a question whether there are sufficient assets in the hands of C.[7]

---

[6] John Roemer's chapter, in the *Alternatives to Capitalism* collection that Rawls cites, concludes with Roemer's "intuition that mechanisms that obey the necessary postulates for public ownership will be considerably more welfare egalitarian in their consequences than private ownership mechanisms are. This does not mean, in practice, that markets cannot be used to implement a conception of public ownership. It means, rather, that there would have to be *frequent or continuous redistributions to adjust for the private property externalities* that come about from the use of markets" (1989, 178; emphasis added). Among the private property externalities, for Rawls, will be effects on the fair value of political liberty and the public perception of reciprocity.

[7] Thad Williamson asserts, without elaboration, that "[o]nce the background institutions for allocating property are established, the system should operate of its own accord to produce a less concentrated, far wider distribution of property, with no 'interference' in the everyday operations of the economy required beyond that present in the existing system of periodic taxation." He quickly adds, however, that "this virtue could be claimed only on behalf of an already-established POD [property-owning democracy]" and confesses that in any case "[i]t is less clear that a society of this sort would fully solve the structural constraints problem (2009, 449), viz., "that certain public policy options that might be endorsed by popular majorities are effectively taken off the table by the dependence of policymakers on the investment decisions of capitalists; public policies that might alienate or constrain investors are thus not adopted even by relatively 'liberal' leaders" (2009, 438). Williamson thus glosses over a key task that Rawls sets property-owning democracy: the task of assuring fair value. It is irrelevant that a

Assume, however, for the sake of argument, that a property-owning democracy can operate with a set of rules that involves no greater interference in the stream of commercial and economic events than do presently existing systems of taxation. Even so, having to judge even only on a periodic basis whether *C* is adequately capitalized does not "allow us to abstract from the enormous complexities of the innumerable transactions of everyday life" or "free[] us from having to keep track of the changing relative positions of particular individuals" (*JF* 54). To the contrary, a record of the distribution of productive capital in private hands – and an assessment of its fairness – would have to be ongoing. Not only that, it would require processing quantities of hard-to-get-at information, such as *C*'s desires and intentions with respect to future, perhaps innovative productive projects, without the assistance of a market pricing mechanism. In this respect, property-owning democracy would recapitulate the futility of state socialism with a command economy, which (wholly apart from its disregard for basic, first-principle liberties) "is discredited – indeed, it was never a plausible doctrine" (*LHPP* 323).

Maintaining even a rough equality of private holdings in productive capital assets would thus require restricting transfers, whether by sale, trade in-kind, pledge, loan, or gift. Restrictions as extensive as this are inconsistent with the ordinary association of a property right with free alienability. Moreover, they arguably would require a vast bureaucracy that would itself tend to diminish the fair value of political liberty (Vallier 2014).[8]

Most importantly, one of the advantages of pure procedural justice – "it is no longer necessary to keep track of the endless variety of circumstances and the changing relative positions of particular persons" (*TJ* 76) – could not be captured by a property-owning democracy. A property-owning democracy thus cannot sustain the claim that "acceptance of the two principles constitutes an understanding to discard as irrelevant as a matter of social justice much of the information and many of the complications of everyday life" (*TJ* 76). The publicity condition favors liberal socialism.

Express Reciprocity Condition

Rawls's third condition for a stable constitutional democracy "is that its basic institutions should encourage the cooperative virtues of political life" (*JF* 116). In the first fundamental comparison, Rawls shows that "the two principles of justice express an idea of reciprocity that is lacking in the principle of utility" (*JF* 117). Reciprocity

---

property-owning democracy that fails to secure fair value could consist of institutions that do not minutely supervise economic life.

[8] Krouse and McPherson (1988, 84, 94) seem to discount the degree to which property-owning democracy requires continuous interference in the economy (see Vallier 2014). They recognize that "Rawlsian justice in political economy . . . requires, as well, the continuing redistribution of market outcomes (within as well as between generations)" (1988, 94), but suggest that the requirement is not already built into the concept of a property-owning democracy which Rawls supposes.

fosters the cooperative virtues, for it expresses the nature of society as a fair system of cooperation between free equals. Seeing that the basic structure conforms to a design that assures mutual benefit, citizens grow in confidence in themselves and in their fellows, trusting that all are engaged in a fair mutual endeavor.

The expressive dimension is one that Rawls's colleague and critic Robert Nozick came to appreciate in his thinking subsequent to *Anarchy, State, and Utopia*, his 1974 critique of Rawls:

> The libertarian position I once propounded now seems to me seriously inadequate, in part because ... [i]t neglected the symbolic importance of an official political concern with issues or problems, as a way of marking their importance or urgency, and hence of expressing, intensifying, channeling, encouraging, and validating our private actions and concerns toward them. ... If symbolically expressing something is a way of intensifying its reality, we will not want to truncate the political realm so as to truncate the reality of our social solidarity and humane concern for others. I do not mean to imply that the public realm is only a matter of joint self-expression; we wish also by this actually to accomplish something ... and we would not find some policies adequately expressive of solidarity with others if we believed they would not serve to help or sustain them. The libertarian view looked solely at the purpose of government, not at its *meaning*; hence, it took an unduly narrow view of purpose, too.
>
> (Nozick 1989, 287–288)

Nozick does not say this by way of making any specific concession to justice as fairness, and certainly not to socialism.[9] Rawls speaks of "social union" and "reciprocity" rather than "solidarity," but the ideas are much the same. Krouse and McPherson (1988, 102) suggest that the "desire to bring more sense of membership to the immediate economic life of an egalitarian society is one strong reason to consider introducing some socialist element into the Rawlsian ideal." In acknowledging their "instructive discussion," (*JF* 135 n. 2) Rawls does not discourage this thought.

Recall from Chapter 6 the hallmarks of a reciprocal arrangement. Reciprocity requires (a) a starting point of equal division of common assets, (b) no departures from an equal division unless for good reasons, and (c) a reference point – ideally, a natural focal point – for determining whether the degree and manner of departure are justified. Both liberal socialism and property-owning democracy begin with a starting point of common ownership of the means of production. But common ownership is untenably wasteful, as political scientist Garret Hardin showed in his celebrated article, "The Tragedy of the Commons" (1964)(cf. *LHHP* 147). So, there is compelling reason to restrict rights to the commons by creating an exclusive but jointly exercised right of property in them. Equality is preserved in each citizen if

---

[9] But one is reminded of the biblical warning, "Where there is no vision, the people perish" (*Proverbs* 28:18).

each is the beneficial owner of an equal share in the asset and its proceeds and has an equal say in how it is to be deployed. Much greater productive activity is possible, and indeed there is a product. The need for incentives supplies a compelling efficiency ground for an unequal division of the social product. The limit is the point at which the unequal division ceases to benefit all. This is the D point on the OP curve (see Figure 6.1, page 99). But what reason is there to warrant an unequal division of the productive assets themselves, as distinct from the product? To put it differently, what reason warrants unequal "pure ownership" of productive means?

Again, the demands of efficiency offer a reason. Some will be better able to make use of any given capital asset, and incentives may be needed to induce the more able to channel their activities in the direction of using them. If this is to the benefit of the least advantaged, all is well. But what reason is there to provide incentives in the form of ownership, rather than a greater share of the profits of using the productive means? Admittedly, there might be able people who would be more responsive to incentives in the form of ownership. In the simple case of a pastoral society, the ablest shepherd might demand an exclusive right to certain pasturage. But presumably there is some exchange rate such that the abler citizen would be willing to forgo a demand of ownership and be satisfied with a greater share of revenue. The same problem presents itself in other guises. Some citizens would be willing to exercise greater productive efforts in return for an assurance that they could convey the bulk of their earnings to their offspring. Or, as Mill contemplated, some might not be willing to work harder unless they were assured they could "entail" their estates, so that what they leave at death will "stay in the family" in near-perpetuity (Mill 2006 [1848] vol. 2, 223).

At first glance, it can seem that the incentive argument for allowing private ownership of productive assets knows no obvious stopping point. Certainly, under property-owning democracy, none is suggested. But liberal socialism insists that the major means of production must remain public property. The distributive function of rents for capital assets is "greatly restricted," that is, confined to non-major means. The major means are those that everyone, practically speaking, must have access to because they depend on them in leading a full, if ordinary, productive life. What Rawls intends to be understood by the concept of means of production are not the everyday necessities such as food, clothing, and shelter, but rather the further necessities that a decently clothed, well-housed, and well-nourished citizen needs in order to realize her role as a productive citizen. Rawls recognizes the natural division of these means into the category of human capital, that is, education and specialized training on one hand and everything else – transportation, credit, insurance, natural resources, health services, and other infrastructure – on the other. Recall the discussion in Chapter 2 about the non-rigid character of the designation. The key idea is this: the means of production are those capital assets that, if not owned by everyone jointly, are known to lend themselves to relations of dominance and subordination between those who own and those who do not own, and between those who collect rents and those who must pay them.

One might think that a property-owning democracy also expresses reciprocity by its determination to assure that each owns sufficient productive capital at the beginning of each period. Thus, the regime type that best expresses reciprocity is the one that the parties should, *ceteris paribus*, choose. Recall, from Chapter 6, Rawls's example of the Dunkin' Donuts franchise agreements (*JF* 118–119 n. 39). The franchiser has to decide whether to offer its franchisees either a variable percentage of revenue or a fixed rate. The latter is preferable on the ground that it more clearly expresses reciprocity between all who are part of the overall project. Rawls's analogy points the same way if the variable-terms strategy provides not a higher take for the franchiser from the better-performing franchisees, but a lower take from the less-well-performing franchisees. This strategy puts greater productive resources into the hands of the needier franchisees "at the beginning of each period, so to speak," but it would invite franchisees to engage in destabilizing strategic behavior at the end of each period in order to appear to be in greater need of a replenishing supply or a supplement. Among the reasons Rawls cites for disapproving a lump sum head tax on native endowments is that "once established, the tax is public knowledge and people will have a strong incentive to conceal their endowments" (*JF* 158). A publicly known program for replenishing people's individual capital stake would presumably be essential to maintaining a property-owning democracy. But such a program would be likewise objectionable for incentivizing strategic behavior.

Similarly, the basic structure of society faces a choice. It can offer its citizens separate allotments of productive assets, with periodic but continual adjustments to assure adequacy and rough equality. Alternatively, it can maintain the major productive means in joint ownership, while regarding the distribution of non-major productive assets, just as it does the distribution of wealth and income generally, as a matter of pure procedural justice. The latter, democratic socialist strategy "fixes once and for all the terms of agreement," while the former, the property-owning democracy strategy, perpetuates uncertainty "and the continuing suspicion and distrust which that uncertainty would cause" (*JF* 119 n. 39). The attempt to perform the redistributions required in a property-owning democracy, and to defend their empirical bases, would be "socially divisive" in the same way as the application of the "principle of proportional satisfaction" and similar principles that Rawls, for that very reason, rejects (*PL* 330). On similar grounds, Rawls objects to the principle of restricted utility, in pairwise comparison to the difference principle, as discussed in Chapter 6.

Property-owning democracy, considered as a strategy for ensuring the fair value of political liberty, is open to devastating objections. John Tomasi represents Rawls as committed to adopting it, even as Tomasi articulates a fundamental flaw in taking such an approach:

> [Rawls's] strategy for realizing fair political equality generates a feedback problem. The more significant the economic issues that [Rawlsian] regimes place on the legislative agenda, the more significant the exposure of their citizens to the danger

of political domination. To prevent this domination, [Rawlsian] regimes seek to equalize wealth by placing further economic issues on the legislative agenda, thus further exposing their citizens to the danger of political domination.

(2012, 252)

The constitution of a property-owning democracy might declare that private ownership on the "commanding heights" shall not be allowed to undermine fair value. But this is infeasible. The same kinds of reasons that disqualify the difference principle from serving as a constitutional essential likewise disqualify any usable element of the ideal description of property-owning democracy as a constitutional essential. The aim of putting productive assets into everyone's hands at the beginning of each period – an undefined period that might coincide with each legislative term – is, like the difference principle itself, a guideline for legislators but not itself capable of serving as a judicially enforceable standard.

Constitutionally entrenched joint ownership of the major means of production is not subject to the feedback problem. In contrast to the obscure and complex question whether holdings across society as a whole are equal enough, the question whether or not all the chief productive assets are socially owned, and *pro tanto* subject to free and equal democratic control, seems easy to ascertain. If the answer is yes, then it is reasonable to think that the grounds of excusable envy have been removed or at least minimized. Of course, because the efficient management of the means of production can require the use of differential wages and salaries as incentives, liberal socialism does not and need not guarantee equality of income and wealth: it can employ the difference principle to regulate these inequalities, confident that the structural guarantee of social ownership of the means of production secures reciprocity.

There will, of course, be questions whether an enterprise in possession of significant market power – though short of a monopoly, and not providing a basic service – should be treated as one standing upon the "commanding heights." Line-drawing judgments about what does and does not stand on the "commanding heights" of the economy will be needed, but these are significantly more amenable to the strictures of public reason. Compare Rawls's remarks about the social minimum:

> What determines the level of well-being and education below which … people simply cannot take part in society as [equal] citizens … is not for a political conception to say …. But that does not mean that *the constitutional essential itself is not perfectly clear; it is what is required to give due weight to the idea of society as a fair system of cooperation* between free and equal citizens.

(*PL* 166; reordered, emphasis added).

Public ownership of the means of production not only possesses this clarity, it is also an idea capable of being stated in justiciable terms. Rawls endorses his Harvard colleague Frank Michelman's (1979, 680–685) view that a textual constitutional basis makes it easier to overcome misgivings about judicial overreaching, which sets back the principle of participation.

Let me enlarge on the claim that liberal socialism's insistence on public ownership of the means of production "meets the desideratum that . . . a constitutional essential should be [one] that courts should be reasonably competent to assess" (*JF* 162; see also Michelman 1973, 995–996 for an articulation of Rawlsian grounds to limit sharply the scope of judicial review). Courts in the United States, for example, are regularly called upon to determine whether or not certain businesses wield market power. See *Hanover Shoe v. United Shoe Mach. Corp.*, 392 U.S. 481, 486 n.3 (1968); *United States v. Grinnell Corp.*, 384 U.S. 563, 580 (1966); and cf. *Fortner Enterprises v. United States Steel Corp.*, 394 U.S. 495, 510 (1969) (White, J., dissenting, distinguishing "market" and "monopoly" power). In bankruptcy cases in the United States, administrative courts routinely decide whether or not to put private corporations into public receivership. Justiciability is the first virtue of legal rights generally, and it is especially vital to constitutional rights, whose enforcement via judicial review necessarily involves interfering with legislative enactments or contractual arrangements whose terms will normally be more precise than the constitutional language that the court must apply (see Michelman 1973, *passim*). As Michelman has argued, because judicial review that appeals in an unmediated way to moral notions "seems to carry greater threats to the self-respect cherished by the equal-liberty principle than review strictly anchored to specific constitutional text," the constitutional framers would "try to minimize any harm to self-respect by making premises explicit in the constitution when they could" (Michelman 1973, 1001–1002).

Rawls was familiar with the legal methods available as means to constitutionally entrench socialism. By way of underlining the continuing significance of Marx, Rawls approvingly cites economist John Roemer's book, *A Future for Socialism* (1994), on the "features" of "liberal socialism":

This illuminating and worthwhile view has four elements:

(a) A constitutional and political regime, with the fair value of the political liberties.
(b) A system of free competitive markets, ensured by law as necessary.
(c) A scheme of worker-owned business, or, in part, also public-owned through stock shares, and managed by elected or firm-chosen managers.
(d) A property system establishing a widespread and a more or less even distribution of the means of production and natural resources. [footnote to Roemer 1994]

Of course, all this requires much more complicated elaboration. I simply remind you of the few essentials here. (*LHHP* 323 n. 8).[10]

---

[10] Thus, O'Neill and Williamson somewhat overstate when they say that Rawls "does not engage with various recent efforts by left political economists such as John Roemer . . . to specify the institutional form of a workable form of market socialism. . . ." (2014, 3–4).

The list compounds elements of what Rawls later factors into property-owning democracy and liberal democratic socialism – I will not recapitulate the analysis I presented in Chapter 2. The Roemer book that Rawls cites as *Liberal Socialism* appeared in print under the title *A Future for Socialism* – a fact that suggests that Rawls may have looked at the book in manuscript. In the book, Roemer proposes

> a statute requiring nationalization of private firms that reach a given size – a size at which their erstwhile owners would become wealthy from the state's purchase of their firm. Allowing a private sector under these conditions should provide almost the same incentives that exist in capitalism for those who form new firms in order to bring innovations to market. Nationalizing firms at a certain level would prevent the emergence of a class of capitalists capable of influencing politics and economic policy by virtue of their economic control of significant sectors of the means of production.
>
> (1994a, 78–79)

Roemer's proposal is more complicated than this short excerpt conveys, but the key point is that Rawls wrote the *Restatement* while cognizant of a variety of liberal socialist mechanisms designed to protect fair value by means of nationalization of firms that arrive at a position on the commanding heights. The ordinary statute Roemer proposes would, as Rawls could readily agree, be more properly cast in terms of a constitutional provision, which would take the issue of public ownership of the means of production "off the table" of ordinary legislative disputation. As Roemer (1994a, 110) goes on to propose, "[A] regime of market socialism might well be characterized by its constitution, which might limit the permissible degree of accumulation of private property in productive assets." This would encourage long-term planning and avoid the costs associated with privatizing and renationalizing, as Roemer notes.

More importantly, a constitutional provision would also better enable the political conception to perform its educational role.

> Those who grow up in [a well-ordered] society will in good part form their conception of themselves as citizens from the public political culture .... They will see themselves as having certain basic ... freedoms they can not only claim for themselves but ... must also respect in others. Doing this belongs to their conception of themselves as sharing the status of equal citizenship.
>
> (JF 146)

In Rawls's contemplation, much of moral and civic education will depend on the family and on associations such as churches and private and parochial as well as public schools. But the educational role requires more.

> The idea behind the educational role of a political conception of justice suitable for a constitutional regime is that by being embedded in political institutions and procedures, that conception may itself become a significant moral force in a society's public culture.
>
> (JF 147)

By creating a permanent public world, in which the major means of production belong to everyone, liberal socialism educates citizens to regard themselves as reciprocally related, productive co-venturers. Because "certain features of a political conception importantly affect the political sociology of the basic institutions that realize it" (*JF* 146), those institutions' educational role cannot be dismissed as a mere matter of political sociology, rather than one implicating essential justice.[11] The same kinds of grounds that favor a constitutional regime over a "procedural democracy" (*JF* 145) favor liberal socialism over its competitor.

Property-owning democracy cannot similarly express reciprocity between citizens. Rawls faults welfare-state capitalism for its focus on the redistribution of income "at the end of each period, so to speak," but property-owning democracy similarly contemplates periodic reallocations of productive means, albeit "at the beginning" (*JF* 139). But, as time unfolds, the beginning of one period is but the end of another. Rawls is committed to preserving the "present time-of-entry interpretation of the original position" (*JF* 160) and so the parties should be prepared to test candidate principles regardless of whether they suppose themselves to be at the beginning or at the end of any arbitrarily stipulated measurement interval. In liberal socialism, citizens, as co-owners of publicly held means of production, can readily recognize themselves as standing in a permanent relationship of reciprocity. Unlike those living under a regime of property-owning democracy, citizens have no occasion to be disturbed by or suspect the fairness of periodic transfers of productive assets. "[S]implicity is itself desirable in a public conception of justice" (*TJ* 479), and this factor too favors liberal socialism.

Other Aspects of Stability

Recall from Chapter 6 the discussion of the "conflict segment" that the principle of restricted utility encourages parties to explore. The conflict zone is that segment of the OP curve in which losses to some might be outweighed by a gain in average utility (see Figure 6.1 on page 99, above). The difference principle does not allow inequalities that fall within the conflict segment, where average gains mean that

---

[11] As Rawls presses the point in the posthumously published *Lectures on the History of Moral Philosophy*:

> If citizens of a constitutional democracy are to recognize one another as free and equal, basic institutions must educate them to this conception of themselves .... This task of education is part of the role of the political conception. In this role, such a conception is part of the public political culture: its first principles are embodied in the institutions of the basic structure ... acquaintance with and participation in that public culture is one way citizens learn that conception of themselves, a conception which, if left to their own reflections, they would most likely never form, much less accept and desire to realize.
>
> (*LHMP* 366–367)

> The principles of justice are worked up from ideas latent in the public political culture, but just institutions carry out the task of raising these ideas, in a determinate form, to consciousness.

some gain while others lose in absolute as well as relative terms. Under restricted utility, the already more-advantaged are licensed to argue for policies that create further inequality, on the ground that the average index will be increased thereby. This is destabilizing in several ways. Most importantly, those who put forward such proposals will do so from a standpoint of personal gain, or will at any rate be suspected of doing so. No "average citizen" will step forward, but someone who is likely to be motivated by a more concrete prospect of improving her situation. Rawls takes McClennan's point about the destabilizing tendency of ambiguous proposals in the context of distributive issues. Because the difference principle does not permit entry into the conflict segment, it is to be preferred, on grounds of stability, to the principle of restricted utility, in the second fundamental comparison.

Similar concerns are in play when it comes to deciding which of the two ideal regime-types to adopt: liberal socialism or property-owning democracy. Both implement the difference principle, so neither would authorize proposals in the conflict segment D-B of the O-P curve. But property-owning democracy authorizes proposals in a conflict zone of a different sort. Because property-owning democracy seeks continually and gradually – or at least periodically – to even out differences in the capital holdings of citizens, and the major means of production are subject to private ownership, there is a permanent incentive for all to make legislative proposals with regard to them. Whatever is publicly held is always for sale, in the sense that it is a candidate for privatization. Those who are better off already are in a better position to advance the complex arguments that would justify such sales, and their proposals – although they be nominally in the spirit of the difference principle – are likely to be viewed with suspicion. Less well-off citizens normally lack the capital to make competing offers, and a collective-action problem has to be overcome for them to pool capital to make a higher bid.

Obviously, for the less-well-off, the political solution of simply voting down a privatization bill in the legislature is more appealing than scrambling to mount a counteroffer. But this simply brings the point of stress into the political arena itself. If the fair value of political liberty is truly guaranteed, opponents of privatization need not fear: a majority must be persuaded that the major means of production in question can better serve all if privately owned. But it is not the "average citizen" who advances a concrete proposal within the conflict segment under restricted utility. Rather, it must be some actual individual or group of individuals who must be assumed to have a "special" interest. So, too, it is not the public personified who advances a concrete proposal for major productive means to become or remain private property. Rather, it is some party who must be assumed to have an interest, financial or personal. And recall the feedback problem Tomasi describes. Even if private ownership of the capital asset in question were certain to be more efficient, a transfer of ownership of this magnitude has an incalculable effect on the value of political liberty. Property-owning democracy introduces instability.

Liberal socialism disallows proposals in this conflict zone and, therefore, is to be preferred as the more stable regime. This is not to say that no conflicts and destabilizing suspicions are possible under liberal socialism. Bureaucrats and managers have an incentive to maintain public ownership of capital assets that are not truly major, and to extend state ownership into areas where unequal private ownership would indeed better benefit all. Political and even judicial oversight is at best a partial corrective; there is no panacea for what economists call the agent/principal problem, any more than there is one for the more general problem of "incentive-compatibility" (*JF* 136 n. 4). But there is a crucial difference between the two cases. Bureaucrats and managers cannot extract rents – their role is never that of pure owners. Their proposals never involve that very significant kind of ambiguity.

To summarize, there are three headings between which Rawls divides the essentials for the stability of a constitutional regime. First is a reconciliation requirement: divisive issues are kept off the public agenda to the extent possible. Second is a publicity condition: there are clear, reliable, and therefore workable criteria that citizens can apply to determine whether the regime under which they live measures up to its principles. Third is an express reciprocity condition: the institutions of the basic structure create a public world that in its design and detail expresses the free equality of citizens and the mutual benefit each realizes from the restrictions that govern their lives. The stability in question is, of course, not a matter of brute endurance. What is at issue is stability for the right reasons: a well-ordered constitutional regime endures because of the virtues of its political conception of justice. In terms of each of these essentials, it is evident that liberal socialism is decisively superior in terms of its aptness to stabilize a constitutional regime. Insofar as Rawls would apply the same modes of reasoning to the choice of regime type as are utilized in arguing for justice as fairness itself, the case for socialism is made.

It is interesting to compare what Rawls says about equal political rights in *The Law of Peoples*. In the context of international justice, Rawls wants to allow non-liberal but decent peoples as members of a just Society of Peoples. He describes the conceptual possibility of a "decent consultation hierarchy" that rejects the formal political equality insisted on by constitutional democracies. Rawls anticipates the criticism that "only liberal democratic governments are effective in protecting even those human rights specified by the Law of Peoples. According to critics who take this line, this is a fact confirmed by the history of many different countries around the world" (*LP* 79). The form and phrasing of his reply is telling:

> Should the facts of history, supported by the reasoning of political and social thought, show that hierarchical regimes are always, or nearly always, oppressive and deny human rights, *the case for liberal democracy is made*.

> (*LP* 79; emphasis added)

Rawls did not convey a sense of skepticism about those facts, and in his recognition of the fact of domination had in effect already credited them. To flesh out even the

conceptual possibility of a human-rights-respecting consultation hierarchy, Rawls
had to stipulate that the rulers of his imaginary Islamic republic, Kazakistan, "do not
allow themselves to be corrupted . . . by favoring the rich" (*LP* 70). He neither raised
nor addressed the question of the *stability* of a decent consultation hierarchy as a
respecter of human rights.

CONCEIVING SOCIETY AS A COOPERATIVE SCHEME FOR MUTUAL ADVANTAGE

The expressive significance of social ownership of the means of production flows
directly from Rawls's most fundamental conception: that of society as a cooperative
scheme for mutual advantage (*JF* 5; *TJ* 4).[12] Compare the "bourgeois" conception
typified by two passages quoted by Arthur DiQuattro, in an unjustly neglected
1983 article that was among the first to recognize Rawls's hostility to capitalism.

> For [Chicago School economist Milton] Friedman, "Despite the lip service that we
> all pay to 'merit' as compared to 'chance,' market distribution is akin to a game or
> lottery which everyone agrees to enter with the anticipation of winning a jackpot
> prize." "Most differences of status or position or wealth can be regarded as the
> product of chance at a far enough remove," and redistribution of these goods after
> people play the game of economic life is "equivalent to denying them the oppor-
> tunity to enter the lottery."
>
> (DiQuattro 1983, 58; quoting Friedman 1962, 165–166)

Society, as Friedman conceives it, is a regulated lottery that allows presumptively
efficient voluntary exchanges. Non-voluntary redistribution is disallowed because it
undoes the outcome. If players at a poker table were forced to disgorge their
winnings, they would be deprived of the liberty to play for stakes. For the lover of
capitalist liberty, it is no answer to say that some measure of the winners' winnings
are attributable to chance rather than skill, and that both skill and chance were not
ex ante distributed fairly.

Rawls's conception of society is radically different. It is not a cooperative scheme
for mutual sport and amusement, but a cooperative scheme for mutual advantage. It
is not a lottery that free and equal citizens enter by staking independently gotten

---

[12] Samuel Scheffler writes that Rawls's

> focus on the basic structure represents, among other things, an attempt to incorporate
> into liberal theory what Rawls sees as the legitimate insights not only of utilitarianism but
> also of the socialist tradition [each of which] has emphasized the extraordinary and
> transformative significance of modern social and economic institutions."
>
> (2008, 73).

Clearly, though, the conception of society's basic structure as a scheme of cooperation between
freely associated producers further narrows this focus; and the conception more naturally derives
from the socialist, as distinct from the utilitarian, tradition.

assets. It is a productive enterprise that generates those very assets. Speaking of Austrian economist Friedrich von Hayek, DiQuattro points out that

> Hayek's acceptance of [the lottery] view prompts him to wonder whether "we ought to encourage in the young the belief that when they really try they will succeed, or rather emphasize that inevitably some unworthy will succeed and some worthy will fail."
>
> (1983, 58; quoting Hayek 1976, 74)

Hayek might well wonder that. Rawls would first ask why, in the original position, one would choose to enter those one represents in such a lottery, rather than to enroll them in a cooperative productive scheme for mutual advantage. Having chosen the latter, we need not hesitate to assure the young that the basic structure of the society they are born into has been designed to assure that all have access to the necessary means for making their lives productive ones, that, as far is possible, all have a roughly equal chance to influence the fundamental decisions that affect their lives, and that any resulting inequalities will be to their benefit.

But then, which ideal regime type better expresses this choice: property-owning democracy or liberal democratic socialism? If there is one that better expresses that choice, it will be the one that better serves the educational role expected of a political conception of justice. The defining difference is between a regime that allows private ownership of the means of production on which all depend and a regime in which those centrally vital means of production are held publicly, so that each citizen has a roughly equal chance of determining how they are to be developed and deployed, and that any surplus they produce is a common asset. To pose the question is almost to answer it. To show everyone that their society is indeed a cooperative scheme for mutual benefit, it makes sense to establish everyone an owner of the essential means of producing those benefits. Insofar as we have chosen to reject the idea that social life is simply a playing-out of the natural lottery, it makes no sense to allow the major means of production to be owned privately. The only reasons to favor leaving this legislative option open are the very reasons that would favor taking that option if it is constitutionally available.[13] These all must boil down to reasons of expediency, to the idea that private ownership will lead to greater total wealth that will "raise all boats." But the value of efficiency – even as leavened by the difference principle – is orthogonal to the public expression of society's conception of itself as a cooperative, productive scheme for mutual benefit.

Recall once again the defining difference between the two regimes. Liberal socialism insists that ownership of the means of production remain in public hands.

---

[13] John Gardner (2014, 16) makes the general point that "depending on the circumstances, nationalization ... may not be the right cause to support. For it may be but a roundabout way of giving extra windfalls and levers of power to future asset-strippers." Applied to the present case: in a property-owning democracy, nationalization risks becoming a mere prelude to re-privatization, primarily benefitting private rather than public interests.

Property-owning democracy does not. "While property in productive assets is permitted" in a property-owning democracy, he writes in the first lecture on Marx, "that
right is not a basic right, but subject to the requirement that, in existing conditions, it
is *the most effective way* to meet the principles of justice" (*LHPP* 321; emphasis
added). Rawls does not state what those conditions might be. Property-owning
democracy aspires to spread productive assets widely, but so does liberal socialism.
As noted in Chapter 2, Meade (1964, 75) proposed his version of property-owning
democracy not as a substitute for social ownership, but as a supplement to it.[14] The
natural duty of respect requires that we "be prepared to give reasons for our actions
whenever the interests of others are materially affected ... in the belief that they are
sound reasons as defined by a mutually accepted conception of justice" (*TJ* 297).
What public reason can be offered for privatizing, or allowing to remain private, the
major means of production, which, in the original position are a common asset?
What "evident intention" (*JF* 196) could be ascribed?

One reason might be that public ownership must inevitably lead to corruption, or
to undue political power vested in the hands of a managerial elite. But there is no
admissible ground for either belief. If contingent circumstances reveal that either
evil has come about, or is impending, the political process should be capable of
remedying it. Another public reason might be that productive assets must be more
efficiently employed if privately owned. This may be, but it is not a reason Rawls
accepts. Rawls makes plain his opinion that public ownership is fully compatible
with realizing market efficiencies (*TJ* 241–242, 248). No other reasons favoring
privatization are handy.[15] But a powerful public reason for retaining public

[14] Of Meade, Krouse, and McPherson write that he notes that his "proposals for creating a property-
owning democracy are needed 'to supplement rather than to replace the existing Welfare-State
policies'" (1988, 99; quoting Meade 1964, 75). When, in 1964, Meade refers to "welfare-state
policies" he is in fact intending to refer to the socialized British economy that was built under
Attlee, which was largely intact until the 1980s. Meade is not referring to a social minimum or
relief programs of the kind that Rawls's welfare-state capitalism contents itself with. Meade indeed
calls for *further* "measures for the equalization and socialization of property ownership" (1964,
75). What Meade's proposals supplement, rather than replace, is socialism.

[15] It is fairly certain that Rawls would endorse this view, recently advanced by Avihay Dorfman
and Alon Harel:

> Privatisation is not only the transformation of detention centres, trains, tax inquiry offices,
> forestry operations, and so on, considered one service at a time; it is also the transformation of
> our political system and public culture from ones characterised by robust shared responsibility
> and political engagement to ones characterised by fragmentation and sectarianism.

(2015, 27)

I dissent from Alan Thomas's claim that in "a property-owning democracy it is guaranteed
that we all know that it explicitly implements 'deep reciprocity'" (2016, 300) and that it "cannot
fail to express the principle of reciprocity" (2016, 304). A regime that permits the major means
of production to devolve to private ownership is not one that expresses or implements
reciprocity even of a shallow kind. Such privatization can only be justified on the kind of
consequentialist ground that Thomas otherwise rejects as incompatible with his, and with
Rawls's, egalitarian republicanism.

ownership of the means of production is ready to hand: public ownership expresses the reciprocal relation of free equality between citizens and manifests their mutual assurance that unequal power over productive forces will not be permitted to translate itself into unequal political power.

GROUNDS DISFAVORING PROPERTY-OWNING DEMOCRACY

Rawls explicitly cautioned that his description of the ideal of property-owning democracy raises the possibility that it "generates political and economic forces that make it depart all too widely from its ideal institutional description" (*JF* 178). Some of these have already been discussed. Others emerge when one tries to picture other aspects of the ideal description in operation. Presumably, one who uses potentially productive assets to support a nonproductive lifestyle, such as amateur surfing, will not be entitled to their replenishment should they become exhausted. James Meade welcomed the advent of an age of amateurism; but for Rawls, the nonproductive are no more entitled to productive assets than they are to any other form of public subsidy. What, then, of the means of production of things that are unlikely to be valued in the market? Will a property-owning democracy have to keep staking every would-be professional surfer, and every would-be craftsman who wants to work with precious metals and stones?

Kenneth Arrow posed to Rawls the question of someone whose upbringing causes him to crave "plover's eggs and pre-phylloxera clarets": Does Rawls's index of primary goods unfairly ignore this person, whose special need is not his fault? Rawls's answer is that it does not: "[V]ariations in preferences and tastes are seen as our own responsibility ... whether or not they have arisen from our actual choices ... this is something we must learn to deal with" – this is merely the corollary of the taking "responsibility for our ends [which] is part of what free citizens may expect of one another" (*PL* 185). Rawls does allow that therapeutic treatment – but not subsidy – might be provided legislatively. The task of legislatively subsidizing nonessential productive means would seem to have to be treated in parallel fashion. Those who have expensive productive tastes had better learn to deal with it – that is, to get along without subsidized productive means – and should they fail, seek retraining and perhaps therapy.[16]

But these ambitions cannot be dismissed as mere "expensive tastes" (*PL* 184–186). For one thing, they are not tastes for consumer goods, but ambitions to supply a consumer market. For another, successful professional surfers and goldsmiths can earn handsome livings. But, proverbially, "though many are called, few are chosen." Must one qualify for a first shot? And is one entitled to a second-chance? A third? At what point does a persistent but unsuccessful professional surfer become another just surf bum who wants to "surf off Malibu" (*JF* 179) at public expense?

---

[16] Compare Rawls's dismissal of the "principle of equal proportionate satisfaction" (*CP* 281–285).

This raises the question why Rawls did not explicitly include means of production among the primary goods. I say "means of production," rather than "access to the means of production," for two reasons: one, because it is shorter; and two, access is implicit in the idea, whereas "pure" ownership of and access to means of production are importantly distinct ideas in Rawls. The primary goods come into play in the original position to make the parties' choice task determinate. They are conceived as all-purpose means not yet subject to rights of ownership, and whose subsequent distribution will not necessarily take the form of ownership – that is to say, "pre-legal" ownership rights are recognized in the original position only if the parties would not chance anything else. The right to bodily integrity, for example, is not one that can validly be violated by any subsequent legislative act.

Fair access to whatever means of production exist at a particular historical stage is already encompassed in the guarantee of fair equal opportunity and the difference principle. The question arises: In what way does the idea of a property-owning democracy make more concrete the guarantees of justice as fairness? The principles already assure an adequate measure of primary goods and fair equality of opportunity to occupy productive roles in society. Yet a property-owning democracy is characterized in terms of a distributive role. But what does it distribute? Does a property-owning democracy distinctively operate a "branch" or agency that equalizes the distribution not of political influence or of primary goods, but specifically, of *privately owned means of production*? In *Theory*, Rawls outlines a figurative "stabilization branch" of government, which assures "reasonably full employment" by bringing about conditions such that "the free choice of occupation and the deployment of finance are supported by strong effective demand" (*TJ* 244). I do not take Rawls to mean that government will be in the business of "making a market" for products and services that will otherwise fail. As Meade (1964, 67) points out, state ownership of productive assets has a decisive efficiency advantage over a regime in which equalizing private holding of productive assets is the mechanism by which holdings, generally, are equalized.

The means of production are either among the primary goods or they are not. If they are, then the business of equalizing the distribution of one type of primary good, considered in isolation from the whole bundle, is fraught with uncertainty and the potential for generating excusable envy. On the other hand, if means of production are not within the primary-goods category, some agency has to look not only at the primary goods a citizen could exchange to secure ownership of productive means but also at whether the "business plan" is one that is sufficiently promising to assure that what the means are put to can properly be called "production" rather than waste, or even consumption. In either case, property-owning democracy, on top of its other destabilizing features, unnecessarily introduces regular occasions for excusable envy, the main worry that arises in Part Two of the original position procedure. Of course, decisions about what private projects to finance have to be made anyway, but the ambition of justice as fairness is to settle issues about distributive justice at the level of background institutions, rather than to inject them into routine administrative decision-making. If, for example, by ordinary legislation, loans at a favorable rate are to be offered to those who propose to develop energy-efficient appliances, there is no occasion for excusable envy. But if loans at a favorable rate are to be offered to those who can show they are unhappy with their share of private means of production, there is trouble ahead for everyone. The same reasons Rawls gives for refusing to guarantee the fair value of the non-political liberties apply. If operating a property-owning democracy means that "income and wealth are to be distributed according to the content of certain interests regarded as central to citizens' plans of life ... then it is socially divisive" (*JF* 151).

JUST SAVINGS AND REGIME TYPE

Additional grounds for choosing socialism are found in the requirement that the parties choose a just-savings principle in Part One of the original position procedure. This principle is separate from those governing relations solely within a generation. It is intended to achieve justice between generations. To do so, it governs relations within each generation: different generations are conceived here as not interacting in the same sense. Behind the veil of ignorance,

> the parties, who are assumed to be contemporaries, do not know the present state of society. They have no information about the stock of natural resources *or productive assets*, or the level of technology beyond what can be inferred from the assumption that the circumstances of justice obtain. The relative good or ill fortune of their generation is unknown.
>
> (*PL* 273; emphasis added)

Given that the circumstances of justice obtain, the parties are assured that (only) moderate scarcity exists in any of the relevant generations. That means that cooperation is both profitable and worthwhile. It also assures them that the conditions are suitable for liberal constitutional government, if there is the will to have it.

> [S]ince society is a system of cooperation between generations over time, a principle of savings is required ... [thus] the parties can be required to agree to a savings principle subject to the further condition that they must want all *previous* generations to have followed it. Thus, the correct principle is that which the members of any generation (and so all generations) would adopt as the one their generation is to follow and as the principle they would want preceding generations to have followed (and later generations to follow), no matter how far back (or forward) in time.
>
> (*PL* 274)

Again, we must remind ourselves that all the variations in the material circumstances of society across the distances into past and future time remain within the band of moderate scarcity that characterizes the circumstances of justice. We need not imagine, for example, what savings principle we would want our troglodytic forebears to have followed. Nor ought we blithely assume that in the future ours will be a society of superabundance that is "beyond justice."

Within the band of development defined by the circumstances of justice, Rawls allows the parties to imagine an incremental progressive development. The parties

> are to ask themselves how much (what fraction of the social product) they are prepared to save at each level of wealth as society advances, should all previous generations have followed the same schedule.
>
> (*JF* 160)

Notice the assumption that society is progressively advancing. What the parties do not know is where they will find themselves on this upward slope when the veil of ignorance is fully lifted.

> Each generation must not only preserve the gains of culture and civilization, and maintain those just institutions that have been established, but it must also set aside in each period of time a suitable amount of real capital accumulation. This saving may take *various forms* from net investment in machinery and other *means of production* to investment in learning and education.
>
> (*TJ* 252; emphases added)

Rawls does not expressly say that a just-savings principle ought to, if appropriate, address the "various forms" savings might take – whether, in particular, the major means of production ought to be conveyed to successive generations in social ownership or as privately held. His immediate point was not even to derive quantitative limits on the savings rate, but to make the general point that the difference principle, which applies intra-generationally, does not require setting the social minimum so high that future generations inherit nothing. To make that point Rawls did not need to address the "qualitative" just-savings question. By "the qualitative just-savings question" I mean the property question, viewed inter-generationally. But the method he describes is fully up to the task of answering it.

We certainly hope that the previous generation will have conveyed the means of production to us intact. In receiving them, we are not mooching off the sacrifices of our forebears. As Rawls says, "It is a natural fact that generations are spread out over time and actual economic benefits flow in only one direction. This situation is unalterable, and so the question of justice does not arise" (*TJ* 254). But the way institutions "are set up to take advantage of historical possibilities" can be just or unjust. The question of justice is decided by our considered preference, formed behind the veil of ignorance, as to the form in which the means of production are bequeathed to our generation. Would we prefer that the previous generation conveyed them to us in the form of social ownership, or in whatever mixture of private and public ownership seemed best, or would we perhaps even prefer that all capital assets come down to us as private property? Or are we indifferent?

We cannot simply assume that a uniform answer is to be given. Within the relevant circumstances-of-justice band there are different stages of development, and these certainly have a bearing on the *quantitative* version of the question:

> It is essential to note that a savings principle is a rule that assigns an appropriate rate (or range of rates) to each level of advance, that is, a rule that determines a schedule of rates. Presumably different rates are assigned to different stages. When people are poor and saving is difficult, a lower rate of saving should be required; whereas in a wealthier society greater savings may reasonably be expected since the real burden of saving is less. Eventually, once just institutions are firmly established and all the basic liberties effectively realized, the net accumulation asked for falls to zero. At this point a society meets its duty of justice by maintaining just institutions and preserving their material base. The just savings principle applies to what a society is to save as a matter of justice. If its members wish to save for other purposes, that is another matter.
>
> *(TJ* 255)

For Rawls, what "withers away" is not, *pace* Marx, the state, but the requirement of net capital saving. That is Rawls's stated, though nonspecific, answer to the quantitative question. The strains of commitment rule out certain extreme possibilities. A poor society cannot be expected to save deeply simply because a later generation will be glad they did. The parties must "ask what is reasonable for members of *adjacent generations to expect of each other* at each level of advance" *(TJ* 255; emphasis added). For convenience, I will call this the "adjacent generations test."

Before applying the adjacent generations test, we had better consult what Rawls has to say about the relevant extremes of development, including the rate.

> [T]he last stage at which saving is called for is not one of great abundance. This consideration deserves perhaps some emphasis. Further wealth might not be superfluous for some purposes; and indeed average income may not, in absolute terms, be very high. Justice does not require that early generations save so that later ones are simply more wealthy .... It is a mistake to believe that a just and good society must wait upon a high material standard of life. What men want is meaningful work in free association with others, these associations regulating their relations to one another within a framework of just basic institutions. To achieve this state of things great wealth is not necessary. In fact, beyond some point it is likely to be a positive hindrance, a meaningless distraction at best if not a temptation to indulgence and emptiness.
>
> *(TJ* 257–258)

This language tells us perhaps more about Rawls the man, and about what he later would discount as his personal comprehensive conception of the good, than about the precise question put to the parties. But his remarks remind us that in addition to the strains of commitment, already taken into account in Part One of the original position procedure, the parties will, after making a tentative choice, proceed to Part

Two, where the choice of savings principle, and its schedules, is tested again in light of the special psychologies.

Still, the adjacent generations test remains indeterminate. I will tentatively stipulate that the relevant adjacent generations are located in conditions of industrial or postindustrial development, and that the rate of technological change is not so great that the major means of production are rapidly obsolescent. In other words, the stages of development are not so rapid that what were for the earlier generation major means of production are of little or no use to its successor. Each generation expects to receive, more or less intact, the basic productive and social infrastructure that its predecessor enjoyed.

With this stipulation, a tentative answer to the qualitative property question is evident, applying the adjacent-generations test. The parties would prefer to bequeath and receive their endowment of major productive assets in the form of assured public ownership. Look at it first from the recipient's side. Bear in mind that there will already be strict taxation of receipts of individual gifts and bequests. Those inter-generational controls are already part of the background of both liberal socialist and property-owning democratic regime types. The question is whether or not the receiving generation would like to find the possibility of privatizing socially owned productive capital on its political agenda. Given the destabilizing tendencies inherent in putting these vital social assets on the block for private sale, the answer must be: not unless there is a compensating gain. But, from Rawls's perspective, no such compensating gain appears, or if it does, it is of lower priority. Given his view that justice does not require an especially high level of social wealth, a party heeding Rawls's counsel would be unwilling to take destabilizing risks for the mere chance of accelerating economic wealth.

Looked at from the prior generation's side, justice does not require it to convey its major productive assets in a constitutionally unencumbered form. Justice does not require the predecessor generation to hold its productive assets in a form that will facilitate their liquidation immediately upon transfer to the next generation. In other words, justice does not require that the "dead hand" of public ownership be lifted for each succeeding generation. The reasonable preference of the successor generation is that its productive inheritance be public property. The adjacent generations agree. The just-savings principle requires that each generation save in the form of public ownership those productive assets that are vital to its successor's flourishing as a stable, just society. The parties will adopt liberal socialism as a requirement of justice between generations.

There are several elements of Rawls's overall theory that confirm this argument. The result is the only one that conforms with Rawls's view of the realizability of a steady-state or stationary-state economy, in which real capital accumulation ceases. Now, such an economy is not itself a demand of justice. As Rawls says, there may be reasons other than justice for generations to continue to accumulate. I want ask whether a steady state can be maintained if major productive means are privately ownable. One of Rawls's lines of defense of the difference principle appeals to the effervescence of economic growth in a property-owning democracy (*JF* 67–69); yet he also holds that a Millian "stationary state" economy would be eligible (*LP* 106–107 n. 33; *JF* 64) and even desirable (Rawls and van Parijs 2003; Little 2014, 519–521). By what means? Simply put, a property-owning democracy having an economy exuberant enough to trivialize the inequalities tolerated by the difference principle is irreconcilable with maintaining a stationary-state economy. By contrast, a liberal democratic socialist state, by dint of owning the means of production, can rather straightforwardly maintain a cap on overall growth. Inequalities exist, but the public world of a socialist society is more capacious than the noncomparing groups to which the less-advantaged members of a property-owning democracy are referred.

Finally, citizens of a liberal socialist regime are far likelier to be a "satisfied people" (*PL* 19, 46–47) eligible for membership in the realistic utopia of the Society of Peoples. Rawls borrows French political theorist Raymond Aron's idea of "peace by satisfaction," in which nations do not "seek to extend themselves, either to increase their material or human resources, to disseminate their institutions, or to enjoy the intoxicating pride of ruling" (*LP* 47). Liberal peoples can satisfy Aron's conditions.

> These peoples … are not swayed by the passion for power and glory, or the intoxicating power of ruling. These passions may move a nobility and a lesser aristocracy to earn their social standing and place in the sun; yet this class, or caste rather, does not have power in a constitutional regime …. Domination and striving for glory, the excitement and conquest and the pleasure of exercising power over others, do not move them against other peoples.
>
> (*LP* 47)

It was not mere coincidence that Britain foreswore its empire under Attlee's socialist leadership. Is it mere coincidence that Britain's retreat from socialism coincided with a certain restless, even reckless, urgency to reassert itself as a global power?

SUMMARY AND CONCLUSION

Rawls's emphasis on stability, publicity, and reciprocity elevates socialism as the regime type uniquely suited to realizing justice as fairness. Rawls granted that reasonable minds, applying the original position procedure and drawing differently from the fund of ideas latent in the political culture of a constitutional democracy, might reach different and incompatible but still liberal conceptions of justice. It is for this reason that he approached the question of stability with the understanding that justice as fairness was but one of a family of reasonable liberal political conceptions (*PL* xxxviii; 1). This raises the question: "[H]ow specific is the [constitutional] consensus, or how wide is the range of the liberal conceptions defining it?"

(*PL* 167). We also want to ask: Is this consensus specific enough to single out liberal socialism as its embodying regime type? Rawls discusses two considerations.

> One concerns the range of views that can plausibly be elaborated from the fundamental ideas of society and person found in the public culture of a constitutional regime. Justice as fairness works from the fundamental ideas of society as a fair system of cooperation together with the conception of the person as free and equal. These ideas are taken as central to the democratic ideal. Are there other ideas equally central, and if there are, would they give rise to ideals and principles markedly different from those of justice as fairness?
>
> (*PL* 167)

By "central ideas" Rawls means to include at least the conception of free and equal citizens in a society that conceives itself as a fair system of productive cooperation.[17] Any "other ideas equally central" are meant not to displace, but to complement, these central ideas. The argument of this chapter has been based on requirements of stability, publicity, and reciprocity that would be equally incumbent upon any proposed alternative. This is confirmed by Rawls's next consideration: What might account for differences between these conceptions?

> The second consideration is that different social and economic interests may be assumed to support different liberal conceptions. The differences between conceptions expresses [*sic*], in part, a conflict between these interests. Let us define the relevant interests for each conception as those it would encourage and be supported by in a stable basic structure regulated by it. The width of the range of liberal conceptions will be determined by the degree of opposition among these interests.
>
> (*PL* 167)

I take this to express Rawls's acknowledgment that members of the family of liberal conceptions of justice may be distinguished by their relative solicitude for the interests of different social classes. The case for justice as fairness rests on its superiority, with respect to other liberal conceptions, in terms of narrowing class conflicts and thus in terms of stability. Justice as fairness can claim "to specify the center of the focal class" only if it is most clearly "correctly based on more central fundamental ideas" and "stable in view of the interests that support it and are

---

[17] Here, I disagree with Rawls's former student Paul Weithman's reading, which endorses the possibility of a liberal political conception of justice that dispenses with the fundamental idea of society as a fair system of cooperation, and instead builds on, e.g., a Thomistic idea of the common good (Weithman n.d., citing *LP* 77 n. 19 and *LP* 142 n. 29). Rawls certainly acknowledges that the veil-of-ignorance device is one that is variously interpretable – as, for example, admitting knowledge of "natural abilities and skills" or "ambitions and aspirations" (*LHPP* 19). It is thus natural to interpret the veil as allowing the parties to know that common-good conceptions are among the comprehensive conception of the good represented in society. But it does not follow that such conceptions count as liberal political conceptions of justice, rather than as comprehensive conceptions that may be housed within a suitable political conception.

encouraged by it" (*PL* 168). Rawls does not here state, though he transparently intimates, that justice as fairness fulfills these conditions.

> [I]f the liberal conceptions correctly framed from fundamental ideas of a democratic public culture are supported by and encourage deeply conflicting political and economic interests, and if there be no way of designing a constitutional regime so as to overcome that, a full overlapping consensus cannot, it seems, be achieved.
>
> (*PL* 168)

The idea of a full – that is, *stable* – overlapping consensus is not objectionably utopian because, and evidently only because, a constitutional regime *can* be designed that will sufficiently dampen political and economic – that is to say, *class* – conflict in a way that is democratic, liberal, and "open to view." As I have argued, Rawls believed that justice as fairness is the conception best suited to this demand, and liberal democratic socialism – though Rawls was reluctant to say so – is the regime type best capable of realizing justice as fairness.

> The decision of the persons in the original position hinges … on a balance of various considerations. In this sense, there is an appeal to intuition at the basis of the theory of justice. Yet when everything is tallied up, it may be perfectly clear where the balance of reason lies. The relevant reasons may have been so factored and analyzed by the description of the original position that one conception of justice is distinctly preferable to the others. The argument for it is not strictly speaking a proof, not yet anyway; but, in Mill's phrase, it may present considerations capable of determining the intellect.
>
> (*TJ* 108)

But if I am right that Rawls was aware that his system presents considerations that determine the intellect in favor of socialism, why did he not say so? This is the subject of the next chapter.

11

Religion and Reticence

I have argued that the gradual unfolding of Rawls's thinking brought him to the verge of declaring that justice as fairness is realizable only in a liberal democratic socialist regime. The reader is entitled to ask why Rawls himself did not say so, and why, after creating numerous occasions in which it would be natural to make a declaration, he persistently refused the chance. He posed what I have called the property question in its sharpest form in the *Restatement*, published shortly before his death. He had already posed the question in the *Guided Tour*, a version of which had been circulating at least since 1989. In both, he raised decisive objections to welfare-state capitalism, the regime type he had, since 1971, been understood to have been defending. He cleared the field of all but two candidates, liberal socialism and what he calls property-owning democracy. But he says little more about socialism other than that it is as capable, ideally, of realizing justice as fairness as property-owning democracy is. Then he goes on to talk about property-owning democracy with not another word about socialism, other than to say that the issue between these two surviving candidates turns on their relative stability, and that property-owning democracy in practice might unleash destabilizing political and economic forces.

And that is all he said. But, as I have argued, the question he left hanging admits of but one answer within the system of thought Rawls had painstakingly erected and continually refined. Liberal socialism possesses all of the stabilizing essentials, and property-owning democracy does indeed, just as Rawls hinted, unleash destabilizing forces. The destabilizing forces have their source in the distinctive feature of property-owning democracy: its resolve to leave open the possibility of private ownership of the basic means of production on which all citizens depend. But, within Rawls's system, there is no reason to take this chance, and many reasons not to. The only reason to leave the possibility of private ownership open is to have the benefit of possibly greater efficiencies if private financiers and entrepreneurs can be offered the incentive of what Rawls calls pure ownership. But Rawls is consistently adamant that the pursuit of ever-greater social wealth cannot justify putting justice in jeopardy.

It does not require a rehash of the preceding chapters, I hope, to remind the reader that Rawls's dearest goal as a political philosopher was to deny the claims of utility in order to create a space for justice.[1] One need only recall that the most central aim of *Theory* was to present an alternative to utilitarianism, which Rawls took to be the dominant theory of justice in contemporary political philosophy.[2] Nor do I need to recapitulate what I have said to remind the reader that the importance of stability, that is, *stability for the right reasons*, and the related virtues of publicity and reciprocity, became increasingly central to Rawls's thinking throughout the thirty-year interval between 1971 and 2001.

So why the reticence? In the third lecture on Locke, "Property and the Class State," Rawls works it out that Locke's view was compatible with the adoption of a liberal socialist regime (*LHPP* 150). As a jaunty preliminary, he remarks:

> The idea of thinking political conceptions through is less familiar to us than, say, thinking through conceptions in mathematics, physics, and economics. But perhaps it can be done. Why not? We can only find out by trying.

(LHPP 139–140)

The property question is not one that Locke faced, and in that sense working out what Locke was committed to is "merely academic." But the property question, as Rawls confronted it, was not academic, nor is it the easy or trivial kind of problem appropriately left as "an exercise for the reader." The problem is not easy and, far from being trivial, it is the most momentous question in the history of modern political philosophy. Millions of lives have been shaped or ended because of contention surrounding it. Did Rawls leave off because he believed he had taken the subject to a point beyond which, given the times, it could not "be fruitfully discussed" (*LHPP* xiv)? That cannot be right either, because Rawls in fact deliberately sets us the task of discussing it.

In the Introduction, I quoted what Rawls said about his needing coaching from Burton Dreben, to "be clear, to write forcefully and sharply, to be less guarded and muffled," and to be less like those (unnamed) philosophers whose style was "muffled and cramped, somehow they held back" (Rawls 2000a, 426). Many readers of Rawls, sympathetic or not, would agree that such coaching was needed, and many of these might doubt that it took. The style is in certain ways consistent with the character of the man. His former student and then colleague Tim Scanlon once described him

---

[1] I paraphrase Kant, who, in the preface to the second edition of the first *Critique*, says, "I had to deny *knowledge* in order to make room for *faith*" (Bxxx).

[2] In his 1972 review of *Theory*, the politically engaged philosopher Bernard Williams refers to justice as fairness as an "Attlee-like alternative" to utilitarianism (2014, 86). Attlee himself was delighted to proclaim himself a Socialist, even to the joint assembly of the U.S. Congress (Harris 1982, 280–281).

as "famously modest as a person" (Ponce 1999). This is consistent with his essentially Southern upbringing, in Baltimore, just south of the Mason-Dixon line. The Princeton of 1939 was still very much the "northernmost outpost of the Southern gentleman" when he matriculated, and Rawls proudly thought of himself a "Princeton man" who could smile at Harvard's (Yankee?) pretentiousness (Rawls 2000a, 417).

Rawls extols as an ideal the person who acts "with grace and self-command" (*TJ* 514), but his writing evokes the latter more often than the former. Not only did Rawls's writing style suggest that he "held back"; so did his demeanor. Rawls's obituary in *The Guardian* speaks of his "bat-like horror of the limelight" (Rogers 2002). Ben Rogers, the obituarist, continues, "As a child, he was traumatised by the deaths of two brothers from infections they had contracted from him; Rawls later admitted that this tragedy had contributed to the development of a severe stutter, which afflicted him for the rest of his life." Rawls was a determined avoider of interviewers. With few exceptions, he declined honors. And he worked mostly from his home in suburban Lexington, rather than from his office in Emerson Hall, a mere eight miles away. Rogers may exaggerate in describing him as "rather tortured" (1999, 5), but it is fair to say that Rawls left the impression of being a man who always had far more on his mind than he was ready to discuss.

One need look no farther than his record of military service in New Guinea and the Philippines to be persuaded that Rawls was a courageous man. But Rawls was also aware that voicing advanced moral opinions could impose a personal cost while achieving little. The cost comes regardless of how correct and how, in retrospect, predictably triumphant the opinion may be. Rawls writes that because Mill voiced advanced opinions, "his contemporaries thought him a fanatic . . .. He was viewed as simply unbalanced on these topics; people shook their heads and stopped listening" (*LHPP* 298). The equality of women and population control are the topics Rawls refers to, not socialism; but the example of Mill's reception, combined with Rawls's innate aversion to unnecessary controversy, could have discouraged explicitness, especially as Rawls's contemporaries recoiled from the leftish extremes reached during the late 1960s.[3] Already by the early 1970s one Harvard colleague, Hilary Putnam, had publicly resigned from the (Maoist) Progressive Labor Party, while

---

[3] In his first lecture on Hobbes, Rawls notes that

> It was a matter of personal affront in some circles if someone took you to be a Hobbist. That was an accusation against which many felt they had to defend themselves, much as people felt around 1950 in this country that they had to defend themselves from being thought to be a communist. Locke thought that Newton took him for a Hobbist, and this was something that they had to straighten out before they could be friends. It was a very serious matter to have others regard you in this light.
>
> (*LHPP* 25)

> There is no evidence that Rawls ever, even in the 1950s, harbored worries of this type about how others might regard him.

another, Robert Nozick, was mounting a libertarian challenge to basic assumptions that Rawls might have regarded as fairly uncontroversial. Rawls's not wanting to be careless with the literally incendiary power of ideas was no doubt another factor. The manuscript of *A Theory of Justice* had nearly perished in a radical firebombing in 1970, an incident I will return to in the next chapter.

RAWLS'S DEVELOPMENT AND MILL'S: A COMPARISON

It is interesting to compare Rawls's socialism with Mill's in terms of its transparency and its development. Within a certain range, there are parallels. This is not the place to make a detailed comparison of Rawls's and Mill's specific doctrines. To do so would be illuminating and fruitful, but would require more care in expounding Mill than is fitting for a book that is not on the subject of Mill's influence on Rawls – which was considerable – nor on the relative strengths of the two views, but on Rawls alone. I therefore borrow, at its face value, Joseph Schumpeter's account of Mill's socialist development, which is an account with which Rawls himself was likely to have been familiar.[4] Speaking of Mill's *Principles of Political Economy*, Schumpeter (1954, 531) writes:

> For the sociologist of capitalism . . . nothing can be more revealing of the character of bourgeois civilization – more indicative, that is, of its genuine freedom and also of its political weakness – than that the book to which the bourgeoisie accorded such a [warm] reception carried a socialist message and was written by a man palpably out of sympathy with the scheme of values of the industrial bourgeoisie. J.S. Mill was exactly what is meant by an evolutionary socialist.

The following substitutions can be made in the paragraph *salva veritate*, that is, without altering its truth: we understand the book to be *Theory*, rather than *Principles of Political Economy*, the author to be Rawls, not Mill, and we replace "industrial bourgeoisie" with, simply, "bourgeoisie." In Mill's case, as in Rawls's, it was not only the bourgeoisie who were fooled. Mill's "admirable modesty" – indeed, his whole "judicial" habit of thought and expression – lent itself to misapprehension by Marx, who complained that "Mill never says a thing without also saying its opposite" (Schumpeter 1954, 531). In Rawls's case, the obstacle is not so much a perception of "many tergiversations" as it is an accumulation of qualifications, disclaimers, postponements, and avoidances woven throughout a "strangely unpoetic mantra" (Rogers 1999, 1) of iterated phraseology: "well-ordered society," "fact of reasonable pluralism," "values of public reason," "background culture," and

---

[4] An adequate discussion would require addressing Richard Arneson's interpretation, which emphasizes Mill's trepidations about socialism's compatibility with the fullest compossible liberty (Arneson 1979).

so on. These, on top of the intimations I cited in the Introduction and elsewhere, that although "some form" of socialism can satisfy the principles of justice as fairness, so can some forms of capitalism.

In both cases, there are successive writings. It would be a mistake, Schumpeter says, to take Harriet Taylor's working up, after her husband's death, of "exploratory sketches" that consist of "little more than critical appraisals of the French and English socialist literature prior to 1869 and of current socialist slogans" as the book on socialism that Mill would have written had he lived. Mill's "socialism went through a steady development, the traces of which are but imperfectly discernible in the successive editions of the *Principles*" (Schumpeter 1954, 531). Schumpeter identifies four stages:

> Emotionally, socialism always appealed to him. He had little taste for the society he lived in and plenty of sympathy with the laboring masses. As soon as he had gained intellectual independence, he readily opened his mind to the socialist – mainly French – ideas of his time. But, being a trained economist and thoroughly practical-minded, he could hardly fail to perceive the weaknesses of what a little later was labeled Utopian Socialism by Marx.
>
> (Schumpeter 1954, 532)

In this second stage[5] of development, Mill dismissed as "beautiful dreams" all but the Saint Simonian, "instruments-of-production" conception of socialism, while also concluding that private ownership of land could not be justified (Mill 2006[1848] vol. 2, 201–203, 210–214, 227).

The third stage of Mill's socialist development was the announcement in the preface to the 1852 edition of *Principles* "to the effect that he never intended to 'condemn' socialism 'regarded as an ultimate result of human progress'" that had only to wait upon "'the unprepared state of mankind'" (Schumpeter 1954, 532; citing Mill 2006 [1852] vol. 2, xciii). Schumpeter cites the following passage in the 1852 edition as one "really amount[ing] to *explicit* recognition of socialism as the Ultimate Goal" (1954, 532):

> When I speak, either in this place or elsewhere, of "the labouring classes," or of labourers as a "class," I use those phrases in compliance with custom, and as descriptive of an existing, but by no means a necessary or permanent, state of social relations. I do not recognize as either just or salutary, a state of society in which there is any "class" which is not labouring; any human beings, exempt from bearing their share of the necessary labours of human life, except those unable to labour, or who have fairly earned rest by previous toil. So long, however, as the great social evil exists of a non-labouring class, labourers also constitute a class, and may be spoken of, though only provisionally, in that character.
>
> (Mill 2006 [1852], vol. 3, 758)

---

5 Schumpeter calls it the first, but I depart from his way of numbering the stages.

A classless society – or, at least, a society not divisible into a class of pure owners and a class of workers – is plainly the ultimate goal, insofar as justice is. The final stage, according to Schumpeter, was Mill's increasing optimism that "'progress' was accelerating wonderfully and that this 'ultimate end' was coming rapidly within view" (Schumpeter 1954, 532; but cf. Arneson 1979).

Let me summarize Schumpeter's stages this way: (1) there is a pre-analytic ground-floor stage, in which young Mill orientates himself with respect to society as he finds it; (2) there is an analytical stage, at which the economically sophisticated Mill is receptive to but critical of utopian socialism; (3) there is a corrective stage, in which Mill completely rewrites the property-question chapter in *Principles*, and explicitly declares his approval of socialism as goal; and (4) there is a final, prospective stage, in which the mature Mill perceives a rapid progressive improvement in social conditions and projects this movement into the future that will survive him.[6] Rawls's development can be divided into roughly the same stages.

The Youthful Stage: A Brief Inquiry

Mill's education was entirely secular and he was a lifelong freethinker. His opinion of society was therefore entirely this-worldly. Rawls, in contrast, was brought up in the Episcopal Church, and was sent to Kent School, a boarding school operated by clergy of the Order of the Holy Cross, in rural New England. The posthumously published *Brief Inquiry* tells us a great deal about Rawls's conception of society at the time when he was finishing his undergraduate degree at Princeton and preparing to enlist in the military, and considering whether to enter the clergy after the war's end. In December 1942, the undergraduate Rawls wrote:

> [T]he capitalist seems merely to use his employees. He treats them as so many cogs in the machine which piles up wealth for him. Hence, he seems merely to be an egoist; he seems to want nothing more than concrete wealth, bodily comfort, to which ends those he hires are means.

(*BI* 194)

There is nothing uncommon here. Rawls is unlikely to have been adverting to the theory of surplus value, but he does add one of his surprisingly few citations to Kant. He implies that Kant did not grasp the heart of the matter, and he goes on:

> But all the time this use of persons is justified by a tacit abuse of them. In the mind of the capitalist those persons are inferior, while he is superior. Further, the employees are not being used as means to concrete egoism, that is, to help amass large properties and estates; no, the end is not purely appetitional, but is spiritual. The capitalist takes great pride in his wealth; he loves to show it off. He likes to walk

---

[6] It is this last stage that perhaps justifies Isaiah Berlin's remark that Mill "had scarcely any prophetic gift" (1970, 183).

about his estate inwardly praising himself on his success. He likes to imagine his estate as a kingdom in which he is the most important figure. He keeps a host of servants not to serve his needs, but to swell the ranks of those who must obey him. All of his activities go to build up this petty kingdom by virtue of which his consuming vanity can congratulate itself. The entire activity of his life, all the feverish rushing in and out of town, all the unending worries of business, all these efforts which exhaust body, mind, and soul are aimed at this indeterminate end of silent, self-congratulatory self-worship. Underlying all this sinful striving is the egotist lie, namely, that he is a person distinct and superior. The purely egoistic sin of using other people, of turning personal relations into natural relations, is justified by the deepest of all sins, the egotist's lie.

(*BI* 194–195)

Lest the reader get the wrong idea, young Rawls immediately adds, "[W]e should remark that we have no particular dislike for capitalism. We are not spreading Marxist propaganda" (*BI* 195). By his own later account, Rawls in his teens was "concerned with moral questions and the religious and philosophical basis on which they might be answered," but it was only with his military service that he came "to be also concerned with political questions" (Pyke 1995). Rawls never intended to publish the *Brief Inquiry*, and within the space of three and a half years he had lost the Christian faith that the *Brief Inquiry* was designed to expound. Not a single word of it can simply be assumed to reflect anything durable about Rawls's opinions or worldview. But on the other hand, none of it should be ignored if it is useful in understanding his orientation toward society and subsequent intellectual development.

I want to draw attention to the distinction between "egoism" and "egotism," as Rawls uses it in the *Brief Inquiry*, and his later emphasis on the distinction between the rational the special psychologies. There is an alignment that is hard to mistake. The "egoist" is one who is concerned to satisfy his appetites, that is, to pursue the natural objects of his appetites. The "ego*t*ist," on the other hand (I italicize the first "t" in "ego*t*ist" to aid the reader), is one who denies an equal relationship to other persons. An ego*t*ist is normally also an egoist, but egoism does not inexorably tend to ego*t*ism. Rawls credits Paul Leon with the terminology, and it helped Rawls expound what he believed to be the nature of sin, and to correct the mistaken views of Augustine, Aquinas, and other theologians. They confuse sinfulness with egoism; but, Rawls insists to the contrary, the great sin is not egoism, but ego*t*ism.

On Rawls's retelling, the Christian fathers were misled by the Greek notion that virtue is knowledge. This is correct, he says, if we think of man as an appetitive creature. Knowledge is a virtue if what you want is some object that you need to know how to achieve. "The rational" was not the term Rawls used, but he well might have. Later, he stipulates that parties in the original position are rational. They want to do as well as they can for those they represent, in terms of primary goods. With a slight amount of wedging, we can think of the primary good consisting in the social bases of self-respect as an appetitive, object-involving rather than personal-relationship-in-the-true-sense-involving good. The parties take no interest in the interests of others. But they are also reasonable. That is, they choose principles by which those for whom they choose will justify themselves to each other. Those whom they represent are assumed to want to live together justly, if they can, and not simply to live egoistically. Thus, it is the represented persons' reasonableness, not their rationality, that makes it possible to propose principles to them even tentatively. But what if the citizens are not only egoists but egotists? Egotists not only want to get as much as they can, like egoists; they also care how much others get. "It is not enough to succeed," as Oscar Wilde quipped, "others must fail." Can the principles chosen stand the additional stress this kind of attitude brings into the mix?

The later division of the original position procedure into its two parts, Part One and Part Two, can be understood in these terms. In Part One, the parties are rational and reasonable, and those for whom they choose are conceived as being able, provisionally, to live by the principles chosen. But Part Two is necessary because the parties have to consider that those they represent will exhibit the special psychologies, which are much the same vices Rawls assigned to the egotist in his undergraduate thesis: "envy, vanity, pride . . . the perverse desire for height . . . [what] we may term, if we care to, Original Sin" (*BI* 191, 193). The question in Part Two is whether the reasonableness of the principles the parties chose in Part One can stand up to and stabilize a society of egotists – who are not merely, but may be also, egoists. The proof of the principles is in the institutions, and the proof is not complete until what we generally know is brought to bear on the question whether the institutions needed to realize the principles can handle the additional strains of commitment that egotists, as well as mere egoists, will be expected to bear.

This development lay far ahead. The key point is that the young Rawls saw the point of creation to be salvation, and saw salvation as consisting in union with other human persons in a community of mutual love. The great sin is egotism. The property question is nowhere mentioned, nor is production, nor is cooperation for mutual advantage in the mundane sense. Political questions will not arise for Rawls until he has seen combat and lost his faith. There is a long tradition of Christian socialism (see Gray 1968 [1946]), which Rawls, even as an undergraduate, was unlikely not to have known to exist. But there is no evidence that Rawls was influenced by it or even interested in it.

Analytical Stage: A Theory of Justice

At this stage, an ideal society is no longer conceived in theological terms, as a community of believers striving for salvation through mutual love. Rawls has steeped himself in the economic literature of the time, much as Mill had done. Society is now conceived as a cooperative scheme for mutual advantage. The success of the scheme depends on the public availability of fair terms defining a conception of justice to which all members of society may appeal to settle conflicting claims to a share of the benefits produced by the scheme. It does not need a divine sanction, and would be no different if it had one.

The property question is now not only unavoidable; it is paramount. It is interesting to compare Mill's way of approaching it.

> In considering the institution of property as a question in social philosophy, we must leave out of consideration its actual origin . . .. We may suppose a community unhampered by any previous possession; a body of colonists, occupying for the first time an uninhabited country; bringing nothing with them but what belonged to them in common, and having a clear field for the adoption of institutions and polity which they judged most expedient; required, therefore, to choose whether they would conduct the work of production on the principles of individual property, or on some system of common ownership and collective agency.
>
> (Mill 2006 [1852] vol. 2, 201)

For Rawls, the task is to choose rules on the basis of not mere expediency, but of fairness. To assure that, Rawls, like Mill, sets aside all thought of "previous possession," but Rawls also introduces a veil of ignorance that would deny Mill's colonists of all knowledge of their particular gifts and desires.

It is unnecessary to recapitulate here the position Rawls arrives at on the property question, as expounded in *Theory*. Unlike Mill, Rawls does not undertake any extensive exposition of the then-current state of socialist theorizing, and thus has no occasion to make criticisms that could lead the reader to assume that socialism was not realistic or desirable. Rawls does rule out one-party systems of all kinds as inconsistent with first principle liberties, and he also, by implication at least, rejects non-market varieties of socialism. As I recounted in the Introduction, Rawls left the unintended impression that he was friendly to welfare-state capitalism. Unlike Mill, the impression he is later concerned to correct is not one of hostility toward socialism, but of friendliness toward capitalism.

Corrective Stage: The Restatement

Let me first quote Mill's own assessment of where he stood at the end of his corrective stage:

> The only objection [to socialism] to which any great importance will be found to be attached . . . is the unprepared state of mankind in general, and of the labouring classes in particular; their extreme unfitness at present for any order of things, which would make any considerable demand on either their intellect or their virtue. It appears to me that the great end of social improvement should be to fit mankind by cultivation, for a state of society combining the greatest personal freedom with that just distribution of the fruits of labor, which the present laws of property do not profess to aim at. Whether, when this state of mental and moral cultivation shall be

attained, individual property in some form (though a form very remote from the present) or community ownership in the instruments of production and a regulated division of the produce, will afford the circumstances most favorable to happiness, and best calculated to bring human nature to its greatest perfection, is a question which must be left, as it safely may, to the people of the time to decide. Those of the present are not competent to decide it.

(Mill 2006 [1852] vol. 2, xciii)

It is impossible not to be struck by the similarity between this passage and those in *Theory* and the *Restatement* in which Rawls expresses his reluctance to say more. But Rawls's question is quite other than Mill's.

Rawls's question, in the original position, conceives of persons as free equals who are fit to live by ideal principles, and are equally prepared to do so, whatever their actual abilities and cultural level happens to be. There is no question of unreadiness. There are strains of commitment, and burdens of judgment, but they affect all, and not merely a backward laboring class. For Rawls, the question is one of justice rather than happiness or perfection. He is only later to conclude that his account of stability in *Theory* relies on a perfectionist, at least partly comprehensive conception of justice and of the good, and in need of recasting. Finally, the principles of justice Rawls derives have to withstand the destabilizing effects of the special psychologies introduced in Part Two of the original position procedure. Rawls is aware already of the pressure the fact of domination places on the achievement of democratic stability. Mill, by contrast, seems complacent. For example, Mill proposes limits on inheritance as a means of apportioning award to virtue. For Rawls, limits on inheritance are grounded quite differently. For him, it is a matter of preserving the fair value of political liberty, and of reducing destabilizing occasions for excusable envy.

The last contrast I will draw at this stage is this. For Mill, the property question is for another day. For Rawls, the question must be adressed in light of a country's level of development, resources, and traditions, but it is a question for today – that is, for us to ask now. The principles that determine how it is to be addressed are to be decided, once and for all, to the extent possible, by us, you and me, now. As I explained in Chapter 10, Rawls left the property question for us to decide, here and now, but to decide according to the guidance and within the framework of the original position procedure, Parts One and Two.

The Prospective Stage

Mill was optimistic that as the property notions handed down from the past progressively lost their hold, and the working class improved intellectually and morally, the day would come when socialism in a suitable form would be realized. Futurity would elect either some hitherto unexampled form of private ownership, or public ownership of the means of production, or perhaps some hybrid, as will appear likeliest to promote spontaneity, happiness, and perfection. Mill was not, as Rawls says, interested in propounding a system (*LHPP* 251), and so the optimism of Mill's prospective stage was not tarnished with the obsessive theorist's anxiety that all events unfold according to a predetermined scheme.

Rawls's mind was always engaged in improving and reworking a theory of large proportion. He was also pessimistic about the practical influence of his work, and increasingly so as he neared the end of his life. Rawls's development did not really include a prospective stage: his corrective essay, the *Restatement*, was published only a year, more or less, before his death in 2002. Unlike Mill, he did not have the opportunity to observe the decades unfolding after the publication of his corrected view, much less to observe the long arc of history bending in his direction.

Rawls's corrective stage involved adjustments of various and seemingly uncon-nected kinds. Beginning in the 1980s and continuing into 1990s, Rawls was working to recast the account of stability that he had given in *Theory*, to make it "political" rather than "metaphysical" or comprehensive. Simultaneously, and less conspicu-ously, he was reconfiguring the argument for the two principles. To achieve the latter, he reduced Part One's reliance on the maximin principle and separated the argument into what he called the two fundamental comparisons: the first, justice as fairness versus average utility; and the second, justice as fairness versus restricted utility. All this was set out in earlier chapters. It was against this background that we must place his repudiation of welfare-state capitalism and his reluctance to declare that justice as fairness culminates in socialism.

FETISHIZING THE MEANS OF PRODUCTION

The word "socialism" is fraught with historical associations that, for many people, are unpleasant. The Cold War (1947–1991) encouraged journalistic practices in the West such that "'socialism' sometimes means little more than that a country is ruled despotically and that no political opposition is allowed" (Kołakowski 2005 [1978], 1181). The dissolution of the Soviet Union and of the Warsaw Pact did little to rehabilitate the word. The triumphant "shock therapy" the West imposed in the former Soviet states privatized the means of production: it was a humanitarian disaster, yet no regret or apology has been thought necessary. Rawls never shied from using the term *socialism* to designate a type of regime capable of justice. "[W]hile central command socialism, such as reigned in the Soviet Union, is discredited ... the same is not true of liberal socialism[, t]his illuminating and worthwhile view" (*LHPP* 323). But it is a step further to declare that what is illuminating and worthwhile is also a demand of justice. And reflective equilibrium is harder to reach if the claim is that the public political culture of constitutional democracies contains fundamental ideas that can best be worked up into a set of principles that only socialism can realize.

Chapter 2 recounted the history of struggles within the British Labour Party over Clause Four of its original constitution. The issue was fundamentally one concerning whether or not to demand public ownership of the means of production. Revisionist politicians have not been alone in wishing that this term, and the baggage it carries, would go away. But Rawls is likelier to have been in mind of Marxian economist John Roemer's complaint:

> My view is that socialists have made a fetish of public ownership: public ownership has been viewed as the *sine qua non* of socialism, but this judgment is based on a false inference. What socialists want are the three equalities I enumerated [viz.] equal opportunity for
>   (1) self-realization and welfare,
>   (2) political influence, and
>   (3) social status[;]
>
> [socialists] should be open-minded about what kinds of property rights in the MP [i.e., the means of production] would bring about those three equalities.
>
> (Roemer 1994a, 11, 21; reordered)

Rawls would have no reason to dissent from this and, as I have already noted, he cited Roemer's book approvingly, though in a general way. Magnanimously, Rawls would have ignored Roemer's warning that "self-realization ... is a specifically Marxist conception of human flourishing ... to be distinguished, for instance, from philosopher John Rawls's notion of fulfillment of a plan of life" (1994a, 11).[7] But Rawls does not share Roemer's further view that it is not an urgent task for socialists to set priorities between desiderata (1), (2), and (3). In fact, justice as fairness can be read as an expression of the three, but in a definite lexical ordering, and Rawls's political philosophy is, primarily, an argument for those principles standing in a definite order of priority.

As noted in Chapter 10, Roemer nonetheless goes on to advance a case for what is in essence a constitutional guarantee that the major means of production be publicly held. Rawls, for reasons I detail also in Chapter 10, has framed the property question in a way that requires the same conclusion. Of course, there will be reasonable disagreement about the precise dimension of this guarantee, especially if it is reduced to terms in a written constitution. As Cardinal Newman said in a different connection, even ten thousand difficulties do not make a doubt.

---

7   Roemer carelessly misreads (and mis-cites) *TJ* (1st ed.) 426 (correctly, 432; cf. *TJ* 379–380) as conveying Rawls's endorsement of "counting blades of grass" as a plan of life. Rawls's "fanciful example" is of someone who "manages to survive by solving difficult mathematical problems for a fee" and of whom we conclude "there is no feasible way to alter his condition."

STAYING TRUE TO THE POLITICAL

The most discussed of the developments in Rawls's thinking, post-1971, was his recasting justice as fairness as a political rather than a comprehensive doctrine. He struggled to re-center the argument in such a way that the primacy of the political values could be freely assented to by citizens who embrace religious doctrines that posit higher values than those of autonomous equal citizenship in the temporal world. Remarkably, Rawls suggests that some components of justice as fairness, the comprehensive doctrine set forth in A *Theory of Justice*, might "seem ... and may actually be" religious, as well as moral and philosophical in the comprehensive sense (*PL* xliii). He does not specify which these are: he could be alluding to his Kantian conception of moral autonomy. In light of his posthumously published senior thesis, a likelier surmise is that Rawls came to recognize his 1971 conception of a well-ordered society to be too continuous with his youthful – and aggressively Christian – conception of a community of faith (*BI* passim). Rawls emphatically does not want a well-ordered society to turn out, under the microscope of analysis, to be a secularized community bonded and stabilized by a controversial religious conception of society.

What is society? The answer one gives to this question pretty much determines the outline and content of one's political philosophy and one's politics. One way to understand the trajectory Rawls's thinking took is to contrast his changing conceptions of what society is. The young Rawls of the *Brief Inquiry* was drawn to – or, really, in the grip of – a conception of society as a stage on which certain virtues can be performed. The most pertinent of these is the virtue of humility. The mature Rawls conceived society less monolithically. It has a basic structure and it has a background culture and intermediate between these is an assortment of more-or-less voluntary associations. But the key idea is that society is a cooperative productive enterprise.

> We reject the idea of allocative justice as incompatible with the fundamental idea by which justice as fairness is organized: the idea of society as a fair system of social cooperation over time. Citizens are seen as cooperating to produce the social resources on which their claims are made
>
> (*JF* 50).

Once society is conceived this way, joint ownership of the means of production, at least at some level of abstraction, is almost presupposed. Compare this with what Rawls says of Marx: "His ideal: a society of freely associated producers" (*LHPP* 354). Marx's ideal and the mature Rawls's idea are essentially indistinguishable. It is not easy to explain why the youthful Rawls's idea of community is comprehensive and the mature Rawls's idea is not. I do not say there is no explanation that can be given. The point is that Rawls would rather emphasize that his mature conception of society is one latent in our shared, public political culture. The fact that it may also feature in a comprehensive view does not close off that possibility. In fact, the motivational efficacy of the political conception will, to some degree, depend on its resonance within different, incommensurable but equally reasonable comprehensive viewpoints.

Those who consider themselves to be socialists frequently adhere to socialism as a fully or at least partially comprehensive doctrine. Not all socialists do, and it is certainly possible to argue for socialism without appealing to any comprehensive doctrine. One has to admit that Rawls vouches for this, even if one dissents from the thesis of this book. Even so, points of analogy between socialism and religion are commonplace. If, like Rawls, one is trying to detach a political conception of justice from the comprehensive doctrines from which it historically derives – principally, those of Kant and Mill – then one might want to be quiet about putting forward a theory sporting, as it were, a sticker that reads "Socialism Inside!"

THE MOTIVATIONAL WORRY

One of the concerns that led Rawls to recast justice as fairness as a political rather than comprehensive doctrine was disclosed in a rare interview he granted in 1998, late in his life:

BP: *[I]*n your recent work ... religion has become ... a major focus .... What's the motivation ...?

JR: Well, that's a good question. I think the basic explanation is that I'm concerned for the survival, historically, of constitutional democracy. I live in a country where 95 or 90 percent of the people profess to be religious. (CP 616)

By "survival" Rawls means, of course, stability – that is, survival for the right reasons. He is acutely conscious that a large majority of his compatriots are responsive to religious discourse. He had amended his account of public reason to make room for appeals to religious belief, subject to "the proviso" that equivalent secular reasons always be made available "in due course" (*LP* 144). His acknowledgment that comprehensive doctrines make for more effective rhetoric is already unmistakable, as his discussion of Martin Luther King, Jr. (*PL* 250 n. 39), and Abraham Lincoln (*PL* 254) merely amplifies.

In the United States, at least, the resonance of socialist ideals is far weaker than that of religious ones. A remark by Bernard Williams, speaking of himself, Charles Taylor, and Alasdair MacIntyre, is pertinent here:

All three of us ... accept the significant role of Christianity in understanding modern moral consciousness, and adopt respectively three possible views about how to move in relation to that: backward in it, forward in it, and out of it.

(Williams 2005, 54)

Parallel remarks apply to the role of Christianity in modern political consciousness. Rawls, obviously, recognized the significance of Christianity in both spheres. But it is less easy to state which way he was orientated with respect to it. The undergraduate Rawls looked to be ready to move backward in Christianity. The Rawls of *A Theory of Justice* went out of it. And the late Rawls seemed increasingly to have wondered whether he had gone out of it at all. Michael Walzer (2013, 7–8) remarks:

> For many years now, I have been worrying about what might be called the cultural reproduction of the left. [I]n comparison with the different religious communities, the secular left does not seem able to pass on to its next generations a rich intellectual culture or an engaging popular culture. The tradition is thin. I worried about this with regard to the American left and also, in greater anxiety, with regard to the Zionist left.

One could interject a quibble about the "red diaper babies," who include Hilary Putnam and Rawls's determined critic, Jerry Cohen, and Walzer himself. But these exceptions are beside the point.

> Indeed, the problem is general . . . . [C]ompare[] three national liberation movements – in India, Israel, and Algeria. In each case, the movement was secular and leftist; in each case, it succeeded in establishing a secular state; and in each case, this secular state was challenged some 30 years later by religious zealots. Three different religions but three similar versions of zealotry: modernized, politicized, ideological. The leaders of the secular liberationists, people like Nehru, Ben-Gurion, and Ben Bella, were convinced that secularization was inevitable – the disenchantment of the social world. But they did not succeed in creating a rich cultural alternative to the old religion. They thought they didn't have to do that; modern science was the alternative. Modern science, however, does not produce emotionally appealing life-cycle celebrations or moving accounts of the value and purpose of our lives. That's what religion does, and secular leftism, though often described on analogy with religion, has not been similarly creative.

> (Walzer 2013, 8)

It is impossible to avoid being reminded of Attlee's socialist Britain failing to reproduce itself. But, as Roemer (1994a, 19) points out, of course public ownership of the means of production is "a rather weak concept" if it can be swept away at the next election. Constitutional entrenchment can achieve quite a lot even in the absence of life-cycle celebrations.[8] The citizens of Wyoming perform no uniform observances, for example; and yet their state is assured its equal representation in the U.S. Senate so long as the grass shall grow.

The trick is to achieve that entrenchment without destroying democracy. Wholly apart from the practical or procedural problems that form barriers to constitution

---

[8] On the use of constitutional debt ceilings to elevate "market justice" over "social justice," see Streek 2014, 58, 117.

making and amending, there is the more fundamental problem of popular will-formation. Rawls was troubled by the realization that his was a professedly religious people, and that his secular socialism might be without the mythic *oomph* necessary to reproduce itself. This, I conjecture, was why he was unwilling to take on the baggage of secular socialism, which had failed to take root in Britain – or, as Walzer points out, in India (set free by Attlee), or Algeria, or Israel, despite its kibbutzim raised from the nursery with a socialist ethic. Property-owning democracy has even weaker credentials in this respect, of course. But why declare at all, unnecessarily?

Non-Ideal Theory: The Transition to Socialism

John Rawls's ideal theory of justice, justice as fairness, is realizable only in a democratic socialist state. For us, who are not citizens of well-ordered democratic socialist states, the questions of non-ideal theory are unavoidable. The history of socialism is preponderantly a history of political violence intended to achieve or to maintain a socialist regime – that is, to use political power to transfer the means of production from private to public ownership and to keep it there. Rawls was no doubt as distressed by the thought of more of this as he was at the thought of a revival of the religious wars of the sixteenth century. But Rawls was no pacifist. The process of transition is subject to the moral constraints that belong to non-ideal theory, although, depending on the distance to be traveled, ideal theory too has a role.

CIVIL DISOBEDIENCE AND POLITICAL VIOLENCE

Rawls's closest personal encounter with specifically political violence was as victim, rather than as a perpetrator or a sympathizer:

> During the 1969–1970 academic year, Rawls intended to finish his book at Stanford University's Center for Advanced Study in the Behavioral Sciences. The year almost ended in disaster when the Rawlses received an early morning phone call informing them that the Center had been bombed. "Jack's first reaction," says Margaret Rawls, "was to turn pale and say, 'I can't do it again.'" But the manuscript, while soaked, was still legible.

> (Ponce 1999)

The front page of the *Stanford Daily News* of April 27, 1970, was divided between the firebombing story and a report on a campus-wide strike called to demand that the Stanford administration oust ROTC, the Reserve Officer Training Corps. An inside page ran a Jules Feiffer cartoon, depicting two sleek, adult white men, tête-à-tête, whose dialogue suggested that, because ecology requires socialism, ecology is not a discussable issue. It was a wild time.

Philosopher Amelie Rorty was also at the Center, and she recalls Rawls's deportment:

> When we heard that the Center had been attacked overnight, we all rushed up the hill in the early morning to see what had happened. The fire was limited to the wing that held Rawls's study and that of the anthropologist M.N. Srinivas. Srinivas's study was completely burnt ... a lifetime of research notes on class and caste in an Indian village were entirely destroyed, lost. He was walking around in a daze when Jack came up. Before going into his own study (next door to Srinivas's) to see what damage had been done to the only revised copy of *Theory of Justice*, Jack took Srinivas off for a long walk in the hills behind the Center. Only after they returned from the walk about an hour later, did Jack go into his study to see that his manuscript was waterlogged but intact. It was completely characteristic of Jack to help someone in grief before turning to his own concern.

(Rorty, personal e-mail correspondence, 2016)

The revised copy of *Theory* was the copy Rawls had been working on for the entire academic year. This was before photocopying machines became standard office equipment, and before the personal computer made it easy to "back things up." Philosopher and biographer David Reidy recalls Mardy Rawls telling him that the Rawlses "gathered the typescript and spread it out throughout their living quarters to dry and then proceeded to retype the entire thing" (Reidy, personal e-mail correspondence, 2016). There is no evidence that Rawls was specifically targeted.

Rawls himself rebounded almost instantly, after absorbing the initial shock of the telephone call in the night. But the gulf between academic intellectuals and militant activists has never been wider than it was on the morning of April 26, 1970. It is no wonder that, in the *Restatement*, Rawls assigns to political philosophy a task of reconciliation alongside the problem of order (*JF* 1–5):

> [P]olitical philosophy may try to calm our frustration and rage against our society and its history by showing us the way in which its institutions, when properly understood from a philosophical point of view, are rational, and developed over time as they did to attain their present, rational form. This fits one of Hegel's well-known sayings: "When we look at the world rationally, the world looks rationally back." He seeks for us reconciliation – *Versöhnung* – that is, we are to accept and affirm our social world positively, not merely to be resigned to it.

(*JF* 3)

Imagine: Rawls, almost fifty years of age, peeling apart and dealing out, like oversized playing cards, the hundreds of sodden, faintly malodorous leaves of the only copy of his magnum opus, covering the available surfaces in his temporary California apartment, as the world looks rationally back.

Among those pages – sections 53 to 59 to be exact – was Rawls's discussion of civil disobedience, which was a topic he had addressed earlier, in articles published in 1964 and 1969. It is the only aspect of non-ideal theory that *Theory* purported to treat in detail.

Ideal theory deals with a well-ordered society, in which everyone "is presumed to act justly," while non-ideal or "partial compliance theory" deals in "principles that govern how we are to deal with injustice ... the pressing, urgent matters ... in everyday life" (*TJ* 8). The value of ideal theory consists essentially in the guidance it provides in non-ideal circumstances, which are the only circumstances we will ever witness.

It is a common mistake to confuse a well-ordered society with a society of saints or even angels. But Rawls writes that

> even in a well-ordered society the coercive powers of government are ... necessary for the stability of social cooperation ... [for citizens] may lack full confidence in one another ... and so may be tempted not to do [their part] ... [but] sanctions are not severe and may never need to be imposed.
>
> (*TJ* 211)

Pace Marx and Engels, there will be no withering away of the state. Rawls divides non-ideal theory itself into two parts: "One consists of the principles for governing adjustments to natural limitations and historical contingencies, and the other of principles for meeting injustice" (*TJ* 216). It is worth taking care to explore the structure of Rawls's non-ideal theory.

The "Perfectly-Ordered Society"

In what Rawls calls the "perfectly-ordered society" (*TJ* 310) there is a just consti-tution, and all laws happen also to be just. There is, therefore, "no difficulty" (*TJ* 308) in deriving a duty to comply with every law "given favorable conditions" (*TJ* 309). Unfavorable conditions demand "adjustments to natural limitations," and the "ideal conception of justice applies" (*TJ* 309). What Rawls has in mind, I believe, is a natural catastrophe or epidemic that creates an emergency. Under these circum-stances, "regulation of liberty of conscience" and "limitation of the scope of majority rule" may be required to restore public order (*TJ* 309). Rawls says very little about this kind of case. Rawls's remark, that in "many historical situations a lesser political liberty may have been justified" (*TJ* 217), may be apposite, but I leave this aside.

Injustice in the Well-Ordered Society

In a well-ordered society, not only will there be disobedience and sanctions; there will also be the permanent possibility of unjust laws being enacted. The burdens of judgment alone are sufficient to create conditions in which good-faith adherence to just procedures results in laws that are not only suboptimal but unjust. Lawmaking is, in general, a case not of perfect but of imperfect procedural justice in a well-ordered society. The fact that matters of specifically distributive justice are ones of pure procedural justice must not be allowed to obscure this. To avoid confusion, Rawls designates this kind of case as that of a "reasonably just" society: some laws are unjust, but unjust laws are binding within "certain limits" (*TJ* 308). In such cases, "[s]ome principles counsel compliance ... others direct us the other way," and therefore the competing "claims of duty ... must be balanced by a conception of priorities" (*TJ* 308). But there is a further problem that can arise when unjust laws not only find their way "onto the books" but shape institutions. In that event, there are "unjust arrangements" (*TJ* 308, 309). "We must ascertain how the ideal conception applies, *if it applies at all*" (*TJ* 309; emphasis added). The problem is that the assumptions that enabled the derivation of the principles of justice are no longer fully operative, and an argument is needed to show how the ideal conception they embody is even applicable. In other words, what would make a principle of average utility, or some other principles, inapplicable?

This inquiry belongs to what Rawls calls, less than illuminatingly, the "partial compliance part of non-ideal theory" (*TJ* 308, 309). The terminology is not meant to suggest that there is also a partial compliance part of ideal theory, nor that there is a full compliance part of non-ideal theory. The topic is meant to include punishment, compensation, just war theory, civil disobedience, conscientious refusal, militant resistance, and revolution (*TJ* 8). From this point forward, I will simply call this the non-ideal theory. But "even here" we assume that the basic structure is "nearly just, making due allowance for what is reasonable to expect in the circumstances" (*TJ* 309). This assumption presumably justifies us in applying the "ideal conception," but bear in mind that for Rawls the "principles of right" always balance against political duties and obligations generally – the weight given to "existing arrangements," and their "laws and institutions" varies according to their distance from ideal justice. To acknowledge the significance of the intuitive idea of distance, Rawls introduces a further division to be made within non-ideal theory.

There are two ways in which laws and institutions can depart from justice. In the first way, current arrangements depart in degrees from just standards (*TJ* 309). In the second way, arrangements conform to an *unreasonable* conception and "in many cases are clearly unjust" (*TJ* 309). First-way departures allow for justified civil disobedience. Second-way departures do not. For "when a society is regulated by principles favoring narrow class interests, one may have no recourse but to oppose the prevailing ... institutions ... in such ways as promise some success" (*TJ* 310). Civil disobedience, as I will explain more fully, involves a public appeal to a just constitution. Where there is no just constitution, there is nothing to appeal to – there is only the possibility to make what John Locke called an "appeal to heaven," that is, to use whatever means "promise some success" to remedy injustice.

The "Badly Ordered" Society

Rawls does not give a name to a society that lacks a just constitution. For convenience, I suggest the term "the badly ordered society." Although there may be other
ways of falling into this category, the only one Rawls mentions is a society captured,
so to speak, by a politically privileged class. Presumably this class enjoys social and
economic privileges as well. In a badly ordered society, not only is the fair value of
equal liberty absent, or not taken seriously – recall from Chapter 5 Rawls's rueful
observation that steps needed to achieve fair value seem never to have been taken
seriously – but the political processes are rigged to serve to protect the politically
privileged class and to perpetuate its rule.

It is interesting to contrast the badly ordered society with what in *Law of Peoples*
Rawls's calls a "decent society," whose political structure may instance what he calls
a "decent consultation hierarchy." A badly ordered society is unlike a decent society
in two respects. A decent society generates genuine political duties of obedience,
while a badly ordered society does not. A decent society is not obligated to become
liberally just, while a badly ordered society is obligated to become liberally just, that
is, to organize itself according to principles like those of justice as fairness. The
reason for this difference, presumably, lies in the difference in history and traditions
that exists between badly ordered and decent societies ("peoples"). There are traces
here of Hegel's influence, but Bernard Williams has also expressed much the same
idea: once a society has started down a liberal path, it must pursue it.[1]

But a badly ordered society lacks a just constitution, and liberal justice cannot be
expected to eventuate within it with the mere passage of time. The strictures of
public reason, which limit appeals to comprehensive moral and philosophical
values in a well-ordered society, are inapplicable.

---

[1] Williams, like Rawls, acknowledges that "there manifestly have been, and perhaps are, [legit-
imate] non-liberal states" (2005, 4). But Williams adds:

> Now and around here the [basic legitimation demand, which is equivalent to Rawls's
> liberal principle of legitimacy] together with the historical conditions permit only a
> liberal solution: other forms of answer are unacceptable. In part, this is for the
> Enlightenment reason that the other supposed legitimations are now seen to be false
> and ideological. It is not, though it is often thought to be, because some liberal
> conception of the person, which delivers the morality of liberalism, is or ought to be
> seen as correct. (2005, 8)

Williams's formulation dramatizes the dilemma Rawls faced. The later Rawls disavows "the
liberal conception of the person" of Part III of *Theory*. But he is also unwilling to rely on "the
Enlightenment reason." His hope is that an overlapping consensus of reasonable comprehensive
views –including both "the liberal conception of the person" and the "Enlightenment" view, along
with suitably reasonable religious conceptions –will form and stabilize. Rawls never says why a
badly ordered liberal society has an obligation to become a well-ordered liberal society. His
increasing interest in Hegel is an indication that he shared Williams's conclusion that "now and
around here," sliding into mere decency (a "decent consultation hierarchy") is not an acceptable
solution even if it were a "live" option.

[I]t may happen that for a well-ordered society to come about in which public discussion consists mainly in the appeal to political values, prior historical conditions may require that comprehensive reasons be invoked to strengthen those values.

(*PL* 251 n. 41)

Rawls goes on to say, in another connection, that socialism is "one of the most comprehensive political doctrines ever formulated" (*PL* 346). But "comprehensive" is not, in the context, intended to be taken as contrasted (as it often is) to "political." If the best theory of political justice for an advanced industrial or postindustrial society requires socialism, then socialism is pro tanto a political conception, and advocacy of socialism is an appeal to political values. (So also is advocacy of property-owning democracy.)

A badly ordered society has no right to expect obedience: "[T]o employ the coercive apparatus in order to maintain manifestly unjust institutions is itself a form of illegitimate force that men in due course have a right to resist" (*TJ* 342). Resistance in due course is not the limit of the rights of members of badly ordered societies. Militant and violent revolutionary actions are also justified, within the bounds of right, to the extent that they promise success. Militant action means "well-framed ... acts of disruption and resistance ... to prepare the way for radical or ... revolutionary change" (*TJ* 323). If no means promise success, or the promising means require violating duties or obligations in the theory of right, then one must bide one's time. The principles of the theory of right applicable in this case are other than those comprising the ideal conception. They might be intuitionistic or utilitarian or, of course, contractualist principles.

The Nearly Just Society: Well but Not Perfectly Ordered

The non-ideal case that Rawls devotes by far the most attention to is that of what he calls "a well-ordered" but not "perfectly ordered" society. It is not badly ordered, for it has a just constitution. Legislative majorities "are bound to make mistakes ... from a lack of knowledge and judgment [or] partial and self-interested views" and sincerely held "opinions of justice are bound to clash" (*TJ* 312). Moreover, "tendencies of general social facts will often be ambiguous and difficult to assess" (*TJ* 314). Recognizing that "even the ideal legislature is an imperfect procedure" (*TJ* 316), the parties in the original position adopt a "principle of political settlement," which can at best render the case one of "quasi-pure procedural justice" (*TJ* 318).

The principle of political settlement is not spelled out, but it contains a strand entailed by the natural duty of justice: "Being required to support a just constitution, we must go along with one of its essential principles, that of majority rule" (*TJ* 311). Another strand is "a natural duty of civility not to invoke the faults of social arrangements as a too ready excuse for not complying ... nor to exploit inevitable loopholes in the rules" (*TJ* 312). There is a companion principle that Rawls does not name. It could be called the "principle of political progression," for want of something euphonious. It gathers up the following remarks. "The aim of a well-ordered society, or one in a state of near justice, is to preserve and strengthen the institutions of justice" (*TJ* 325). This strand is the counterpart of the duty of a badly ordered society to become, if you like, better ordered, or more nearly just. It is not only an institutional duty but also an individual one, for "we have a natural duty to remove any injustices, beginning with the most grievous ... guided by the priority indicated by the lexical ordering" (*TJ* 216). The lexical ordering is in force, meaning that, for example, the fair value of equal political liberty principle is to be satisfied before the second principle is consulted. There is a further distributive component: "[I]n the long run the burden of injustice should be ... evenly distributed" (*TJ* 312).

Justifying Civil Disobedience in a Nearly-Well-Ordered Society

Rawls gives a precise, stipulative definition of civil disobedience: it is "a public, nonviolent conscientious yet political act contrary to law usually done with the aim of bringing about a change in the law or policies of the government" (*TJ* 320). The qualifier "usually" serves to mark the fact that sometimes disobedience may be so unlikely of success that the actor "aims" not so much to bring about a change as to register a protest, or to disassociate herself from official injustice. Civil disobedience is public and nonviolent because it "expresses disobedience to law within the limits of fidelity to the law" which is in turn "expressed by the willingness to accept the legal consequences of one's conduct" (*TJ* 322). An act of disobedience is pro tanto inconsistent with the duties associated with the principle of political settlement, and is therefore in need of a justification. In the original position, the parties would recognize justified civil disobedience "to address the sense of justice of the majority" (*TJ* 335), as "a final device to maintain the stability of a just constitution" (*TJ* 337). Rawls painstakingly sets out the form it must take, as necessary but possibly insufficient conditions.

First of all, justified civil disobedience is "limit[ed] to circumstances of clear and substantial injustice," such as the denial to minorities of the voting franchise or freedom of movement, or religious discrimination or persecution. "The establishment of these wrongs does not presuppose an informed examination of institutional effects" – unlike issues involving the difference principle, for example, tax laws, "unless clearly designed to ... abridge a basic equal liberty." Second, "normal appeals to the majority have already been made in good faith and have failed." Third, there is no risk that "serious disorder" due to multiple, equivalent claims will result in "lasting injury" to the "just constitution." Fourth, due "allowance [is] made for the possibility of injury to third parties." Fifth, and finally, the resort to civil disobedience is "wise and prudent" (*TJ* 326–330).

This is a fairly exacting list of prerequisites. Rawls also discusses in lesser detail the cases of militant action, conscientious refusal, and covert conscientious evasion, but I set those aside. Rawls's reputation as an apologist for the status quo, and for welfare-state capitalism derives in no small part from his writings on civil disobedience. Belonging to non-ideal theory, it has a practical bearing that brought it a certain notoriety in anti–Vietnam War circles. Let me cite an instance, involving two brothers, both Catholic priests at the time:

> [O]n May 17, 1968 ... Daniel and Philip Berrigan, entered a ... local draft board ... seized hundreds of draft records ... and set them on fire with homemade napalm. The Berrigans were convicted of destroying government property and sentenced to three years ... [T]hey were to begin serving their terms on April 10, 1970. Instead, they raised the stakes by going underground. ... As Daniel explained ..., he was not buying the "mythology" fostered by American liberals that there was a "moral necessity of joining illegal action to legal consequences." [B]oth ... were tracked down and sent to prison.
>
> (*New York Times*, May 1, 2016)

(Coincidentally, the Berrigans went underground only a few weeks before Rawls's office building at the Stanford Center was firebombed.) Rawls's theory does not entail that the Berrigans were morally required to submit to serve their terms in prison, nor that they were unjustified in going underground, but their avoiding prison does not fall within his admittedly narrow and stipulative definition of civil disobedience.

The meticulous theoretical apparatus obscures which side Rawls was on. Rawls was outspoken in his criticism of the draft law, which issued four-year deferments to college students, and he went so far as to state that there was a duty to oppose conscription administered in this discriminatory way. Conscription is "a drastic interference with the basic liberties" which can only be imposed, even democratically, on the condition that it involves "no avoidable class bias" (*TJ* 334). If a war's aims and methods are dubious enough, "one may have a duty and not only a right to refuse" (*TJ* 335).

IS WELFARE-STATE CAPITALISM BADLY ORDERED?

What I have called a badly ordered society is a society that conforms to an unreasonable conception of justice, and thus lacks a just constitution. Its arrangements are plainly unjust in numerous respects. Its hallmark is that it is "regulated by principles favoring narrow class interests" (*TJ* 310). Recall the reasons Rawls gives in the *Restatement* for rejecting welfare-state capitalism as incapable of realizing justice as fairness, or, by implication, any reasonable political conception of justice. Welfare-state capitalism rejects the first-principle requirement that the fair value of the equal political liberties be guaranteed. It does not pursue the policies needed for equal opportunity.

It permits very large inequalities in the ownership of real property (productive assets and natural resources) so that the control of the economy and much of political life rests in few hands.

(*JF* 138)

Finally, its provision of a social minimum – however stingy or generous the level – does not respect a principle of reciprocity.

For Rawls, a welfare-state capitalist society is a badly ordered society. Although justice in certain other senses – such as between equally matched parties in a civil dispute – may occur within the operation of these institutions, these occurrences, however numerous, do not add up to a condition of near-justice of the basic structure. Being badly ordered, a welfare-state capitalist society lacks a just constitution. Therefore, civil disobedience, which consists in an appeal to a just constitution, is not even possible. The conflict of duties faced by citizens of a badly ordered society is unlike the conflict of duties that citizens of nearly just states confront. In a nearly just state, the duty to support and comply with just institutions that apply to one and its companion duty of civility come into conflict with the natural duty to correct and remove injustices. In a badly ordered society, there is no such conflict. The conflict that one faces is one between one's natural duty to create just institutions, when one can do so without unreasonable sacrifice, and the principles of right that generally restrict one's pursuit of permissible or even mandatory ends. Ideal theory tells us what a just constitution must look like, but it tells us far less than what we would like to know about how we might justly get there.

Rawls says that "after an ideal conception of justice has been chosen … the parties ask which principles to adopt under less happy conditions" (*TJ* 216); but he never details how the original position procedure could be extended to cover such cases. He denies that the original position procedure is even possible in the case of merely decent societies, for their political culture does not contain the requisite fundamental ideas (*LP* 70). In a badly ordered society, the original position procedure is apposite, but "the measure of departures from the ideal is left importantly to intuition" (*TJ* 216). If close enough to a just constitution, the remaining gap is to be closed under the guidance not of principles for the non-ideal, but of the priority principles adopted for the ideal case. Intuitionism without priorities may have to serve those who find themselves in "a less fortunate society" (*TJ* 217) far from near-justice.

The overlapping consensus of reasonable political conceptions that figures prominently in *Political Liberalism* must not be mistaken as intended as any part of a theory of transition. "In part III, *Theory* supposes that the well-ordered society of justice as fairness is possible and *somehow comes about*. It then asks whether that society is stable" (*PL* xlii; emphasis added). Rawls makes an illuminating reference, in passing, as he makes clear that the strains of commitment to be considered in Part One of the original position procedure do not arise from a desire to preserve the benefits of previous injustice. Strains such as these belong to the process of transition but questions connected with this are covered by nonideal theory and not by the principles of justice for a well-ordered society. Allen Buchanan has an instructive discussion of these points.

(*PL* 17–18 n. 19)

Typically, when Rawls writes that someone else has an "instructive discussion" of something, he does so by way of endorsing its content, rather than as a way of merely clarifying a position Rawls himself would not endorse. This is especially so when what the other writer has written is itself an interpretation of Rawls. Here is what political philosopher Buchanan says, about Rawls, in the passage Rawls cites:

> Marxians often charge that the liberal's priority on civil and political rights, especially on the right to free speech and to vote, can serve as a barrier to the revolutionary transformation of society because it may be necessary to violate these rights temporarily, during the transition to a classless society. But because Rawls lacks a developed theory of transition, he is not committed to a well-defined prohibition on the abridgment of civil and political rights. Indeed Rawls's condition on the priority of his first principle explicitly recognizes that such abridgment may be necessary, while only stating in an extremely vague way the circumstances under which it may be abridged.

(Buchanan 1982, 149)

Those who think Rawls intended the priority of the first-principle liberties, or the justification of civil disobedience, as obstacles to revolutionary action in the transition to a just society have mistaken his meaning.

The question now arises whether our contemporary circumstances place us in a welfare-state capitalism or other type of comparably badly ordered regime. For if our circumstances do so place us, they are profoundly unjust, and we therefore, in Rawls's view, have not only a right but a duty to oppose the status quo, within the boundaries of natural right, by whatever means promise success.

THE "NEW PARTY" AND STABILITY FOR THE WRONG REASONS

Later in his life, Rawls became increasingly despondent about the prospects for justice in the United States. But this is in part because there was an earlier period in which, like Mill, he was hopeful. Real progress was made during the decade of the 1960s in many areas: civil rights for African Americans, women's rights, voting rights for eighteen-year-olds, and further progress seemed assured. But not all was well. In 1980, Rawls confesses that "[o]ur society is not well-ordered ... a basis of public justification is still to be achieved," and he widens the scope of a possible basis to a "conception of the person and of social cooperation conjectured to be implicit in

[our] culture, or at least congenial to its deepest tendencies when properly expressed and presented" (*CP* 355). (One is reminded of Stephen Daedalus forging in the smithy of his soul the uncreated conscience of his race.) Rawls writes in 1993 that

> I assume as sufficiently evident that in our country today reasonably favorable conditions – [including "culture ... traditions, ... acquired skill in running insti- tutions, [and] level of economic advance (which need not be especially high)] – do obtain, so that for us the priority of the basic liberties is required. Of course, whether the political will exists is a different question entirely. While this will exists by definition in a well-ordered society, in our society part of the political task is to help fashion it.
>
> (*PL* 297)

The task of fashioning the political will can be facilitated or obstructed by existing institutions and the educational role they assume. The "exemplar of public reason" (*PL* 231), the Supreme Court of the United States, had already disappointed Rawls in its *Buckley v. Valeo* decision, described in Chapters 5 and 9; and the wider, background culture was tending in a direction that was undoubtedly distressing to Rawls. He complains in his 1995 "Reply to Habermas,"

> [T]he present system woefully fails in public financing for political elections, leading to a grave imbalance in fair political liberties; it allows a widely disparate distribution of income and wealth that seriously undermines fair opportunities.
>
> (*PL* 407)

Concern about the justice of economic equality was conspicuously absent among the leadership of the Democratic Party during the 1990s (Stoller 2016). The United States was not approaching but in fact drawing farther away from even "reasonably just" or "nearly just" proximity to the principles of justice as fairness.

In October 1995, Rawls returned to California to address a conference at the University of Santa Clara to mark the twenty-fifth anniversary of the publication of *Theory*. The list of speakers consisted of many of his closest and most eminent contemporaries: Bernard Williams, Michael Sandel, Jürgen Habermas, Thomas Nagel, Amy Gutmann, and Ronald Dworkin. In his remarks,

> Rawls expressed his concerns about developments in the US with surprising force. He is [*sic*] especially exercised by the way in which the lack of limits on political donations is being allowed to distort the political process; in Rawlsian terms, the value of political liberty is now almost infinitely greater for some than it is for others. "I think," says Joshua Cohen, "his hopefulness has been shaken by the world. His feelings have soured."
>
> (Rogers 1999, 6)

The souring was due in part to the collaboration between the administration of Democratic President Bill Clinton and the Republican Speaker of the House, Newt

Gingrich, whose "Contract with America" set the legislative agenda.[2] The shaking was due to the effective destruction of the New Party, a political party that Rawls had quietly lent financial support.

The New Party was formed in 1993 to promote an alternative to the so-called "two-party system," the de facto political duopoly in the United States. It was founded in the hope of establishing the constitutional right of all political parties to have the willing candidate of their choice to appear on official election ballots. This entailed challenges to the so-called anti-fusion laws operative in most of the United States, which essentially restrict candidates to a single-party affiliation on the ballots voters use. Anti-fusion laws have been commonly used to minimize the chances of third parties.

One with an acquaintance with constitutional law would think that, as content-based restrictions of political expression, these laws would be subject to the heightened "strict scrutiny" test that the Supreme Court has devised and applied with fatal effect to Congress's efforts to level the political playing field by limiting campaign spending. One would be wrong. That reasoning did prevail in the Court of Appeals for the Eighth Circuit but, in the case of *Timmons v. Twin Cities Area New Party*, the Supreme Court reversed. In an opinion announced on April 28, 1997, the Court held that not only could an anti-fusion statute be justified on the ground that it promotes stability; it could be presumed to have that effect. Moreover, the U.S. Constitution allows the states, and by implication also the federal sovereign, actively to promote a two-party system. John Rawls was not mentioned in the opinion or in the dissenting opinions of Justices Stevens and Souter. (John Rawls has never been cited in any opinion of the Supreme Court, or in any concurrence, or in any dissenting opinion.) The Republican Party had filed a brief amicus curiae for affirmance of the Eighth Circuit: the Democratic Party did not.

---

[2] Rawls's tone sinks from sour to bitter in some of his asides. For example, in his posthumously published lectures on Hegel:

> [T]hese social forms [viz., the three estates: the hereditary landed gentry, the business class, and the civil service] represent the rational interests of their members in what Hegel views as a just *consultation hierarchy* ... having the purpose of moderating the influence of the competitive market and the aspirations of the business class .... The modern industrial economy would otherwise be a danger to and corrupt political and civil life. His constitutional scheme with its three estates no doubt strikes us as quaint and out of date, and teaches us little. But does a modern constitutional society do better? Certainly not the United States, where the purchase of legislation by "special interests" is an everyday thing.
>
> (*LHMP* 357; emphasis added).

As if the comparison of the contemporary United States to 1820 Germany were not invidious enough, readers of *The Law of Peoples* will be reminded of Rawls's imaginary Kazanistan, his example of a "decent" but illiberal consultation hierarchy (*LP* 75–78).

Rawls was aware of the outcome in *Timmons*, but it is not known what he thought of its invocation of stability.[3] The Supreme Court's conception is quite other than the "stability for the right reasons" to which the final one-third of *Theory* is devoted, and which is the pivotal idea in the later development of Rawls theory. For Rawls, the maintenance of stability in this guise is simply the oppressive use of political power. The misuse of the idea of stability by the Supreme Court would have been keenly vexing to him, and it would have been a relief to him to have avoided possible misattributions. "[P]olitical philosophy is always in danger of being used corruptly as a defense of an unjust and unworthy status quo" (*JF* 4 n. 4; also *LHPP* 10).

This is too bleak. Until we have, with Hegel, looked at the world rationally, we need not "ask, with Kant, whether it is worthwhile for human beings to live on the earth" (*LP* 128). The Austrian Marxist economist, Rudolf Hilferding, argued that, in late capitalism, the financial sector and major industries stand alone on the commanding heights. As Leszek Kołakowski, the eminent theorist and historian of Marxism, describes Hilferding's doctrine, "The state need not and should not expropriate all medium-sized and small enterprises .... The state has only to take over the big banks and industrial firms to control production" (Kołakowski 2005 [1978] 599). Unforeseen by Marx, this development has meant that the transition to socialism is much less difficult and disruptive than we tend to assume. We have only to think of Attlee's Britain, still vivid during Rawls's time at Oxford, or of the aftermath of the global financial apoplexy of 2008, which Rawls did not live to see. The financial sector, the automotive industry, and the re-insurance industry of the United States simply settled into public hands, like exhausted children after too much play. President Obama, deferring to the strong national tradition of private ownership, determined that the People were not ready to keep possession of what history had returned to them.[4] The formation of the political will, which depends on jettisoning the sense of false necessity that our social world cannot be other than it is, is all that remains to be done.

Still, one has to wonder, why was Rawls unwilling to prepare the way in more explicit terms? The observations of political philosopher David Estlund are worth pondering. Writing shortly after Rawls's death in 2002, Estlund – a former student – had this to say:

---

[3]   Rawls had written but not yet published the observation that "it is obvious that the party that can raise the most money will have less desire for reforms [of campaign financing laws], and if it is in power, can block reforms. If both parties in a two-party system are corrupt and can raise large funds, such efforts at reform may be practically impossible without a major political change via, say, a third party" (*LHPP* 18).

[4]   "[W]e also have different traditions in this country. Obviously, Sweden has a different set of cultures in terms of how the government relates to markets and America's different. And we want to retain a strong sense of that private capital fulfilling the core – core investment needs of this country." "Obama: No Easy Out for Wall Street," Feb. 10, 2009, http://abcnews.go.com/ Politics/Business/story?id=6844330&page=1 (cf. Williamson 2015, 412)

The greatness of John Rawls's work depends on its relevance for its time, but (again) *A Theory of Justice* did not say anything – not a word – about Jim Crow, women's liberation, or the Vietnam War. Paradoxically, its relevance has consisted partly in its drawing attention away from fights over specific practical political goals. By steering clear of many of the particular issues of the day in their temporary contexts (without in any way deriding them), Rawls leaves us a model of political philosophy that will retain its value over time. Social progress toward justice remains urgent, and it never happens without activism, conflict, and contextually specific arguments very different from Rawls's work. But we will pursue the goal of social justice more clearly and effectively if, as just one stratagem in the struggle, we reflect on deeper principles that we share. The point is not to avoid or deny the disagreements, but to shed light on them. Rawls's work was hardly nonpartisan. He pursued a deeply egalitarian liberal political agenda, but in that patient and indirect way.

(Estlund 2003, 91)

I have argued that the phrase "deeply egalitarian liberal political agenda" is itself an understatement. Rawls's agenda leads us toward a socialist society. But let Estlund finish:

This remote or reticent approach to political philosophy can easily look like a symptom of Rawls's legendary personal humility. At other times, in its hope of philosophy's making any difference at all, it looks positively audacious.

(Estlund 2003, 91)

The world has understandably wearied of its most overtly audacious socialists. We ought to be grateful for having one who was patiently reticent in calling us to build the common world that is implicit in how we would want to be treated if we did not know which of God's or fate's children we happen to be.

Bibliography

Anderson, Elizabeth 1999. What is the point of equality? *Ethics* 109: 287–337.
    forthcoming. Rawls's difference principle. In Matthew Williams and Andrew Clayton, eds. *The Cambridge Companion to a Theory of Justice*. Cambridge: Cambridge University Press.
Arneson, Richard 1979. Mill's doubts about freedom under socialism. *Canadian Journal of Philosophy*, supp. 5: 231–249.
    1986. Comment on Krouse and McPherson. *Ethics* 97(1): 139–145.
Baumol, W. J. 1974. The transformation of values: What Marx "really" meant (an interpretation). *Journal of Economic Literature* 12(1): 51–62.
Bell, Daniel. 1972. On meritocracy and equality. *The Public Interest* 29: 29–68.
Berlin, Isaiah. 1970. *Four Essays on Liberty*. Oxford: Oxford University Press.
Bernstein, Eduard. 1993 [1899]. *The Preconditions of Socialism*. Henry Tudor, ed. Cambridge: Cambridge University Press.
Blackburn, Simon. 2001. Taking the veil. *Times Literary Supplement*, September 28, 11.
Bowles, Samuel, and Herbert Gintis. 2002. The inheritance of inequality. *Journal of Economic Perspectives* 16(3): 3–30.
Brighouse, Harry 1997. Political equality in justice as fairness. *Philosophical Studies* 86(2): 155–184.
Brudney, Daniel. 2014. The young Marx and the middle-aged Rawls. In Jon Mandle and David A. Reidy, eds. *A Companion to Rawls*, pp. 450–471. Oxford: Wiley Blackwell.
Buchanan, Allen. 1982. *Marx and Justice: The Radical Critique of Liberalism*. Totowa, NJ: Rowman & Allenheld.
Coates, David. 1975. *The Labour Party and the Struggle for Socialism*. Cambridge: Cambridge University Press.
Cohen, Joshua 1989. The economic basis of deliberative democracy. *Social Philosophy and Policy* 6: 25–50.
    2003a. For a democratic society. In Samuel Freeman, ed. *The Cambridge Companion to Rawls*, pp. 86–138. Cambridge: Cambridge University Press.
    2003b. Deliberation and democratic legitimacy. In Derek Matravers and Jon Pike, eds. *Debates in Contemporary Political Philosophy: An Anthology*, pp. 342–360. London: Routledge and the Open University.
Dahl, Robert. 1989. *Democracy and Its Critics*. New Haven, CT: Yale University Press.
    1956. *A Preface to Democratic Theory*. Chicago: University of Chicago Press.

Daniels, Norman. 1975. Equal liberty and unequal worth of liberty. In Norman Daniels, ed. *Reading Rawls: Critical Studies on Rawls's A Theory of Justice* pp. 253–281. New York: Basic Books.

Dillon, Robin S. 1997. Self-respect: Moral, emotional, political. *Ethics* 107: 226–249.

DiQuattro, Arthur. 1983. Rawls and Left criticism. *Political Theory* 11(1): 53–78.

Doppelt, Gerald. 1981. Rawls' system of justice: A critique from the Left. *Noûs* 15(3): 259–307.

Dorfman, Avihay, and Alon Harel. 2015. Against privatisation as such. *Oxford Journal of Legal Studies* 2015: 1–28.

Dunn, John. 1984. *The Politics of Socialism: An Essay in Political Theory.* Cambridge: Cambridge University Press.

Elliott, Gregory. 1993. *Labourism and the English Genius: The Strange Death of Labour England?* London: Verso.

Elster, Jon. 1986. Comments on Krouse and McPherson. *Ethics* 97: 146–173.

Elster, Jon, and Karl Ove Moene, eds. 1989. *Alternatives to Capitalism.* Cambridge: Cambridge University Press.

Estlund, David. 2003. The audacious humility of John Rawls. *Dissent* Spring 2003: 89–91.

Fieldhouse, Andrew. 2013. A review of the economic research on the effects of raising ordinary income tax rates: Higher revenue, unchanged growth, and uncertain but potentially large reductions in the growth of inequality. *Economic Policy Institute/The Century Foundation.* Issue Brief #353.

Freeman, Samuel, ed. 2003. *The Cambridge Companion to Rawls.* Cambridge: Cambridge University Press.

  2007a. *Justice and the Social Contract: Essays on Rawlsian Political Philosophy.* New York: Oxford University Press.

  2007b. *Rawls.* New York: Routledge.

  2013. Property-owning democracy and the difference principle. *Analyse & Kritik* 9(1): 9–36.

Friedman, Milton. 1962. *Capitalism and Freedom.* Chicago: University of Chicago Press.

Galston, William. 2010. Realism in political theory. *European Journal of Political Theory* 9(4): 385–411.

Gardner, John. 2014. The evil of privatization (June 20, 2014). Available at SSRN: http://ssrn.com/abstract=2460655 at 16.

Gaus, Gerald. 2011. *The Order of Public Reason.* New York: Cambridge University Press.

Geuss, Raymond. 2005. *Outside Ethics.* Princeton: Princeton University Press.

Gilens, Martin, and Benjamin I. Page. 2014. Testing theories of American politics: Elites, interest groups, and average citizens. *Perspectives on Politics* 12: 564–581.

Gray, Alexander. 1968 [1946]. *The Socialist Tradition: Moses to Lenin.* New York: Harper & Row.

Gray, John. 1989. *Liberalisms: Essays in Political Philosophy.* London: Routledge.

Green, Jeffrey Edward. 2013. Rawls and the forgotten figure of the most advantaged: In defense of reasonable envy toward the superrich. *American Political Science Review* 107: 123–138.

Gutmann, Amy. 2003. Rawls on the relationship between liberalism and democracy. In Samuel Freeman, ed., *The Cambridge Companion to Rawls,* pp. 168–199. Cambridge: Cambridge University Press.

Harris, Kenneth. 1982. *Attlee.* London: Weidenfeld and Nicolson.

Hayek, Friedrich. 1976. *The Mirage of Social Justice.* London: Routledge & Kegan Paul.

  1984. *The Essence of Hayek,* Chakai Nishiyama and Kurt R. Leube, eds. Stanford: Hoover Institution Press.

Henning, Christoph. 2014. *Philosophy after Marx.* Max Henniger, trans. Chicago: Haymarket Books.

Huberman, Leo. 1968. The ABC of socialism. In Leo Huberman and Paul Sweezy, eds. *Introduction to Socialism*. New York: Monthly Review Press.

Jackson, Ben. 2005. Revisionism reconsidered: "Property-owning democracy" and egalitarian strategy in post-war Britain. *Twentieth-Century British History* 16: 416–440.

2007. *Equality and the British Left: A Study in Progressive Political Thought, 1900–64*. Manchester: Manchester University Press.

2014. Property-owning democracy: A short history. In Martin O'Neill and Thad Williamson, eds., *Property-Owning Democracy: Rawls and Beyond*. Oxford: Wiley Blackwell.

Kant, Immanuel (1793/1996), *Practical Philosophy*, M. J. Gregor (ed.), Cambridge: Cambridge University Press.

Kołakowski, Lesek. 2005 [1978]. *Main Currents of Marxism*. P. S. Falla, trans. New York: W. W. Norton.

Krouse, Richard, and Michael McPherson. 1986. A "mixed" property regime: Liberty and equality in a market economy. *Ethics* 97: 119–38.

1988. Capitalism, "property-owning democracy," and the welfare state. In Amy Gutmann, ed. *Democracy and the Welfare State*. Princeton: Princeton University Press, pp. 79–105.

Kuhner, Timothy K. 2011. *Citizens United* as neoliberal jurisprudence: The resurgence of economic theory. *Virginia Journal of Social Policy and Law* 18: 395–468.

Leiter, Brian. 2015. Why Marxism still does not need normative theory. Analyse und Kritik 2015(37): 23–50.

Lenin, Vladimir Ilych. 1971. *Lenin Collected Works*, vol. 36. Tr. Andrew Rothstein. Moscow: Progress Publishers.

Little, Daniel. 2014. Rawls and economics. In Jon Mandle and David A. Reidy, eds. *A Companion to Rawls*. Oxford: Wiley Blackwell, pp. 504–525.

MacLeod, Colin M. 2014. Applying justice as fairness to institutions. In Jon Mandle and David A. Reidy, eds. *A Companion to Rawls*. Oxford: Wiley Blackwell, pp. 164–184.

Mandle, Jon and David A. Reidy, eds. 2014. *A Companion to Rawls*. Oxford: Wiley Blackwell.

Marx, Karl, and Friedrich Engels. 1978. *The Marx-Engels Reader*, 2nd ed. Robert C. Tucker, ed. New York: W. W. Norton & Co.

McClennan, E. F. 1989. Justice and the problem of stability. *Philosophy & Public Affairs* 18(1): 3–30.

Meade, J. E. 1949. Next steps in domestic economic policy. *The Political Quarterly* 20: 12–24.

1950. Review of Bertrand de Jouvenel, Problems of Socialist England. *The Economic Journal* 60(237): 114–117.

1964. *Efficiency, Equality and Ownership of Property*. London: George Allen and Unwin. Reprinted (with a minor addition to p. 50, fn. 2) in J. E. Meade. 1993. *Liberty, Equality and Efficiency*. New York: New York University Press.

Melzer, Arthur M. 2014. *Philosophy between the Lines: The Lost History of Esoteric Writing*. Chicago: University of Chicago Press.

Metz, Thaddeus. 2002. Review of John Rawls, *Justice as Fairness: A Restatement*. *The Philosophical Review* 111(4): 618–620.

Michelman, Frank. 1973. In pursuit of constitutional welfare rights: One view of Rawls' theory of justice. *University of Pennsylvania Law Review* 121(5): 962–1019.

1979. Welfare rights in a constitutional democracy. *Washington University Law Quarterly* 1979(3): 659–693.

2003. Rawls on constitutionalism and constitutional law. In Samuel Freeman, ed., *The Cambridge Companion to Rawls*. Cambridge: Cambridge University Press, pp. 394–425.

Miliband, Ralph. 1973. *Parliamentary Socialism: A Study in the Politics of Labour*, 2nd ed. London: Merlin Press.

Mill, John Stuart. 2006. *Collected Works of John Stuart Mill*. Indianapolis: Liberty Fund.

Moran, Terry. 2009. Obama chides receding Wall Street: "There is no easy out." Interview with President Barak Obama. *ABC News* (February 9) http://abcnews.go.com/Politics/Business/story?id=6844330 (accessed April 13, 2017).

Nagel, Thomas. 2003. Rawls and liberalism. In Samuel Freeman, ed., *The Cambridge Companion to Rawls*. Cambridge: Cambridge University Press, pp. 62–85.

Neilsen, Kai. 1989. A moral case for socialism. *Critical Review* 3: 542–553.

Nozick, Robert. 1974. *Anarchy, State, and Utopia*. New York: Basic Books.

  1989. *The Examined Life: Philosophical Meditations*. New York: Simon and Schuster.

Nuttall, Jeremy. 2006. *Psychological Socialism: The Labour Party and Qualities of Mind and Character, 1931 to the Present*. Manchester: Manchester University Press.

O'Neill, Martin. 2014. Free (and fair) markets without capitalism: Political values, principles of justice, and property-owning democracy. In Martin O'Neill and Thad Williamson, eds., *Property-Owning Democracy: Rawls and Beyond*. Oxford: Wiley Blackwell, pp. 75–100.

O'Neill, Martin and Thad Williamson, eds.. 2014. *Property-Owning Democracy: Rawls and Beyond*. Oxford: Wiley Blackwell.

Orwell, George. 1941. *The Lion and the Unicorn*. London: Secker & Warburg.

Otsuka, Michael. 2003. *Libertarianism without Inequality*. Oxford: Oxford University Press.

Page, Benjamin I., Larry M. Bartels, and Jason Seawright. 2013. Democracy and the policy preferences of wealthy Americans. *Perspectives on Politics* 11: 51–73.

Peffer, Rodney G. 2014 [1990]. *Marxism, Morality, and Social Justice*. Princeton: Princeton University Press.

Piketty, Thomas. 2014. *Capital in the Twenty-First Century*. Cambridge, MA: Belknap/Harvard University Press.

Pogge, Thomas. 1989. *Realizing Rawls*. Ithaca: Cornell University Press.

  2007. *John Rawls: His Life and Theory of Justice*. Oxford: Oxford University Press.

Ponce, Pedro. 1999. John Rawls. http://www.neh.gov/about/awards/national-humanities-medals/john-rawls (accessed July 4, 2016).

Putnam, Hilary. 1997. A half-century of philosophy, viewed from within. *Daedalus* 126(1): 311–332.

Pyke, Steve. 1995. *Philosophers*, 2nd ed. London: Zelda Cheatle Press.

Rawls, John. 1989. *Justice as Fairness: A Guided Tour*. Unpublished photocopy. [cited herein as *GT*]

  1996. *Political Liberalism*, paperback ed. New York: Columbia University Press. [cited herein as *PL*]

  1999a. *A Theory of Justice*, revised ed. Cambridge MA: Harvard University Press. [cited herein as *TJ*]

  1999b. *Collected Papers*. Samuel Freeman, ed. Cambridge, MA: Harvard University Press. [cited herein as *CP*]

  1999c. *The Law of Peoples*. Cambridge, MA: Harvard University Press. [cited herein as *LP*]

  2000a. Burton Dreben: Afterword, a Reminiscence. In Juliet Floyd and Sanford Shieh, eds., *Future Pasts: Perspectives on the Place of the Analytic Tradition in Twentieth-Century Philosophy*. New York: Oxford University Press, pp. 417–430.

  2000b. *Lectures on the History of Moral Philosophy*. Barbara Herman, ed. Cambridge, MA: Harvard University Press. [cited herein as *LHMP*]

  2001. *Justice as Fairness: A Restatement*. Erin Kelly, ed. Cambridge MA: Belknap/Harvard University Press. [cited herein as *JF*]

  2007. *Lectures on the History of Political Philosophy*, Samuel Freeman, ed. Cambridge MA: Belknap/Harvard University Press. [cited herein as *LHPP*]

2009. *A Brief Inquiry into the Meaning of Sin and Faith*. Thomas Nagel, ed. Cambridge MA: Harvard University Press. [cited herein as *BI*]

Rawls, John, and Phillipe van Parijs. 2003. Three letters on the Law of Peoples and the European Union. *Revue de Philosophie Économique* 8: 7–20.

Robinson, Joan. 1966. *An Essay on Marxian Economics*. London: Macmillan.

Roemer, John E. 1986. *Value, Exploitation, and Class*. New York: Harwood.

    1994a. *A Future for Socialism*. Cambridge, MA: Harvard University Press.

    1994b. *Egalitarian Perspectives: Essays in Philosophical Economics*. Cambridge: Cambridge University Press.

Rogers, Ben. 2002. John Rawls (obituary). *The Guardian*, November 27.

    1999. John Rawls. *Prospect*, June 20.

Ron, Amit. 2008. Visions of democracy in "property-owning democracy": Skelton to Rawls and beyond. *History of Political Thought* 29(1): 168–187.

Scheffler, Samuel. 2008. Cosmopolitanism, justice, and institutions. *Daedalus* 137: 68–77.

    2003. What is egalitarianism? *Philosophy & Public Affairs* 31(1): 5–39.

Schelling, Thomas C. 1960. *The Strategy of Conflict*. London: Oxford University Press.

Schemmel, Christian. 2015. How (not) to criticise the welfare state. *Journal of Applied Philosophy* 32(2015): 393–409.

Schliesser, Eric. 2016. On Rawls and esotericism. http://digressionsnimpressions.typepad.com/digressionsimpressions/2015/07/on-rawls-and-esotericism.html (accessed May 8, 2016).

Schumpeter, Joseph A. 1950. *Capitalism, Socialism, and Democracy*, 3rd ed. New York: Harper & Row.

    1954. *History of Economic Analysis*. New York: Oxford University Press.

Schweikart, David. 1978. Should Rawls be a socialist? *Social Theory and Practice* 5(1): 1–27.

    2014. Property-owning democracy or economic democracy? In Martin O'Neill and Thad Williamson, eds., *Property-Owning Democracy: Rawls and Beyond*. Oxford: Wiley Blackwell, pp. 201–222.

Sedgwick, Peter. 1970. The end of Labourism. *New Politics* 8: 77–86.

Shaw, G. Bernard. 2006 [1884]. The basis of socialism: Economic, in G. Bernard Shaw, ed., *Fabian Essays in Socialism*. New York: Cosimo, pp. 15–45.

Stepan, Alfred, and Juan J. Linz. 2011. Comparative perspectives on inequality and the quality of democracy in the United States. *Perspectives on Politics* 9(4): 841–856.

Stoller, Matt. 2016. How the Democrats killed their populist soul. *The Atlantic*, October 24.

Streek, Wolfgang. 2014. *Buying Time: The Delayed Crisis of Democratic Capitalism*. Patrick Candler, trans. London: Verso.

Taylor, Robert S. 2014. Illiberal socialism. *Social Theory and Practice* 40: 433–460.

Thomas, Alan 2012. Rawls, Adam Smith and an argument from complexity to property-owning democracy. *The Good Society* 21: 4–20.

    2014. Property-owning democracy, liberal republicanism, and the idea of an egalitarian ethos. In Martin O'Neill and Thad Williamson, eds., *Property-Owning Democracy: Rawls and Beyond*. Oxford: Wiley Blackwell, pp. 101–128.

    2016. *Republic of Equals: Predistribution and Property-Owning Democracy*. Oxford: Oxford University Press.

Tomasi, John. 2012. *Free-Market Fairness*. Princeton: Princeton University Press.

Vallier, Kevin. 2014. A moral and economic critique of the new property-owning democrats: On behalf of a Rawlsian welfare state. *Philosophical Studies*, DOI 10.1007/s11098 014 0303 2

van Parijs, Phillipe. 2011. *Just Democracy: The Rawls-Machiavelli Programme*. Colchester: ECPR Press.

Waldron, Jeremy. 2016. *Political Political Theory*. Cambridge, MA: Harvard University Press.

Wall, Stephen. 2006. Rawls and the status of political liberty. *Pacific Philosophical Quarterly* 87(2): 245–270.

Walzer M. 1979. A theory of revolution. *Marxist Perspectives* 2(1): 30–44.

2013. The political theory license. *Annual Review of Political Science* 16: 1–9.

Weithman, Paul 2010. *Why Political Liberalism? On John Rawls's Political Turn*. New York: Oxford University Press.

2013. Review of O'Neill and Williamson, eds., Property-Owning Democracy: Rawls and Beyond. *Notre Dame Philosophical Reviews*, http://ndpr.nd.edu/news/41424-property-owning-democracy-rawls-and-beyond/

forthcoming. Autonomy and disagreement. *Ethics*.

Wenar, Leif. 2004. The unity of Rawls's work. *Journal of Moral Philosophy* 1(3): 265–275.

Williams, Bernard. 2005. *In the Beginning Was the Deed: Realism and Moralism in Political Argument*. Princeton: Princeton University Press.

2014. *Essays and Reviews 1959–2002*. Princeton: Princeton University Press.

Williamson, Thad. 2009. Who owns what? An egalitarian interpretation of John Rawls's idea of a property-owning democracy. *Journal of Social Philosophy* 40: 434–453.

2015. How (not) to criticise property-owning democracy: A response to Schemmel. *Journal of Applied Philosophy* 32 (2015): 410–417.

Index

reconciliation requirement, 142, 144
reflective equilibrium, 1, 120
Reidy, David, 187
relative stability, 91–92, 107
religion, 170
rent, economic, 24–25, 36, 37, 40, 42, 51, 134,
    140, 147, 150, 157, *see also* pure ownership
rent-maximizer's conception, 24
representative citizen, 19
resource constraints, 60
restricted utilitarianism, 92
restricted utility, 92, 96–97, 100–103
restricted utility principle, 155
reticence, 170
right of free speech, 59
risk-averseness, 105
Robinson, Joan, 27
Roemer, John, 32, 140, 147, 153–154, 181, 184
Rogers, Ben, 29, 172
Rorty, Amelie, 187

Scanlon, Tim, 171
Scheffler, Samuel, 158
Schelling, Thomas, 98, 100
Schemmel, Christian, 34, 88, 140
Schumpeter, 174
Schumpeter, Joseph, 29, 36, 39, 173
Schweikert, David, 140
secular socialism, 185
Sedgwick, Peter, 40
self-esteem, 56, 59
self-realization, 181
self-respect, 19, 108, 113, 117, 129, 137
shock therapy, 180
social and economic inequalities, 7
social contract theory, 65
social cooperation, 24, 90, 182
social investment, 138
social minimum, 103, 132, 152, 164, 194
social minimum safety net, 4
social ownership, 35, 152
    right of, 18
    significance of, 158
social surplus, 56, 77
Social Unity and Primary Goods (1982), 67
socialism, 18, 30, 33, 50, 60, 70, 139, 180
    associational, 118
    civil disobedience, 186–188
    comprehensive to political stability, 121–122
    constitutional convention, 122–127
    defined, 36
    original position, mirroring, 124–125
    political violence, 186–188
    prices in, 40

property regimes, 125–127
    sine qua non of, 181
    stability and, 118–127
    transition to, 186–199
socialist leadership, 167
socialist regime, principles of justice, 31
socially dangerous extent, 107
society, exploitation free, 36
special attitudes, destabilizing, 8
special psychologies, 7–8, 12, 21, 61, 68, 84,
    89–90, 105–117, 120, 127, 130, 177,
    179
    envy and, 106–109
    envy and inequality, 109–110
    excusable particular envy, 110–111
    stability of conception, 116–117
    stability of institutions, 116–117
    stability of priority principles, 111–116
Srinivas, M.N., 187
stability
    and constitutional convention, 122–124
    idea of, 99–101
    problem of, 91, 106
stable constitutional regime
    essentials for, 141
    express reciprocity condition, 148
    publicity condition, 145
    reconciliation requirement, 142
    stability aspects, 155
    workability, 145
Stalin, Josef, 21, 23
starting point of equality, 98
super-entrenchment, 80
syndicalism, 32, 49, 118

Taylor, Charles, 183
Taylor, Harriet, 174
testamentary freedom, 134
The Basic Liberties and Their Priority (1982),
    17
The Law of Peoples (1999), 2, 5
The Moynihan Report (1965), 3
The Negro Family: The Case for National Action
    (Moynihan), 3
"The Tragedy of the Commons" (1964), 149
Thomas, Alan, 46, 160
Thomas, Allen, 85
Tomasi, John, 151, 156
totalitarianism, 131
transcendental deduction, status quo, 67
two-party system, 197

unamendable entrenchment clauses, 80
unanimity, 72, 79

Lightning Source UK Ltd.
Milton Keynes UK
UKHW02f2256010818

326651UK00011B/133/P